Haven in a Heartless World

HAVEN IN A HEARTLESS WORLD

The Family Besieged

CHRISTOPHER LASCH

Basic Books, Inc., Publishers

NEW YORK

Parts of chapter 1 first appeared in "Selfish Women: The Campaign to Save the American Family, 1890–1920" in *The Columbia Forum,* volume IV, number 2 (Spring 1975). Copyright © 1975 by The Trustees of Columbia University in the City of New York. All rights reserved. Reprinted with permission.

Parts of chapter 1 have also appeared previously in *Salmagundi,* Fall 1976, number 35 and Winter 1977, number 36.

Parts of chapters 4 and 8 first appeared in "Freud and Women" (October 3, 1974), "The Family and History" (November 13, 1975), "The Emotions of Family Life" (November 27, 1975), and "What the Doctor Ordered" (December 11, 1975) in *The New York Review of Books.*

Library of Congress Cataloging in Publication Data

Lasch, Christopher.
   Haven in a heartless world.

   Includes index.
   1. Family—History. 2. Marriage—History.
3. Socialization. I. Title.
HQ518.L27   301.42   77–75246
ISBN: 0-465-02883-7 (cloth)
ISBN: 0-465-02884-5 (paper)

TO BETSY

"A witty woman is a treasure; a witty beauty is a power."

—Meredith, *Diana of the Crossways*

CONTENTS

4

Culture and Personality   62

5

Doctors to a Sick Society   97

6

The Social Theory of the Therapeutic:
Parsons and the Parsonians   111

7

8

ACKNOWLEDGMENTS

Without the generous support of the Ford Foundation and the Guggenheim Foundation, this work could not have been brought to a successful conclusion. I am grateful also to friends and colleagues who kindly read portions of the manuscript and offered valuable advice and criticism: Norman Birnbaum; Elizabeth Fox-Genovese; Frank F. Furstenberg, Jr.; Eugene D. Genovese; Gerald Graff; Russell Jacoby; William Leach; Steven Marcus; Richard Sennett; and Thomas Spence Smith. I should like to thank Jean DeGroat for typing the manuscript twice, and parts of it three and even four times. My wife, who suffered through the early stages of this undertaking, made a number of suggestions for which I am indebted.

Preface to the Paperback Edition

Praised by right-wing reviewers who misunderstood its political implications; condemned by the infantile left; greeted by the center with a mixture of suspicion, uneasiness, and outrage, *Haven in a Heartless World* has baffled ideologues of every political color. A book that resists assimilation to predigested positions offends those for whom politics consists of ready-made answers and automatic loyalties. To such readers, *Haven* will continue to present itself as a difficult, "obscure," "recondite" book. On the other hand, it has proved readily accessible to those who care more about the problem it addresses—the erosion of family life in contemporary society—than about the mechanical exercise of squaring its approach to the subject with received political pieties.

An Associated Press correspondent has described the book, with more enthusiasm than understanding, as "a rousing defense of traditional values," an "apparent contradiction" of the author's "reputation as a radical." Nathan Glazer finds in it the criticism of state intervention "one might have expected from a conservative or traditionalist, but hardly from a representative of the radical Left." George Gilder, more daring in his analysis of the author's motives, dismisses the "Marxist buncombe" that "disguises" this "marvelously reactionary book"—this "otherwise shrewd and brilliant critique of the pretensions of modern social science"—as a purely rhetorical gesture designed to appease academic readers, for whom the bitter pill of conservatism must be coated with socialist cant.

A number of writers on the left have also found the book, predictably, to be reactionary in its political orientation—though hardly "marvelous" in their eyes. Mark Poster pontificates: "To glorify the old bourgeois family is to idealize the men and women who dominated society during the heroic age of capitalism." "The book is an agenda for restoring the 'bourgeois' family," chimes in Edward Shorter. Even Wini Breines, a radical sociologist who should know better, thinks *Haven* is flawed by "nostalgia" for the patriarchal family.

These progressive-minded critics—whose strictures in any case are outweighed by the appreciative comments of more discerning radicals—have nothing with which to counter the arguments advanced in this book except the clichés of an earlier socialist tradition that has lost its informing power. "The only way to insure democracy for children," says Poster, as if the idea had just occurred to him, "is to provide them with a wide circle of adults to identify with, the ability to select their sources of identification, and a separation between authority figures and nurturant figures such as obtained among some of the early Kibbutzim." But it is precisely the separation of love and discipline that encourages, not merely in the kibbutz but in the middle-class American family itself, the development of personality traits more compatible with totalitarian regimes than with democracy: a strong attachment to the peer group; a marked fear of being alone; more or less complete alienation from the past (since as Bruno Bettelheim notes in his study of the kibbutz, "there is no permanence in human relations except with the peer group"); a strong concern with personal "authenticity" in relations with others, unmediated by conventional forms of politeness or even by respect for the other person's individuality; and a lack of introspection and of a highly developed inner life.

The founders of the kibbutz movement, according to Bettelheim, took Freud to be saying that "parents should never have any but good times with their children." The same fear of ambivalent attachments, based in part on the same misunderstanding of Freudian theory, can be seen in the middle-class American family today. The school, the helping professions, and the peer group have taken over most of the family's functions, and many parents have cooperated with this invasion of the family in the hope of presenting themselves to their children strictly as older friends and companions. Recent child rearing techniques, such as Parent Effectiveness Training, rationalize the retreat from painful confrontations by urging parents and children to talk about their feelings instead of arguing about the rules and principles that provoke confrontations. Much of the current preoccupation with "alternatives to the nuclear family," superficially radical in its willingness to experiment with new social forms, originates in the desire, so prevalent in our culture, to avoid conflicts, to smooth them over, or to deny their existence.

Unfortunately the conflicting emotions parents inevitably

arouse in their children—even enlightened modern parents—
live on at a deep level of unconscious mental life even when
they are denied explicit expression. The attempt to get rid of
conflict succeeds only in driving it underground. Psychiatrists
today see more and more patients whose mental life is dominated by unresolved conflicts dating from the earliest stages of
development. In their most extreme form, such conflicts govern
the mental make-up of the antisocial personalities whose crimes
get so much publicity in a culture hungry for spectacles and sensations.

An understanding of the impact of the family on personality,
and of the political implications of recent changes that have sep-
arated love and constraint, makes it impossible any longer to
equate defense of the nuclear family with reactionary politics or
criticism of it with radicalism. Many radicals in the seventies
have rediscovered the importance of family ties, often without
even reading *Haven in a Heartless World.* Some of them have
come to this position out of a need to put their personal lives in
order, to reject drugs and sexual promiscuity, and to establish
stability and permanence. Others have discovered the value of
the family in the course of their experience as community organ-
izers. Those who embraced this kind of practical activity, after
the collapse of the visionary politics of the new left, although at
first they continued to condemn the family as a bourgeois institution and a bastion of male chauvinsim, soon found that the
working-class family constitutes an important cultural resource in
the working-class struggle to survive. A recent paper by the staff
of the Saul Alinsky Training Institute describes with sympathy
and understanding the pressures that threaten to destroy the
working class family: rising expenses, bad schools, crime and
drugs, television with its alluring images so often "destructive of
healthy family values." The general "expectation that work
schedules are more important than family schedules" forces
women into the job market and leaves their children to be
brought up by day care centers, television, or the culture of the
street. The authors of this report, recognizing that "a strong,
healthy family is essential to personal, individual development,"
dissociate themselves from the "romantic dream that liberation
lies in individualism, isolation, and separation from entanglements." They advocate in place of this outmoded model of liberation a revival of the family and of voluntary associations, the

erosion of which, in their view, has created a vacuum filled all too rapidly by the "huge corporations, mass media, and walrus-like government."

Without fanfare or publicity, a major reorientation of the American left has taken place in the seventies. In the "me decade," the truth of what a few radicals argued even in the sixties—that the so-called counter culture represents a mirror image of consumer capitalism—has come to be widely acknowledged. The outstanding exception to this generalization remains the feminist movement, which still blames the family for much of the injustice inflicted on women. The belief that heterosexual monogamy in any form is inherently oppressive has led some feminists to advocate, and to practice, an extreme form of sexual separatism. More moderate feminists object to the family on the practical grounds that it ties women to the household and prevents them from gaining equality with men in the world of jobs and careers. How can women ever compete successfully with men, they ask, so long as outmoded conventions saddle women with the burden of raising children and taking care of the house?

Even after it is objected that feminist ideas of emancipated womanhood owe too much to the romantic dream of individual self-fulfillment—and to the capitalist vision of individual self-aggrandizement—the justice of women's demand for equality remains too obvious to ignore. Even after it is argued that radicals need to put more emphasis on the family and other associations and less on the individual, the fact remains that economic subordination for women is morally indefensible and that it no longer provides the basis for a good marriage, if indeed it ever did. The trouble with the feminist program is not that economic self-sufficiency for women is an unworthy goal but that its realization, under existing economic conditions, would undermine equally important values associated with the family. While defenders of the family need to acknowledge the justice of the central feminist demands, feminists for their part need to acknowledge the deterioration of care for the young and the justice of the demand that something be done to arrest it.

Feminists have not answered the argument that day care provides no substitute for the family. They have not answered the argument that indifference to the needs of the young has become one of the distinguishing characteristics of a society that lives for the moment, defines the consumption of commodities as the highest form of personal satisfaction, and exploits existing resources with criminal disregard of the future. Feminists have mindlessly denounced every such argument as an expression of blind prejudice; but in its own heedless disregard of the family and of the needs of future generations, the feminist movement, like the cultural radicalism of the sixties that gave rise to it, merely echoes the culture it claims to criticize.

The problem of women's work and women's equality needs to be examined from a perspective more radical than any that has emerged from the feminist movement. It has to be seen as a special case of the general rule that work takes precedence over the family. The most important indictment of the present organization of work is that it forces women to choose between their desire for economic self-sufficiency and the needs of her children. Instead of blaming the family for this state of affairs, we should blame the relentless demands of the job market itself. Instead of asking how women can be liberated from the family, we should ask how work can be reorganized—humanized—so as to make it possible for women to compete economically with men without sacrificing their families or even the very hope of a family. Those who endorse the goals of the women's movement need to look beyond the existing organization of work, and beyond feminism, to a new set of social arrangements in which work becomes itself another aspect of nurture, transcends its present character of individual self-aggrandizement, and comes to serve the needs, not merely of the living, but of generations yet to come.

CHRISTOPHER LASCH
Pittsford, N.Y.
August 1978

INTRODUCTION

As business, politics, and diplomacy grow more savage and warlike, men seek a haven in private life, in personal relations, above all in the family—the last refuge of love and decency. Domestic life, however, seems increasingly incapable of providing these comforts. Hence the undercurrent of anxiety that runs through the vast and growing body of commentary on the state of the family.

Much of that commentary attempts to show that although the family is changing its form and structure, it serves important needs and therefore has a long life ahead of it. Yet the divorce rate continues to climb, generational conflict intensifies, and enlightened opinion condemns the family as a repressive anachronism. Do these developments signify merely the "strain" of the family's "adaptation" to changing social conditions, or do they portend a weakening of the social fabric, a drastic disorganization of all our institutions? Does the family still provide a haven in a heartless world? Or do the very storms out of which the need for such a haven arises threaten to engulf the family as well?

Convinced that much depends on the answer to these questions, I have grown impatient with the quality of the public discussion they provoke. Opinions about the plight of the family clamor on all sides for attention, but they rely too much on vague speculations, vapid pronouncements about "future-shock," and trendy cultural criticism, much of which, ostensibly radical in its condemnation of existing arrangements, is churned out merely to satisfy the demand for cultural novelties. Not only the worst but the best social criticism suffers from a disregard of established traditions of inquiry. It takes the form of isolated perceptions that shine for a time and then fade in the glare of the latest revisionism. Revisionism in American scholarship rarely bothers to master the work it attempts to revise. Even the most original and penetrating of our social critics have cultivated a certain eccentricity. They have deliberately worked in isolation not only from social and political movements but even from the work of other scholars, presenting their ideas as personal judgments on the state of society. These habits explain "the lack of agreement or even clarity about what is being attacked in present-day society and what is to replace it."[1]

The first thing to understand about the present crisis of the family is that it did not materialize overnight. Neofeminists, spokesmen for the so-called counterculture, radical sociologists, practitioners of the "new social history," and the journalists who popularize the ideas of these commentators all treat the plight of the family as a brand-new discovery of their own. They write as if the "sexual revolution," the women's movement, and the decline of parental authority were products of the last fifteen years. Their memories do not extend even as far back as the fifties, a period that stands in current folklore as the heyday of the "traditional" family.

In fact, the family has been slowly coming apart for more than a hundred years. The divorce crisis, feminism, and the revolt of youth originated in the nineteenth century, and they have been the subject of controversy ever since. Popular controversy in turn has given rise to a tradition of sociological study, which still defines the issues that inform most of the current commentary on the family. This book describes and criticizes that tradition, shows how it both reflected and influenced social policy, and analyzes the shattering impact of policy—the impact of the so-called helping professions—on the family. My subject is the intersection of theory, ideology, and social practice. By examining the reciprocal relations between them, by emphasizing the importance of ideas while putting ideas in their historical context, and by rejecting the notion that history automatically unfolds or "evolves," I hope to convince the reader that the contemporary family is the product of human agency, not of abstract social "forces."

The history of modern society, from one point of view, is the assertion of social control over activities once left to individuals or their families. During the first stage of the industrial revolution, capitalists took production out of the household and collectivized it, under their own supervision, in the factory. Then they proceeded to appropriate the workers' skills and technical knowledge, by means of "scientific management," and to bring these skills together under managerial direction. Finally they extended their control over the worker's private life as well, as doctors, psychiatrists, teachers, child guidance experts, officers of the juvenile courts, and other specialists began to supervise child-rearing, formerly the business of the family.

The socialization of production, followed by the socialization of reproduction, has had two contradictory effects. On the one hand, these changes have laid the material basis for a new form of society, in which collective needs rather than private profit determine the form and content of production. On the other hand, they have made people more and more dependent on the managerial and professional classes—on the great business corporations and the state—and have thus eroded the capacity for self-help and social invention. At the very moment when capitalism has not only outlived its usefulness but created the conditions for its own supersession, the will and capacity to replace it have atrophied. The resulting stalemate reminds us again that social change does not occur automatically but requires active human intervention. Men make their own history, although they make it, to be sure, under conditions not of their choosing and sometimes with results the opposite of the results intended.

Anyone who insists on the historical importance of human actions, and who sees history not as an abstract social "process" but as the product of concrete struggles for power, finds himself at odds with the main tradition of the social sciences, which affirms the contrary principle that society runs according to laws of its own. The claim to have discovered these laws is the overriding mystification of social science, which bears the same relation to the later stages of the industrial revolution that the science of political economy bore to the earlier stages. In the eighteenth and nineteenth centuries, the classical economists interpreted industrial capitalism but also provided it with an elaborate apology, which disguised the social relations peculiar to capitalism as universal principles of economics. Whereas those social relations represented the end product of a particular line of historical development in western Europe, political economy mistook them for natural laws, disguised exploitation as the natural order of things, and thus gave class rule an aura of inevitability. Both in capitalist practice and in the theory in which it was mirrored, the relations between men now assumed "the fantastic shape," as Marx put it, "of relations between things."

In the late nineteenth and twentieth centuries, the expansion of the managerial function and the growth of bureaucracy brought into being a new branch of knowledge, social science, which attempted to explain the increasingly dense, opaque network of interpersonal relations so characteristic of advanced societies. Although the social sciences' attack on the commonplace illusion of individual autonomy represented an intellectual advance, their insistence that man is wholly the product of society vitiated this advance and led to new forms of confusion. According to social science, the principle of "interdependence" governs all of modern society. Every part of society is connected to every other part; each part must be understood in relation to the others; the relations among men form a seamless web that defies "monocausal" explanations and sometimes seems to defy explanation of any kind.[2] If political economy failed to see modern market relations as the outcome of a specific historical process (through which peasants and artisans lost control of the means of production and became wage laborers), social science equally fails to see that "interdependence" merely reflects changing modes of class rule: the extension and solidification of capitalist control through the agency of management, bureaucracy, and professionalization.[3] Thus it misrepresents the socialization of reproduction—the expropriation of child rearing by the state and by the health and welfare professions—as an abstract, impersonal social process variously described as the "decline of the extended family," the "transfer of functions," structural and functional "differentiation." The tyranny exercised by these conceptions over historical and sociological studies of the family makes them lifeless and boring. Most studies of the family tell us everything except the things we most want to know. Why has family life become so painful, marriage so fragile, relations between parents and children so full of hostility and recrimination?

A number of historical works have recently enriched our understanding of the "second industrial revolution" of the twentieth century. Carol Gruber's *Mars and Minerva*, Stuart Ewen's *Captains of Consciousness*, Harry Braverman's *Labor and Monopoly Capital*, Russell Jacoby's *Social Amnesia*, and David F. Noble's *America by Design* have analyzed the social transformation implicit in technological change, the transformation of American culture by advertising, the mutual dependence of industry and higher education, and the role of "conformist psychology" in providing ideological support for the prevailing system of social relations. These studies can be read, in part, as a critique of social science and of historical work carried on under its influence—a critique that has become as indispensable to intellectual clarity today as the critique of political economy was to the nineteenth century. Even after these and other works have clarified the socialization of production, however, the socialization of reproduction remains obscure. The "new social history," which has monopolized historical writing on the family, has derived its organizing ideas from the social sciences, whose academic prestige it envies and whose supposed rigor it tries to emulate. In doing so, it perpetuates the misunderstandings about the family that have long flourished among sociologists, anthropologists, and psychiatrists.

Most of the writing on the modern family takes for granted the "isolation" of the nuclear family not only from the kinship system but from the world of work. It assumes that this isolation makes the family impervious to outside influences. In reality, the modern world intrudes at every point and obliterates its privacy. The sanctity of the home is a sham in a world dominated by giant corporations and by the apparatus of mass promotion. Bourgeois society has always held out the promise that private satisfactions will compensate for the reduction of work to a routine, but at the same time it undermines this compromise by organizing leisure itself as an industry. Increasingly the same forces that have impoverished work and civic life invade the private realm and its last stronghold, the family. The tension between the family and the economic and political order, which in an earlier stage of bourgeois society protected children and adolescents from the full impact of the market, gradually abates. The family, drained of the emotional intensity that formerly characterized domestic relations, socializes the young into the easygoing, low-keyed encounters that predominate in the outside world as well.

Whereas in earlier times the family passed along the dominant values but unavoidably provided the child with a glimpse of a world that transcended them, crystallized in the rich imagery of maternal love, capitalism in its late stages has eliminated or at least softened this contradiction. It has reduced conflict between society and the family to a minimum. At the same time, it has intensified almost every other form of conflict. As the world grows more menacing and insecure and the family fails to offer protection from external dangers, all forms of loyalty become increasingly attenuated. The work ethic, nurtured in the nuclear family, gives way to an ethic of survival and immediate gratification. As competition centers on survival rather than achievement, the narcissist replaces the seeker of success and status—the increasingly obsolescent personality type that most social scientists mistake for the still dominant type.

The satire against "privatization," which plays such an important part in recent social criticism, misses the point. The same historical developments that have made it necessary to set up private life—the family in particular—as a refuge from the cruel world of politics and work, an emotional sanctuary, have invaded this sanctuary and subjected it to outside control. A retreat into "privatism" no longer serves to shore up values elsewhere threatened with extinction. Americans can preserve what is valuable in their culture only by changing the conditions of public life itself. Whether they have the energy and imagination to undertake such changes remains to be seen.

Haven in a Heartless World

1

Social Pathologists and the
Socialization of Reproduction

THE MAKING OF
THE MODERN FAMILY

As the chief agency of socialization, the family reproduces cultural
patterns in the individual. It not only imparts ethical norms, providing the child with his first instruction in the prevailing social rules, it
profoundly shapes his character, in ways of which he is not even
aware. The family instills modes of thought and action that become
habitual. Because of its enormous emotional influence, it colors all of
a child's subsequent experience.

The union of love and discipline in the same persons, mother and
father, creates a highly charged environment in which the child
learns lessons he will never get over—not necessarily the explicit
lessons his parents wish him to master. He develops an unconscious
predisposition to act in certain ways and to recreate in later life, in
his relations with lovers and authorities, his earliest experiences.
Parents first embody love and power, and each of their actions con-
veys to the child, quite independently of their overt intentions, the

injunctions and constraints by means of which society attempts to organize experience. If the reproduction of culture were simply a matter of formal instruction and discipline, it could be left to the schools. But it also requires that culture be embedded in personality. Socialization makes the individual want to do what he has to do; the family is the agency to which society entrusts this complex and delicate task.

Of all institutions, the family is the most resistant to change. Given its importance, however, changes in its size and structure, in its emotional organization, and in its relations with the outside world must have enormous impact on the development of personality. Changes in character structure, in turn, accompany or underlie changes in economic and political life. The development of capitalism and the rise of the state reverberate in the individual's inner being. Ever since Max Weber showed the connections between Protestantism and capitalism, and demonstrated, moreover, that the connections lay at the level not of formal religious doctrine but of "psychological sanctions," it has been clear that modern civilization requires, among other things, a profound transformation of personality. The Protestant concept of the calling not only dignified worldly life, insisted on the moral value of work, and legitimized prudent calculation and provision for the future, it also upheld the spiritual dignity of marriage and domesticity. The repudiation of the monastic virtues of poverty and chastity, the upgrading of marriage, and the emergence of a new concept of marriage based on prudence and foresight went hand in hand with the new value attached to capital accumulation. The bourgeois mind conceived of children as hostages to the future and devoted an unprecedented amount of attention to their upbringing. The new style of domestic life created psychological conditions favorable to the emergence of a new type of inner-directed, self-reliant personality—the family's deepest contribution to the needs of a market society based on competition, individualism, postponement of gratification, rational foresight, and the accumulation of worldly goods.

By the end of the eighteenth century, the main features of the bourgeois family system were firmly established in Western Europe and the United States. The distinctive characteristics of this system can be simply, if somewhat schematically, set forth. Compared with practices in most other societies, marriage took place at a late age, and considerable numbers of people remained unmarried. As these demographic facts imply, marriage tended to be arranged by the participants instead of by parents and elders; at best, the elders retained a veto. They allowed young couples to court with a minimum of interference, on the understanding that their own self-restraint would take the place of adult supervision—an expectation that did not appear unreasonable when courting couples were typically young adults themselves and when young women, moreover, had been trained from an early age to accept advances from the other sex without compromising their reputation.

At the same time, men and women did not easily relinquish in marriage the habits of self-inhibition acquired during courtship. The Western marriage system therefore gave rise to much sexual tension and maladjustment, more keenly felt than it would have been felt elsewhere because marriage ideally rested on intimacy and love. The overthrow of arranged marriage took place in the name of romantic love and a new conception of the family as a refuge from the highly competitive and often brutal world of commerce and industry. Husband and wife, according to this ideology, were to find solace and spiritual renewal in each other's company. The woman in particular would serve, in a well-worn nineteenth-century phrase, as an "angel of consolation."

Her mission of mercy extended to her children as well, around whom middle-class family life increasingly centered. A new idea of childhood helped to precipitate the new idea of the family. No longer seen simply as a little adult, the child came to be regarded as a person with distinctive attributes—impressionability, vulnerability, innocence—which required a warm, protected, and prolonged period of nurture. Whereas formerly children had mixed freely in adult society, parents now sought to segregate them from premature contact with servants and other corrupting influences. Educators and moralists began to stress the child's need for play, for love and understanding, and for the gradual, gentle unfolding of his nature. Child rearing became more demanding as a result, and emotional ties between parents and children grew more intense at the same time that ties to relatives outside the immediate family weakened. Here was another source of persistent tension in the middle-class family: the emotional overloading of the parent-child connection.

Still another source of tension was the change in the status of women which the new family system required. The bourgeois family simultaneously degraded and exalted women. On the one hand, it deprived them of many of their traditional employments, as the household ceased to be a center of production and devoted itself to child rearing instead. On the other hand, the new demands of child rearing, at a time when so much attention was being given to the special needs of the child, made it necessary to educate women for their domestic duties. Better education would also make women more suitable companions for their husbands. The new domesticity implied a thoroughgoing reform and extension of women's education, as Mary Wollstonecraft, the first modern feminist, understood when she insisted that if women were to become "affectionate wives and rational mothers," they would have to be trained in something more than "accomplishments" designed to make young ladies attractive to prospective suitors.[1] Early republican ideology had as one of its main tenets the proposition that women should become useful rather than ornamental. In the categories immortalized by Jane Austen, women had to give up sensibility in favor of sense. Thus bourgeois domesticity gave rise to its antithesis, feminism. The domestication of woman gave rise to a general unrest, encouraging her to entertain aspirations that marriage and the family could not satisfy. These aspirations became an important ingredient in the so-called marriage crisis that began to unfold at the end of the nineteenth century.

The bourgeois family system, then, which attained its full flowering in the nineteenth century and now seems to be slowly decaying, rested on what sociologists have called companionate marriage, on the child-centered household, on the emancipation or quasi-emancipation of women, and on the structural isolation of the nuclear family from the kinship system and from society in general. The family found ideological support and justification in the conception of domestic life as an emotional refuge in a cold and competitive society. The concept of the family as a haven in a heartless world took for granted a radical separation between work and leisure and between public life and private life. The emergence of the nuclear family as the principal form of family life reflected the high value modern society attached to privacy, and the glorification of privacy in turn reflected the devaluation of work. As production became more complex and efficient, work became increasingly specialized, fragmented, and routine. Accordingly, work came to be seen as merely a means to an end—for many, sheer physical survival; for others, a rich and satisfying personal life. No longer regarded as a satisfying occupation in its own right, work had to be redefined as a way of achieving satisfactions or consolations outside work. Production, in this view, is interesting and important only because it enables us to enjoy the delights of consumption. At a deeper level of mystification, social labor—the collective self-realization of mankind through its transformation of nature—appears merely as the satisfaction of private wants.

There is an even deeper sense in which mechanization and the introduction of routine degraded the act of work. The products of human activity, especially the higher products of that activity such as the social order itself, took on the appearance of something external and alien to mankind. No longer recognizably the product of human invention, the man-made world appeared as a collection of objects independent of human intervention and control. Having objectified himself in his work, man no longer recognized it as his own. Thus the classical economists described the capitalist economy, the collective creation of human ingenuity and toil, as a machine that ran according to immutable laws of its own, laws analogous to the laws of nature. These principles, even if they had existed in reality (instead of merely in the minds of Adam Smith and Ricardo), were inaccessible to everyday observation. In the lay mind, therefore, the market economy defied not merely human control but human understanding. It appeared as a complex network of abstractions, utterly impenetrable and opaque. John Adams once demonstrated his grasp of modern banking and credit by complaining that "every dollar of a bank bill that is issued beyond the quantity of gold and silver in the vaults represents nothing and is therefore a cheat upon somebody." [2] Jefferson and Jackson held the same opinion. If the governing classes labored under such confusion, we can easily imagine the confusion of the ordinary citizen. He lived in a world of abstractions, where the relations between men, as Marx observed, assumed the fantastic shape of relations between things. Thus labor-power became a commodity, measurable in abstract monetary terms, and was bought and sold on the market like any other commodity.

At bottom, the glorification of private life and the family represented the other side of the bourgeois perception of society as something alien, impersonal, remote, and abstract—a world from which pity and tenderness had fled in horror. Deprivations experienced in the public world had to be compensated in the realm of privacy. Yet the very conditions that gave rise to the need to view privacy and the family as a refuge from the larger world made it more and more difficult for the family to serve in that capacity.

THE CRISIS OF THE FAMILY AT THE
END OF THE NINETEENTH CENTURY

By the end of the nineteenth century, American newspapers and magazines brimmed with speculation about the crisis of marriage and the family. Four developments gave rise to a steadily growing alarm: the rising divorce rate, the falling birthrate among "the better sort of people," the changing position of women, and the so-called revolution in morals.

Between 1870 and 1920, the number of divorces increased fifteenfold. By 1924, one out of every seven marriages ended in divorce, and there was no reason to think that the trend toward more and more frequent divorce would reverse itself.[3]

Meanwhile "the diminution of the birth rate among the highest races," as Theodore Roosevelt put it in 1897, gave rise to the fear that the highest races would soon be outnumbered by their inferiors, who multiplied, it was said, with total disregard for their ability to provide for the rising generation.[4] The better sort of people, on the other hand, allegedly paid too much attention not only to the future but to their own present comfort. In the opinion of conservatives, the middle class had grown soft and selfish, especially middle-class women, who preferred the social whirl to the more serious pleasures of motherhood. Brooks Adams, spokesman for crusty upper-class reaction, described the new woman as the "highest product of a civilization that has rotted before it could ripen."[5] Progressives too fretted about the declining birthrate, but they blamed it on the high cost of living and rising standards of comfort, which led young men either to avoid marriage or to postpone it as long as possible. Women were not to blame for "race suicide," according to a leading women's magazine. The "actual cause" was the "cost of living impelling the masses to pauperdom." The American man, with reason, was "afraid of a large family."[6]

The changing status of women struck the most casual observer as one of the most telling signs of the times. More and more women went to college, joined clubs and organizations of all kinds, and entered the labor force. What explained all this activity, and what did it signify for the future of the family? The feminists had a simple answer, at least to the first of these questions: women were merely "following their work out of the home." Industry had invaded the family, stripped it of its productive functions. Work formerly carried on in the household could now be carried out more efficiently in the factory. Even recreation and child rearing were being taken over by outside agencies, the former by the dance hall and the popular theater, the latter by the school. Women had no choice but to "follow their occupations or starve," emotionally if not in literal fact. Confined to the family, women would become parasites, unproductive "consumers upon the state," as a feminist writer put it in 1910.[7]

Faced with an argument that condemned leisure as a form of parasitism, antifeminists could have insisted on the positive value of leisure as the precondition of art, learning, and higher forms of thought, arguing that its benefits ought to be extended to the American businessman. But an attack on feminism launched from an essentially aristocratic point of view—an attack that condemned feminism as itself an expression of middle-class moralism and philistinism—hardly recommended itself to those who wished above everything else to preserve the sanctity of the home. American critics of feminism preferred to base their case on the contention that woman's usefulness to society and her own self-fulfilling work lay precisely in her sacred duties as wife and mother. The major premise of feminism—that women should be useful, not ornamental—had to be conceded, even while the conclusions feminists drew from this premise—the conclusions, they would have argued, that followed irresistibly—were vigorously repudiated.

For the same reason, critics had to avoid a total condemnation of the feminist movement. Even denunciation of the new woman's "selfishness" was risky. In the mid-nineteenth century, defenders of the home had relied heavily on appeals to woman's duty to sacrifice herself for the good of others, but by 1900 this kind of rhetoric, even when translated into the progressive jargon of "service," had begun to seem decidedly out-of-date. The view that woman lived best by living for others gradually gave way to the view that woman too had a right to self-fulfillment—a right, however, that could best be realized in the home. In a word, the critics of feminism began to argue that motherhood and housewifery themselves constituted satisfying "careers," which required special training in "homemaking," "domestic science," and "home economics." The invention of such terms expressed an attempt to dignify housework by raising it to the level of a profession. By rationalizing the household and child care, some of the opponents of feminism probably hoped also to make the family a more effective competitor with the outside agencies that were taking over its functions. Ironically, the rationalization of housework rendered the housewife more dependent than ever on the help of outside experts.

If feminism disturbed the partisans of domesticity with its criticism of the home's inefficiency and its attempt to provide the "restlessness" of modern women with outlets beyond the family, the movement to liberate sexuality from conventional restraints troubled them more deeply. Feminism at least allied itself with progressivism and with the vision of woman's purifying influence over society; indeed, the very success with which it identified itself with dominant themes in middle-class culture forced antifeminists to refrain from attacking it frontally. The "new morality," on the other hand, directly challenged prevailing sexual ethics. It proclaimed the joys of the body, defended divorce and birth control, raised doubts about monogamy, and condemned interference with sexual life by the state or community.

Yet even here, defenders of the family soon learned that unyielding condemnation by no means served as the best strategy. Instead of trying to annihilate the new morality, they domesticated it—

stripped away everything in the ideology of sexual emancipation that threatened monogamy, while celebrating a freer and more enlightened sexuality within marriage. Incidentally, this operation provided the housewife with another role to complement her new role of consumer-in-chief: the multifaceted role of sexual partner, companion, playmate, and therapist.

Sex radicals, however, did more than call for a revolution in morals; they claimed that such a revolution was already under way. They cited statistical surveys that seemed to show a growing trend toward adultery and premarital sex.[8] Faced with this evidence, the beleaguered champions of marriage once again executed a strategic retreat. The statistics showed, they argued, that American men and women had rejected not marriage but merely the "sex-monopoly ideal" with which marriage had formerly been rather unnecessarily associated. Since "emphasis on exclusive sex possession" actually had a "destructive effect," it could safely be abandoned. Similarly, modern society could dispense with the "virginity standard"—the requirement that the woman be a virgin at marriage. Exclusiveness in sex should be regarded as an ideal to be approximated, not as a standard to be imposed on everyone from without. Each man and wife should decide for themselves whether to consider infidelity as evidence of disloyalty.[9]

Another piece of ideological baggage that had to be thrown overboard was the notion that marriage should be free of conflict and tension. According to the emerging body of authoritative opinion on marriage (and to spokesmen for arrangements that later came to be known as "open marriage"), marital quarrels should be regarded as normal events to be taken in stride and even turned to productive purposes. Quarrels might even have a beneficial effect if properly "stage-managed" and rounded off with "an artistic consummation."[10]

A fierce attack on romantic love played as important a part in the defense of marriage as in the criticism of marriage. Romantic love, it was thought, set impossibly high standards of devotion and loyalty, standards marriage could no longer meet. By undermining "sober-satisfying everyday life," romance wrought as much havoc as prudery, its twin.[11] In the minds of radicals and conservatives alike, romantic love was associated with illusions, dangerous fantasies, and disease; with consumptive heroines, heroes wasting away with fe-

verish desire, and deathbed farewells; with the overwrought, unhealthy music of Wagner, Strauss, and Puccini. Romantic love
threatened both psychic and physical stability. The fashionable talk
of marriage as an art conveyed a conception of marriage and the family that derived not so much from aesthetics as from science and
technology—in particular, from the science of healing. When marriage experts said that marriage represented the art of personal "interaction," they meant that marriage, like everything else, rested on
proper technique: the technique of stage-managing quarrels, the
technique of mutual agreement on how much adultery the marriage
could tolerate, the technique of what to do in bed and how to do it.
The new sex manuals, which began to proliferate in the twenties and
thirties, provided merely the most obvious example of the rationalization of emotional life in the interest of psychic health. Marriage
experts saw "illusion," fantasy, inner life as threats to stability and
equilibrium. They proposed to save marriage at the expense of private life, which they simultaneously expected marriage to foster.
Their program eroded the distinction between private life and the
marketplace, turning all forms of play, even sex, into work. Thus
"achievement" of orgasm, according to medical and psychiatric opinion, required not only proper technique but effort, determination,
and emotional control.

THE PROLETARIANIZATION

OF PARENTHOOD

Those who insisted on the importance of the family—even the
"stripped-down" family created, in their view, by the industrial revolution—adopted self-defeating strategies of defense. At the same
time that they exalted the family as the last refuge of privacy in a forbidding society, the guardians of public health and morality insisted
that the family could not provide for its own needs without expert intervention. Some of them, indeed, had so little confidence in the
family that they proposed to transfer its socializing functions to other
agencies; others wanted merely to improve the quality of family life

through ambitious programs of "parent education," marriage counseling, and psychiatric social work. The difference between these strategies distinguished social democrats and progressives from more conservative practitioners; yet both programs intensified the very "crisis" to which they claimed to hold out the solution.

Historians of the family have paid too little attention to the way in which public policy, sometimes conceived quite deliberately not as a defense of the family at all but as an invasion of it, contributed to the deterioration of domestic life. The family did not simply evolve in response to social and economic influences; it was deliberately transformed by the intervention of planners and policymakers. Educators and social reformers saw that the family, especially the immigrant family, stood as an obstacle to what they conceived as social progress—in other words, to homogenization and "Americanization." The family preserved separatist religious traditions, alien languages and dialects, local lore, and other traditions that retarded the growth of the political community and the national state. Accordingly, reformers sought to remove children from the influence of their families, which they also blamed for exploiting child labor, and to place the young under the benign influence of state and school.

Émile Durkheim, often referred to as the founder of modern sociology, stated in the most sweeping terms the program of educational reformers in all advanced countries and the rationale behind it. Whereas the family specialized in "emotional release and the sharing of affections," the school, according to Durkheim, constituted

a real group, of which the child is naturally and necessarily a part. . . . Consequently, we have through the school the means of training the child in a collective life different from home life. We have here a unique and irreplaceable opportunity to take hold of the child at a time when the gaps in our social organization have not yet been able to arouse in him feelings that make him partially rebellious to common life.

Society itself, according to this logic, would eventually take the place of the private family. "Society is the benevolent and protecting power, the nourishing mother from which we gain the whole of our moral and intellectual substance and toward whom our wills turn in a spirit of love and gratitude." [12]

The principles of *Solidarité* found their American equivalent in the progressive movement, which sought to regulate anarchic business conditions, reduce social and economic inequality through edu-

cational reform and taxation, and promote "cooperation" between
workers and capitalists, government and industry. Convinced that
"interdependence" had emerged as the ruling principle of industrial
society, American progressives hoped to eliminate selfish individualism by exposing children as early as possible to the influence of
the school, the juvenile courts, and other agencies of socialized tuition. "There is no more brilliant hope on earth to-day," wrote Charlotte Perkins Gilman in her critique of the family, "than this new
thought about the child . . . the recognition of 'the child,' children
as a class, children as citizens with rights to be guaranteed only by
the state; instead of our previous attitude toward them of absolute
personal ownership—the unchecked tyranny, or as unchecked in-
dulgence, of the private home." The family institutionalized selfishness, in Gilman's view. "Civilization and Christianity teach us to
care for 'the child,' motherhood stops at 'my child.' "[13]

Opponents of child labor proposed to transfer children from
parental exploitation to the loving care of the school. "The best
child-labor law," said Florence Kelley, "is a compulsory education
law covering forty weeks of the year and requiring the consecutive
attendance of all the children to the age of fourteen years."[14] According to Ellen Richards, one of the founders of professional social
work, the school was "fast taking the place of the home, not because
it wishes to do so, but because the home does not fulfill its function."
The family produced misfits, emotional cripples, juvenile delinquents, and potential criminals, according to this reasoning. "If the
State is to have good citizens . . . we must begin to teach the children in our schools, and begin at once, that which we see they are
no longer learning in the home."[15]

The belief that the family no longer provided for its needs justified
the expansion of the school and of social welfare services. "Social,
political, and industrial changes," educators claimed, "have forced
upon the school responsibilities formerly laid upon the home. Once
the school had mainly to teach the elements of knowledge, now it is
charged with the physical, mental, and social training of the child as
well."[16] "Breakdowns in family morale," according to social workers, underlay crime and "social disorganization."[17] Through children's aid societies, juvenile courts, and family visits, they sought to
counteract the widespread "lack of wisdom and understanding on
the part of parents, teachers, and others," while at the same time

reassuring the mother who feared, with good reason, that the social worker meant to take her place in the home.[18] By the twenties, psychiatric social workers understood the importance of the public relations of mental health and went to great lengths to put such fears to rest. Yet they simultaneously extended the profession's claim to stand in loco parentis. Charlotte Towle, for example, argued that the social worker stood in a "parent-child" relation to her clients. Those who came to her for help experienced a "deep-lying need to be guided by a parental hand," making it necessary for the social worker "to play in secure fashion the mature parent role in social leadership."[19]

In order to justify their appropriation of parental functions, the "helping professions" in their formative period—roughly from 1900 to 1930—appealed many times to the analogy of preventive medicine and public health. Educators, psychiatrists, social workers, and penologists saw themselves as doctors to a sick society, and they demanded the broadest possible delegation of medical authority in order to heal it. The medical profession, they claimed, had learned to prevent disease rather than simply relieving its symptoms, and social pathologists had to master the same lesson. They argued, indeed, that a broad movement to substitute prevention for custody and punishment had already taken shape. Mental asylums, formerly custodial institutions, now emphasized prevention and cure.[20] Social work had abandoned the "case-by-case method" in favor of " 'mass' movements for prevention."[21] Penology no longer punished the criminal but devoted itself to the prevention of crime. "The new penology," wrote the social worker Edward T. Devine, "is not sentimental. . . . It sentences, however, to a hospital by preference rather than to a dungeon. It sentences to cleanliness, good food, and wholesome discipline, and not to infection and degradation."[22]

The reform of juvenile justice in the progressive period best exemplifies the connections between therapeutic conceptions of society, the rise of social pathology as a profession, and the appropriation of familial functions by agencies of socialized reproduction. The juvenile court movement rested on the belief that juvenile delinquency originated in deformed homes. Accordingly, the juvenile delinquent was to be treated not as a criminal but as a victim of circumstances. In order to give him the "protection" of the law, humanitarian reformers created a new type of noncriminal equity, probation, and endowed probation officers with many of the rights of parenthood. They took a broad view of the state's powers as a surrogate parent. According to Jenkin Lloyd Jones, all children were children of the state. "The state is but the coordinated parentage of childhood, yielding to the inexorable logic of civilization that will compel co-partnership, co-operation, corporate life and conscience."[23]

In eliminating the adversary relationship between the juvenile offender and the law, these reformers congratulated themselves on having substituted enlightened medical jurisprudence for the barbarous customs of the past. In fact, however, they made it possible to sentence the juvenile offender, without a trial, to the custody of the very "same probation officer whose testimony had placed them at the court's mercy in the first place."[24] It is not surprising that the incidence of juvenile delinquency rose with the expansion of the probation system. Professional "helpers," ignoring such evidence, attributed the increase in delinquency to public unwillingness to grant the courts full powers of parenthood. Nor did they heed the cries of anguished parents, one of whom wrote to Judge Ben Lindsey, "When my son is so ruthlessly torn away from me, it gives me much pain."[25] Although Lindsey's court in Denver at first had no legal authority to treat juvenile offenders as a special category, Lindsey proceeded to do so anyway, on the grounds that "it is not so much a question of law as a question of doing the thing."[26]

In the twenties, Lindsey shocked respectable opinion with his advocacy of "companionate marriage." He wanted to improve the quality of married life by educating people in sexual hygiene, eliminating the punitive features of marriage and divorce law, and drawing a sharp legal distinction between childless marriages and the "procreative family." By allowing childless couples to divorce by mutual consent, Lindsey hoped to prevent couples who were ill-matched or unfit for parenthood from entering more permanent unions and from raising families. In effect, he wished to professionalize parenthood, disqualifying those who had failed to achieve stable unions. Ultimately, he thought, the state would license parenthood, thereby specializing the child-rearing function in a privileged sector of the population and freeing the rest for childless unions based on sexual companionship alone. Under such a regime, made technologically feasible for the first time by the development of cheap and effective contraceptives, "the unfit of the human species," Lindsey predicted, "would virtually cease to reproduce their kind." [27]

Like other reformers, Lindsey had a low opinion of American parents and hoped to counteract their influence both through the juvenile court and through elaborate programs of sex education in the schools. Just as "Golden Rule" Jones and Brand Whitlock in Toledo had attempted to abrogate whole categories of crime by abrogating the blue laws that made harmless activities illegal, so Lindsey proposed to legalize fornication within the normal course of monogamous relationships, under proper precautions against unwanted births. In both cases, the argument for dissolving the apparatus of "puritanical" repression rested on the premise that the activities in question had become too widespread to stamp out and that intelligent regulation and licensing promised better results than prohibition. According to Lindsey, the practice of living together before marriage was already common, and if it often had pathological consequences, these could be attributed precisely to the attempt to stamp it out. In essence, he asked that legal processes embodying allegedly outmoded concepts such as guilt and sin be converted into medical ones. Along with his obsession with health and eugenics, this adherence to a medical definition of crime and social disorder identified Lindsey as a prime spokesman for the emerging health industry, which hoped to redefine crime and immorality as ignorance, "maladjustment," and "mental illness" and to monopolize their "treatment." He described his clients as misguided, misinformed, and inadequately educated rather than immoral. "The Juvenile Court of Denver," he insisted, "is a hospital, a moral hospital. It deals with the sick and crippled of spirit." Like other interpreters and partisans of the so-called sexual revolution, Lindsey hoped more than anything else to promote a "healthy" attitude toward sex—to get people to "take Sex as much for granted as the weather." [28]

In early modern times, Philip Rieff has observed, the church or cathedral stood as the symbolic center of society; in the nineteenth century, the legislative hall took its place, and in our time, the hospital. [29] With the medicalization of society, people came to equate deviance not with crime (much less with sin) but with sickness, and medical jurisprudence replaced an older form of justice designed to protect private rights. With the rise of the "helping professions" in the first three decades of the twentieth century, society in the guise of a "nurturing mother" invaded the family, the stronghold of those private rights, and took over many of its functions. The diffusion of the new ideology of social welfare had the effect of a self-fulfilling prophecy. By persuading the housewife, and finally even her husband as well, to rely on outside technology and the advice of outside experts, the apparatus of mass tuition—the successor to the church in a secularized society—undermined the family's capacity to provide for itself and thereby justified the continuing expansion of health, education, and welfare services.

Having monopolized the knowledge necessary to socialize the young, the agencies of socialized reproduction then parceled it out piecemeal in the form of "parent education." As two child guidance experts put it in 1934, "Old functions of child welfare and training have passed over into the hands of sociologists, psychiatrists, physicians, home economists and other scientists dealing with problems of human welfare. Through parent education the sum of their experiments and knowledge is given back to parents in response to their demand for help."[30] Having first declared parents incompetent to raise their offspring without professional help, social pathologists "gave back" the knowledge they had appropriated—gave it back in a mystifying fashion that rendered parents more helpless than ever, more abject in their dependence on expert opinion.

The socialization of reproduction completed the process begun by the socialization of production itself—that is, by industrialization. Having expropriated the worker's tools and concentrated production in the factory, industrialists in the opening decades of the twentieth century proceeded to expropriate the worker's technical knowledge as well. By means of "scientific management," they broke down production into its component parts, assigned a specific function on the assembly line to each worker, and kept to themselves the knowledge of the productive process as a whole. In order to administer this knowledge, they created a vastly enlarged managerial apparatus, an army of engineers, technicians, personnel managers, and industrial psychologists drawn from the same pool of technical experts that simultaneously staffed the "helping professions." Knowledge became an industry in its own right, while the worker, deprived of the craft knowledge by which he had retained practical control of production even after the introduction of the factory system, sank into passive dependence. Eventually, industry organized management itself along industrial lines, splitting up the production of knowledge into routinized operations carried on by semiskilled clerical labor: secretaries, typists, computer card punchers, and other lackeys. The socialization of production—under the control of private industry—proletarianized the labor force in the same way that the socialization of reproduction proletarianized parenthood, by making people unable to provide for their own needs without the supervision of trained experts.[31]

Here too, therapeutic modes of thought and practice predominated. Industrial sociologists and personnel managers sought to eliminate labor-management conflicts by translating collective grievances into personal ones, the sense of injustice into personal "problems," ideology into technique. They insisted that friction between workers and owners originated not in irreconcilable conflicts of interest but in the psychology of the individual worker. Therapy replaced politics as the way to "effect improvements" in the worker's condition.[32] When other methods failed, the experts recommended the universal cure-all of consumption, urging the worker to look on consumption as the consolation for deprivations suffered at work. Industrialists began to understand the importance of the worker in his capacity as consumer. The more farsighted among them preached the need to integrate the working class into modern society and culture by means of improved education, mass culture, and advertising. According to a spokesman for the advertising industry, advertising exercised a "civilizing influence comparable in its cultural effects to those of other great epoch-making developments in history." Calvin Coolidge put it more succinctly: advertising, he said, "is the method by which the desire is created for better things."[33]

The propaganda of commodities became in its own right one of the principal agencies of socialized reproduction. Like the helping professions, it undermined puritanical morality and patriarchal authority, subtly allying itself with women against men, children against parents. Consumerism dictated a larger role for women and a limited equality with men. Women had to become equals in the management of household expenditures. They had to become more nearly equal to men in order to enjoy sex and satisfy their husbands. From the moment it began to glimpse its "civilizing" mission, advertising identified itself with the pseudo-emancipation of women, recently epitomized in the slogan "You've come a long way, baby."

Similarly, advertising glorified youth. Advertising men, like psychiatrists and professional experts, claimed to understand the "needs" of the young better than their parents did. On the one hand, advertisers insisted that the needs of the young should occupy the first place in parents' thoughts. On the other hand, they undermined parents' confidence in their ability to provide for those needs. Only modern science and technology, it appeared, could provide the growing child with the proper nutrition, the proper medical care, and the social skills he needed in order to function in the modern world.

In the twenties, the first results of the combined attack on the old-style family began to come into view: the rise of the flapper, the revolt of youth, the "revolution in manners and morals." At the time, many observers saw in these developments the complete collapse of public order, but in retrospect it is clear that they merely facilitated the incorporation of women and youth into the market as full-fledged consumers, perpetually restless and dissatisfied. The combined influence of advertising and the "helping professions" had liberated people from old constrictions only to expose them to more subtle forms of control. These agencies freed personal life from the repressive scrutiny of church and state only to subject it to medical and psychiatric scrutiny or the manipulation of the advertising industry. Insisting on the privacy of sex and marriage, they gave the most intimate acts unprecedented publicity. Upholding the family as the last stronghold of spontaneity, they sought to expel from marriage, love, and sex precisely the irregular, the unpredictable, the unmanageable. The "repeal of reticence" lifted the shroud of sexual ignorance but imposed the new constraint of an allegedly scientific technique, in the light of which sexual "performance" would be judged and usually found wanting.[34] Lawgiver and priest retired from sexual supervision only to make way for the doctor, whose supervision was far more thorough. The older authorities had proscribed acts that threatened the stability of the community; the rest they left to discretion. Doctors, on the other hand, sought to shore up the psychic stability of the individual and therefore omitted nothing from their gaze. The disenchantment of erotic life dispelled many superstitions but reduced it to a routine. The establishment of medical and industrial jurisdiction over marriage thus defeated its own purpose, to strengthen the last bastion of privacy.

2

Sociological Study of the Family in the Twenties and Thirties: "From Institution to Companionship"

THE RISE OF
SOCIAL SCIENCE

The applied science of social control grew up side by side with a pure "science" of society. The two movements exercised a reciprocal influence on each other. Experts in social pathology drew their underlying assumptions from social science; at the same time, practical social therapy defined many of the problems social scientists attempted to solve. No matter how assiduously academic students of society sought to establish the purity of their science and its freedom from assumptions of value, they seldom rose above their preoccupation with questions the urgency of which had already crystallized in the course of clinical practice.

Social science owed its very existence to the rise of new modes of social control. In former times, power surrounded itself with elaborate apologetics, philosophical defenses of the status quo. As religion gave way to law as the principal source of social cohesion, and law to social therapy, the governing classes no longer attempted to mediate their pretensions with appeals to legitimacy. They appealed only to the unmediated authority of the fact. They asked not that the citizen or worker submit to legitimate authority but that he submit to reality itself. Those who wielded power now discouraged inquiries into the principle of its origins. Hence the decay of philosophy and the rise of social science. The new forms of control sought to ground themselves not in the superego—the internalized compulsion to obey—but in the ego's sense of reality. As religion and politics gave way to the new antireligion of mental health, authority identified itself not with what ought to be but with what is. Not the superego's harsh command but the "reality-testing" routinely conducted by the ego was to assure the individual that resistance had become, not unprincipled, but "unrealistic."

The science of society did not fully establish itself as the successor to philosophy and the humanities, in the American university, until the 1940s and 1950s. By the end of the nineteenth century, however, it had already formulated its overriding assumptions: that man is wholly the product of society and culture; that society consists of a network of interpersonal relationships; that social development creates more and more intricate patterns of interdependence; and that this interdependence reveals itself above all in the division and subdivision of labor and the "differentiation" of social functions. In rejecting the idealist illusion that man is the autonomous creator of his own destiny, social science also rejected the truth precariously preserved within the idealist tradition of philosophy—that society represents the collective creation of human intelligence and will, and that for this very reason men retain the collective capacity to understand their own work and even to rise above its historical limitations. Men are both the products of society (more accurately, of the conflict between instinctual drives and the social pressures that seek to repress them) and the creators of society. Men's increasing alienation from their own works, however, obscures the second of these conditions and creates the illusion that society obeys laws of its own and acts like an autonomous organism, totally independent of human will. Social science intellectualized this popular illusion. Just as political economy described capitalism as the product not of historical development but of natural laws, social science described the surface of modern society without penetrating its inner, historical principles.

In modern society, relations among men appear to form a seamless web existing independent not only of human volition but of any recognizable principle of causality. In reality, this "interdependence" merely reflects changing modes of domination. Whereas the lord's domination of the serf was direct and unmediated (the forcible expropriation of the serf's labor by the lord) in modern society, where labor is "free," a complex network of civil institutions mediates the domination of one class by another. Indeed, it was the emergence of "civil society" as something distinct from the state, and the need to understand how it operates, that gave rise to modern social thought in the first place. As the rule of force gave way to the rule of law, social relations became increasingly mysterious and opaque. Political economy and later social science claimed to have unlocked the secret principle of modern society; but the sociological theory of the social order as an organism with a life of its own and as something more than the sum of its parts, in Durkheim's phrase, merely gave scientific standing to an illusion more insidious, in its way, than the commonsense perception of individual autonomy—a perception which, in any case, could not survive the substitution of abstract relations for face-to-face relations of dominance and submission.

The rise of civil society mediated domination; yet beneath the appearance of contractual freedom, individual autonomy, and the rule of reason, domination still continued as the motor of history, class rule as the basis of wealth and economic power, and force as the basis of justice. Social science, ignoring all this, stuck to the surface of society and converted commonplace truisms—the interrelatedness of all social phenomena, the difficulty of assigning causality, the importance of "multicausal" explanations—into the highest principles of its science, where they served, thus elevated from the

dusty plain of the obvious to the empyrean of the recondite and obscure, as elaborate and plausible mystifications.

GENERAL THEORIES OF THE FAMILY'S

ORIGIN AND EVOLUTION

Applied to the study of the family, these sociological principles had
the effect of disguising the socialization of reproduction—the expropriation of parental functions by agencies outside the family—as an
abstract, impersonal, evolutionary process known as the "transfer of
functions." It took a long time, however, to work out the implications of a sociological theory of the modern family. Until the 1920s,
academic sociology in the United States remained almost completely
oblivious to contemporary developments. It fixed its attention on
prehistory and the primitive. It did not distinguish its subject matter
from that of anthropology, and both disciplines, moreover, labored
under the sway of evolutionary theories of social change, which had
brought them together in the first place. Both originated in the
belief, antedating Darwin, that laws of social evolution could be
derived from historical studies conducted on the broadest possible
scale. One of the areas in which the search for evolutionary laws
went on most intensively was precisely the family, around which
scholars waged a controversy far more absorbing to most of them
than the controversy touched off by Carroll Wright's divorce statistics in 1889.[1] The argument raised broad issues touching not just the
family but all of history, and by no means irrelevant to the future.
Adherents of the matriarchal theory of the family, following
Bachofen and Morgan, argued that society had evolved successive
forms of marriage and the family, patriarchal organization having
been preceded by a matriarchal stage in which women dominated
the family and much else besides. These theories, in addition to
their cultural and historical implications, had political implications
congenial to feminists and socialists. If the patriarchal family had
emerged only in the most recent stage of evolutionary time, there

was nothing sacred about it. An opponent of the matriarchal theory accurately observed: "One of the arguments which has been brought forward in support of an extreme form of Communism and State Socialism is, that the Family has been merely the temporary product of a particular stage of economic development, and that with the sweeping away of capitalism and private property the Family also will disappear."[2] The polemical thrust of the matriarchal theory was so obvious that Max Weber habitually referred to it as the "socialistic theory of the family."

The patriarchal theory of the family's origins, as first stated by Sir Henry Maine in 1861—the same year in which Bachofen published his work on "mother-right"—suffered initially from the disadvantage that it reached no further into the past than classical antiquity. The advocates of the matriarchal theory, on the other hand, accumulated a long list of matriarchal "survivals" in primitive societies, which presumably still lived at a much more rudimentary stage of social evolution than the Romans had. In the 1890s, Edward Westermarck attempted to refute the matriarchal theory on its own ground by ransacking the already enormous literature on primitive societies for evidence of the priority not so much of the patriarchal family as of monogamous marriage. According to Westermarck, monogamy had roots in biology—in the prolonged dependence of the human infant and its need for extended parental care. Sexual communism, treated by Morgan and Bachofen as the earliest form of "marriage," did not meet these requirements. By focusing on the universality of monogamy, Westermarck confronted the matriarchal theory at one of its weakest points, without having to defend the antiquity of the patriarchal family as such—a more dubious proposition, it appeared, in light of evidence that many societies had passed through a stage in which descent was traced through the female line. Partisans of the matriarchal theory, meanwhile, had given up the attempt to show that women once ruled the family; they now concentrated on the issue of descent, which both sides mistakenly agreed to be an important index of the status of women.

These disputes enlisted enormous energy and excitement but in the long run proved inconclusive. Disenchantment set in, not only with patriarchal and matriarchal theories of the family's origin but with general theories of all kinds. Without intending to, Westermarck himself contributed to this result by attempting to undermine the idea that all societies passed through the same sequence of evolutionary stages and by invoking special demographic causes—for example, a shortage of men or women—to explain polyandry, polygyny, and other deviations from the monogamic norm. Yet neither Westermarck nor his followers and critics went so far as to question the usefulness of evolutionary modes of explanation. They sought merely to restrict their range. Even Le Play, whose studies of the family were intended to refute evolutionary doctrines, applied an evolutionary framework to the history of Europe.[3] By later standards, Le Play's work, like that of the German scholar Ernst Grosse, remained much too speculative and sweeping, but it looked modest compared to that of Bachofen, Morgan, and Westermarck. Grosse and Le Play cared less to resolve the debate over matriarchal versus patriarchal origins than to analyze the gradual decline of the extended family in Europe. Their writings, though roughly contemporaneous with those of the grand evolutionary theorists, reflected more directly the growing concern about the "instability" of the modern family.

Early twentieth-century sociologists in the United States contented themselves for the most part with summarizing the work of their nineteenth-century predecessors. Elsie Clews Parsons, James Dealey, and Willystine Goodsell all began their studies of the family by rehearsing the controversy between matriarchal and patriarchal theories. Like Westermarck, they rejected both the theory of primitive promiscuity and Maine's theory of the patriarchal structure of the earliest family. Widespread evidence of matrilineal descent, they argued, contradicted Maine but by no means vindicated the theory of a golden age of women—a vision, according to Helen Bosanquet, that "we are forced, however reluctantly, to abandon." Matrilineal descent could coexist with patriarchal power, but that power rested on a brute force "incapable of organising the Patriarchal Family in its fullest sense." For this very reason, however, women held an even lower position in primitive society than under patriarchy proper. In arguing that the history of civilization exhibits a more or less steady improvement in women's condition, early academic sociologists echoed Westermarck once again.[4]

Having dealt with the anthropological background of the modern family, these writers went on to treat, sometimes cursorily, sometimes in much detail, the history of the transition from the extended family to the "modern simple family." The historical studies of George E. Howard, a historian of law and institutions, and Arthur W. Calhoun, a sociologist, also followed this procedure. Howard's *History of Matrimonial Institutions* opens with an elaborate account of the debates among evolutionary theorists, partial to Westermarck, and then traces changes in the law of marriage from prehistory to the present. Calhoun, writing ten years later, devotes the same amount of space (three volumes) to the history of the American family alone—another indication of the retreat from grand theoretical synthesis. A combination of institutional history and a newer type of social history, Calhoun's book still shows the influence of evolutionary thought; its interpretive framework, insofar as it has one, derives from the "socialistic theory of the family." Calhoun argues that the "evolution" of the family follows economic evolution, that "patriarchism and familism" have been rendered obsolete by the passing of the economic arrangements on which they were based, and that the transition from individualism to socialism—the "next stage in social evolution"—can be expected to have profound effects on the family.[5] He restates these socialist commonplaces, however, in a form so general and innocuous that most American progressives would have found them completely acceptable.

By this time, socialist commonplaces had become liberal commonplaces as well, as American liberalism, faced with the growing unreality of many of its traditional beliefs, availed itself of the economic interpretation of history (and of selected pieces of the socialist program) in order to strengthen its position. Free trade, laissez-faire, and rugged individualism ill suited the needs of a social order based on corporations, unions, and organizations of all kinds, in which the pleasant fiction of a self-regulating economy had become untenable. Similarly, the patriarchal family appeared to be "unsatisfactorily adjusted to twentieth-century conditions."[6] The industrial revolution, it was said, had undermined the father's authority, drawing women into industry. Urbanization everywhere reduced the family to "a temporary meeting place for board and lodging."[7] Rising standards of living forced postponement of marriage and strict control of births; educated women refused to settle for economic dependence.

Almost everyone agreed that the family had entered a period of painful "transition." "The old religious-proprietary form of patriar-chal authority is doomed," wrote J. P. Lichtenberger, "and until new spiritual restraints are formed to take the place of those that are passing away a condition which, in the sight of some, will border on chaos is bound to result."[8] Even those who described themselves as optimists did not deny that "the present instability of monogamous wedlock results from imperfect adaptation to modern society and in-dustrial conditions." They argued merely that the community would gradually learn to do things the family could no longer do for itself: enforce housing standards, provide better education, regulate con-ditions of employment, and exercise proper supervision over public places of amusement.[9]

THE OVERTHROW OF EVOLUTIONARY THEORIES

AND THE EMERGENCE OF AN EMPIRICAL

SOCIOLOGY OF URBANIZATION

After World War I, the hold of evolutionary theories began to weaken. W. F. Ogburn's *Social Change* substituted a functional anal-ysis of society for historical and evolutionary analysis.[10] His enumer-ation of the family's functions, economic, educational, religious, pro-tective, and recreational, inspired many similar lists. Ogburn also inspired the sociological profession with his appeals for more rigorous empirical work, which he usually combined with a con-demnation of theory. Sociology had begun its long retreat from its nineteenth-century origins—from history, from theory, from generalization itself.

By the thirties, even socialists had begun to waver in their al-legiance to the matriarchal theory of the family's origins. V. F. Cal-verton dismissed the whole debate about the origins of the family as ideological. If the work of Westermarck—now thoroughly discred-ited, according to Calverton—provided the bourgeois family with a crude "cultural defense," radicals had seized on the ideas of Lewis Henry Morgan not because those ideas "represented the final word in anthropological science" but because "they gave new meaning to the cause of the proletariat." Radical theorists denounced anyone who criticized Morgan as "bourgeois" and accepted *Primitive Society* as uncritically as middle-class writers accepted Westermarck's *The History of Human Marriage*. Yet it was now clear to any fair-minded observer that although Morgan was "much closer to the truth" than Westermarck in rejecting middle-class monogamy and sexual ethics as universal norms, his evolutionary theories had to be dismissed, along with those of his adversaries, as completely untenable.

> We cannot say, as Morgan did, that the marital institution passed through certain stages definitely evolved out of certain others in the history of every tribe. The existence of sexual communism among a certain number of tribes does not furnish us with sufficient evidence to make a sweeping deduction about the entire history of early mankind. . . . If we have enough evidence to show that the family, as we think of it, could not possibly have functioned in the early stages of social organization, . . . we do not have enough evidence to trace adequately the development of sexual relations through precise evolutionary stages, common to all primitive groups. [11]

Calverton dismissed evolutionary theory as more or less useless; Ernest R. Mowrer dismissed all of anthropology. Research among primitive peoples had nothing of importance to say, Mowrer flatly declared, about the origins of the family. Neither anthropology nor, for that matter, any other discipline could bridge the gap between the origin of man and the beginning of written history. The origins of the family, accordingly, had been "irretrievably lost," and further speculation about the subject was a waste of time. [12]

Joseph Kirk Folsom agreed that anthropology had almost nothing to contribute to an understanding of the contemporary family. Citing Calverton, he too dismissed the debate between Westermarck and his critics as ideological. Anthropology itself, Folsom noted, had repudiated the findings of both schools. The proliferation of empirical studies contributed to the growing impression that marriage and family patterns varied enormously from one culture to another. Whereas Westermarck had thought monogamy to be the norm from which other forms of marriage were "pathological variations," in Folsom's words, "present-day theory . . . does not know what the norm is." For this reason, it had to be "frankly stated" that anthropology—more precisely, ethnology—offered to sociology only a negative lesson, "a feeling for the limits of variation of human family patterns."[13]

Surveying the literature on the family in 1926, Ernest W. Burgess came to similar conclusions. Like Folsom, Burgess leaned heavily on the work of the anthropologist Robert H. Lowie. Thanks in large part to Lowie's attack on evolutionary theory, Burgess argued, anthropology had given up the attempt to demonstrate a "fixed succession of maternal and paternal descent." Students of primitive societies had turned "from an attempt to reconstruct social evolution to a description and an analysis of social organization." Similar tendencies were at work in other disciplines. Psychologists, instead of "drawing their conclusions from theories already formulated," now sought to base them on "more or less intensive studies of family situations." In sociology itself, a movement "from historical to sociological description and explanation of family organization" had been begun by W. I. Thomas and Florian Znaniecki, whose study of the Polish peasant in Europe and America showed how the large extended family broke down when transferred to the cities of the New World. Studies of Eastern Europe and China traced "the gradual disintegration of the large family organization." This growing body of work laid down the lines along which "realistic study of American family organization" ought to be conducted—in spite of which, Burgess complained, investigation of the urban American family still "lagged" behind other fields.[14]

Burgess himself had already contributed to the reorientation of sociological study by proposing that the family be treated as a "unity of interacting personalities." Urbanization and the emancipation of women had destroyed the large extended family, but the reduction of the family to the nuclear group, Burgess argued, made it clear that in all societies the "family as a reality exists in the interaction of its members and not in the formalities of the law with its stipulations of rights and duties." The family, like society in general, is held together by the power of imaginative identification, by ideas and "sentiments," and by the development of clearly defined social roles which alone have the power to evoke sentiments and "sympathy." In the long run, the weakening of legal formalities—the evolution of the family "from institution to companionship," in the formula later popularized by Burgess and Harvey Locke—could only strengthen the family by giving greater scope to the personal interaction underlying family life from the beginning. "When an equilibrium is reestablished a new pattern of family life will emerge, better adapted to the new situation, but only a different variety of the old familiar pattern of personal relationships in the family."[15]

The concept of the family as a "unity of interacting personalities" derived from Charles Horton Cooley's sociology of "sympathy"; from the psychology of George Herbert Mead and Harry Stack Sullivan, with its emphasis on roles and role-playing; and, more immediately, from the new school of urban sociology at the University of Chicago. Cooley's influence was the most remote but also the most pervasive, not only over the sociology of the family but over the study of society in general. As the leading American exponent of positivist sociology, Cooley formulated a view of society that has had enduring appeal for American social science. According to this view, which shared many features with that of Spencer, Comte, and Durkheim, society is a living organism, a dynamic equilibrium in which every unit, every individual, plays an appropriate role or function. Mind is a social product; personality, a function of role. Society in turn can be considered as the totality of social roles, the combined interaction of personalities. At bottom, society consists of communication, "the mechanism," in Cooley's words, "through which human relations exist and develop." Social progress is equivalent to the "growth of communication," which begins with face-to-face interaction (the "primary group") and develops ever widening networks. These make it "possible for society to be organized more and more on the higher faculties of man, on intelligence and sympathy, rather than on authority, caste, and routine." The growth of communication unifies life by overcoming both distance and time. It "brings the past into the present" and lays the social and psychological groundwork for what a later theorist, a psychoanalyst whose work drew on the positivist tradition as much as it drew on Freud, would call "more exclusive identities."[16]

The positivist conception of society, it has rightly been said, tends to minimize the importance of conflict in human affairs. In the interpretation of Spencer's "moving equilibrium," the "stress in practice seems regularly to fall on the equilibrium and not on the movement." By giving so much weight to sympathy, positivist sociology correspondingly diminishes the importance of interest. By defining the individual as almost entirely a product of socialization, it rules out in advance the possibility of irreconcilable conflicts between the individual and society. Finally, the proposition that mind is largely social has the interesting corollary that society is largely mental.[17] Society consists of interpersonal relations, but "persons" are merely the ideas associated with their roles, conveyed to others and then reflected by others back to the self. Society is a mirror, and the "images" it projects, as an early exponent of role theory insisted, are the images "of the social suggestion that has surrounded" a given set of roles.[18] Such a conception of society is completely at variance not only with materialist conceptions but with dialectical views of human growth and development, according to which growth results from conflict; but American sociology has modeled itself, for better or worse, on positivist rather than dialectical theories of society. Even Talcott Parsons, who rejected much of positivism, stressed the importance of sentiment and sympathy—of shared beliefs and the interplay of roles—in holding society together.

At the time Burgess began to formulate his idea of the family as a unit of "interacting personalities," the field of psychology was also undergoing revision and redefinition. Much of this revision focused on criticism of various instinct theories. The writings of Harry Stack Sullivan, George Herbert Mead, and their followers appeared to many theorists equally damaging to behaviorism, to psychoanalytic theories based on the primacy of instinct, and to evolutionary ideas that tried to ground the family in biology—for example, Westermarck's famous assertion (only slightly qualified in later editions of his *History of Human Marriage*) that the family is rooted in the "monogamous instinct."[19] The abandonment of instinct theory led to a stress on interpersonal relations and social "roles."

A third influence on the theory of the family was the so-called Chicago school of urban sociology, founded by Burgess himself, Albion W. Small, Robert E. Park, and Thomas Znaniecki, and carried on by their successors, E. Franklin Frazier, Louis Wirth, and John Dollard. For two generations or more, the University of Chicago dominated the emerging field of sociology, even more thoroughly than Boas and his students at Columbia dominated anthropology in the twenties and thirties. The presence in other departments of the university of such important thinkers as Veblen, John Dewey, and

Mead; the enterprise of Jane Addams, Graham Taylor, and other
settlement workers in accumulating empirical data on urban life and
insights into its pathology; the many-sided intellectual awakening
known as the "Chicago renaissance"; the existence of the city itself as
a laboratory of industrial conditions—all these made Chicago almost
inevitably a center of sociological studies. Nor is it surprising that
those studies addressed themselves especially to the sociology of
urban life. From the perspective of Chicago, which had grown from
a frontier settlement to a huge industrial metropolis in less than a
century, completely rebuilding itself after the fire of 1871, rapid urbanization loomed as the central fact of modern society. The city, it
appeared, was "the natural habitat of civilized man." Accordingly,
the city should be studied as a total environment that gave rise to a
distinctive way of life.

The Chicago school seems at times to have expected that the modern city, or at least the smaller communities that made it up, could
be studied with the same techniques that Boas and Lowie had
brought to the study of primitive societies. Yet the work of the
Chicago school turned precisely on a sharp contrast between folk
culture and urban culture. Invoking both the experience of recent
immigrants and the work of such theorists as Durkheim, Simmel,
Cooley, and Max and Alfred Weber, the Chicago sociologists argued
that traditional patterns of life had broken down under the disintegrating impact of urbanism, a theme on which they played innu-
merable variations. In their view, the division of labor, specialization, "differentiation"—all aspects of the general rationalization of
production and administration—had reached their highest development in the modern city, eroding traditional sources of authority and
substituting "formal control mechanisms" for organic "bonds of solidarity." Cooperation gave way to competition, kinship to individualism, "control based on mores" to "control based on positive law."
The authority of the family disintegrated as secondary groups, based
on common interests, replaced primary groups in which customary
and traditional sanctions prevailed. Thus immigrant families maintained themselves only for a single generation, frequently breaking
down in the second generation. Declining fertility rates, according
to Louis Wirth, suggested that "the city is not conducive to the
traditional family life." As kinship ties dissolved, "the individual
members pursue their own diverging interests."[20]

Urban sociology implied that the "transfer of functions" could be understood as part of the breakdown of traditional culture under the "subversive and disorganizing" effect of urbanization. It also helped to explain why the new type of family that was emerging from this process should be studied as a unit of interacting personalities. In the absence of patriarchal authority sanctioned by immemorial tradition, family solidarity, according to Burgess and Locke, now rested on "mutual affection, emotional interdependence, sympathetic understanding, temperamental compatibility, consensus on values and objectives."[21] In Ogburn's formula: as the "institutional" functions of the family declined, the "personality functions" took on greater importance.[22]

The Chicago school succeeded not so much in banishing history from sociological study as in banishing it as an object of explicit analysis. Its work depended at every point on a contrast between folk society and urban society, but it never stopped to examine the historical process through which one evolved from the other. That process remained implicit but unanalyzed. The antithesis between traditional society and urban society served merely as a typology; in the absence of historical analysis, the more that antithesis was elaborated, the more rigid, lifeless, obvious, and banal it became. The worst thing that can be said of generalizations about the disintegrating impact of urban life is not that they seem unconvincing but, on the contrary, that they provoke almost automatic assent. This agreement suggests a paucity of content and a form that makes them impossible to refute. Once we accept the initial antithesis between folk and urban societies—between "traditional" and modern societies—we can hardly object to anything that derives from it. Sociologists might better have concerned themselves with analyzing the validity of the categories than with endlessly elaborating new versions of them.

Vacuous as it was, the theory of urbanism nevertheless contained an important suggestion for the understanding of the family—namely, that each member of the family pursued his own interests. If this was true, even the nuclear family no longer existed in "isolation" from the rest of society. Instead of serving as a refuge, it more and more closely resembled the harsh world of work. Relations within the family took on the same character as relations elsewhere; individualism and the pursuit of self-interest reigned even in the

most intimate of institutions. Parental authority came to rest purely
on the provision of material services, at the same time that industrialization of production and bureaucratization of welfare undermined the family's capacity to manipulate economic rewards.
Parents without property to pass on to their offspring could exact
obedience only by appealing to a sense of duty, deference, or filio-
piety, in other words to hierarchical principles having little place in
a society based on rational self-interest. The spirit of economic ra-
tionality had become so pervasive in modern society that it invaded
even the family, the last stronghold of precapitalist modes of thought
and feeling.

Having hinted at such a view of the family, the Chicago sociologists ignored its implications, probably because these were incompatible with a theory of society that stressed not interests but "sympathy." Instead of showing how the modern child increasingly
judged his parents according to their ability to provide goods and
services, and how the parents in turn attempted to justify their
authority in a way that merely strengthened appeals to enlightened self-interest, the Chicago sociologists forgot self-interest
and concentrated their entire attention on the family's "affectional" function. It was as if the family alone, of all the institutions
in modern society, had managed to escape the drift toward individualism, "egotism," and moral chaos, which even the sociology
of urbanization acknowledged as a powerful tendency in modern
life. It appeared that Louis Wirth's important though unoriginal observation, that as cities develop, "the pecuniary nexus which implies
the purchasability of services and things *has displaced personal relations* as the basis of association," applied to every single institution
except the family. The family, on the contrary, was to be studied
precisely from the point of view of "personal relations," everywhere else "displaced."[23]

MARRIAGE AS A REFUGE
FROM MODERN SOCIETY

The overthrow of evolution, the cultural refutation of "biological determinism," and the emergence of urbanization as the central organizing idea of a sociology that was attempting to substitute analysis of contemporary society for historical speculation—these trends coincided with a growing awareness that sociology might be used to refute predictions of the family's demise. Without for a moment abating its claims to scientific objectivity, sociology began to work out a theory of the family's "functions" that could hardly fail to reassure those who worried about its decline—to reassure them, in part, just because it appeared to rest on an objective analysis having nothing in common either with conservative alarmism or with the attacks of radicals who not only predicted the death of the family but did everything possible to hasten it. Yet the grounds on which sociologists defended the importance of the family—the indispensability of the emotional services it performed—simultaneously justified the transfer of its other functions to other agencies. Sociologists assumed, in fact, that urbanization made such a "transfer of functions" inevitable.

In the mid-twenties, sociological writing on the future of the family still remained anxious and uncertain. An article called "The Lag of Family Mores in Social Culture," published in 1925, analyzed the decline of the family's economic, educational, protective, and recreational functions and conceded that "changes in the social-economic environment" were having a "tremendous and often disastrous" effect. Among other things, the family could no longer claim to be "the stable social unit for the socialization and control of the child."[24] Ernest R. Groves, one of the leading advocates of training for marriage and the expansion of the therapeutic professions, wrote that "marriage faces a crisis and birth control is largely responsible."[25] Most of Ogburn's "Eleven Questions Concerning American Marriages" (1927) clearly originated in popular anxiety about the future of monogamy. Was marriage a desirable state? How often was it broken by divorce? Was marriage "diminishing"? Ogburn's answers were not entirely reassuring. He showed that the marriage rate was actually increasing, contrary to a popular impression, but he could not deny that the divorce rate was increasing too or that urban life had "greatly reduced" the family's functions.[26]

Six years later, Ogburn offered a more encouraging report. Certain functions had declined, but others had taken on new importance. "The family is thought of much less as an economic institution than as an organization for rearing children and providing happiness."[27] Edward Sapir, anthropologist and social critic, had already pointed the way to a more optimistic assessment of the family crisis in an article written for popular consumption and significantly entitled "What Is the Family Still Good For?" Was the family "about to disappear"? Sapir argued that, on the contrary, society could not get rid of the family even if it wanted to. To a superficial observer, the family "seems to stand literally with its back against the wall, faced by an immense crowd known as 'the young,' who are aided and abetted by the figures of the sociologist, the revelations of the psychologist, and the sneers of the anthropologist." A closer look, however, revealed that the family had changed only its form, not its underlying essence, while ideas about the family lagged behind these structural alterations. That the family provided "intimate companionship," he suggested, in itself guaranteed its survival. Sapir went so far as to argue that even child rearing was incidental to marriage. Most couples would continue to want children, and no other institution provided a "more satisfactory matrix" for raising them; but the important fact, to which everything else was merely "incremental," was that marriage provided intimacy between husband and wife.[28]

The next step was to argue that this intimacy took on added meaning in a world from which intimacy had otherwise been excluded. Joseph Folsom noted in 1934 that modern society gave rise to a "generally increased need for intense affection and romance," while increasing the difficulty of satisfying this need. Folsom quaintly referred to this contradiction—implicitly a tremendous indictment of modern society—as a "cultural lag between the increasing need for love and the practical arrangements to promote it."[29] Mowrer put the same idea somewhat differently, but with the same offhand disregard of its disturbing implications: "One of the most pronounced and striking phases of modern life is the repression of the emotions." According to this reasoning, the family became "all the more important as the setting for emotional expression." In the rest of life, emotions had no place. "A business man is supposed to be cold, un-feeling, and 'hard-boiled.' Exchange . . . is unemotional and objective." The family, on the other hand, satisfied what Thomas called "the desire for response."[30] Pent-up rage as well as pent-up love found expression in domestic life, causing unprecedented tensions but also furnishing the source of the family's continuing vitality. Domestic tensions, Mowrer argued, ought therefore to become the primary concern of sociological study, by means of which they could be understood and controlled.

None of these writers had much to say about the family's role in socializing the child. The family, in their view, no longer centered on the child. Children having become an economic liability, small families and even childless families replaced the extended households thought to have existed at an earlier time. So much had been made of the erosion of the family's educative functions by the school that socialization could hardly have looked like a solid basis on which to ground an argument for the continuing importance of the family. In any case, an argument based on socialization would have encountered the objection that children socialized by the isolated nuclear family grew up hopelessly ill-equipped to cope with the realities of modern life. The view that family life alone provided people with the emotional resources necessary to live and work in modern society remained convincing only so long as it ignored the socializing function of the family. Domestic life might be a haven for adults, but what of the children whom it had to prepare to live in precisely the cold and ugly world from which the family provided refuge? How could children raised under the regime of love learn to function in the marketplace? Far from preparing the young for this ordeal, the family, if it operated as sociology insisted, could only cripple the young, at the same time that it offered a psychological haven for the cripples, now grown to maladjusted maturity, whom it had itself produced.

Until the 1940s, sociologists attempted to deal with these problems by ignoring them. In effect, they reduced the study of the family to the study of marriage. Statements to the effect that modern marriage reflected "increasing emphasis upon the personal relationship between husband and wife and decreasing concern over the having of children" provoked no objection whatever. The reduction of the scope of family studies could justify itself on the grounds that it mirrored the "shrinkage" of the family itself. It could also be argued that the marital "situation," in the words of M. F. Nimkoff (whose work on the family was carried out under the influence of Ogburn), was of intrinsically "more moment" than parenthood, "and this in spite of the fact that the basic function of the family is to serve the child." Nimkoff gave two reasons for this strange assertion. During the human life cycle, marriage precedes the family in time, and "the compelling motive for marriage is mutual attraction." He did not mention the "mutual attraction" between parents and their children, so powerful that it colors the child's whole life, including the choice of a marriage partner. Such omissions show, among other things, that students of the family still relied on primitive assumptions about psychology.[31]

In the second place, Nimkoff argued, the quality of family life depends on the quality of married life, not the reverse. "The disastrous effects upon the child of an unstable home situation" are well known.[32] Similar statements can be found throughout the standard sociological writing on the family. When sociologists claimed that their discipline could become a "nomothetic social science" by fastening onto "the conception of the family as a unit of interacting personalities," they almost invariably had in mind the interacting personalities of husband and wife.[33] When they proposed to use "personality enrichment" as a means of measuring marital success, on the grounds that the family's chief function was to serve the "primary-group needs of personality," they referred to the "enrichment" not of the child but of the couple. The happy family came to be regarded as synonymous with the happy marriage, in which the partners achieved a high "degree of marital satisfaction."[34] In sociological theory, parenthood and child rearing, when they were dealt with at all, dwindled to by-products of marriage.

Theory, even bad theory, usually dictates the course of empirical study. Henceforth research on the family concerned itself overwhelmingly with the attempt to define, measure, and predict marital "adjustment." Theory interposed no obstacle, issued no striking challenge, to the continuation of the kind of research already begun not so much by academic sociologists as by practicing social therapists like G. V. Hamilton and Katherine B. Davis, who had based their work, crude as it seemed to later sociologists more skilled in techniques of quantification, on the measurement of marital happiness.[35] The redefinition of the family as a "unity" of interacting personalities merely gave additional support to the already intense preoccupation with the sources of marital conflict and the countervailing "mechanisms of accord." The ultimate object of scientific study of the family, wrote Mowrer, "is, of course, the prediction of what will happen in family relations under a given set of conditions."[36]

Attempts to implement this program produced results once described by Willard Waller, with a good deal of understatement, as "not very impressive."[37] Prediction turned out in practice to mean correlating marriages deemed successful (for no better reason than that they had not yet ended in divorce) with a variety of other information: educational status, gregariousness, tastes, "attitudes." Terman and Buttenwieser found that affirmative answers to such questions as the following held out the promise of marital success:

> Does it make you uncomfortable to be "different" or unconventional?
> Are you easily discouraged when the opinions of others differ from your own?
> Do athletics interest you more than intellectual affairs?
> Do you find conversation more helpful in formulating your ideas than reading?[38]

Burgess and Cottrell argued that a proclivity for joining social groups and a higher level of education were positive "predictors."[39] A later study by Harvey Locke, besides replicating the Burgess-Cottrell study, found that people ranking either near the top or the bottom on a scale of various personality traits tended to get divorces, whereas those who ranked in the middle were more likely to be "happily married."[40] All these studies, as has been pointed out many times, seemed to equate marital "success" with social conformity. They also reinforced the commonsensical belief that happy marriages are founded on shared temperamental affinity and shared interests and tastes—the marriage of like to like.

For these reasons, predictions of marital success are often criticized by writers who would take a more adventurous view of marriage. "The implication is that nonconventional marriages are unsuccessful," a recent textbook complains.[41] A more important objection is that studies of marital success do not tell us why some people resort to divorce and others reject it even in the face of an unhappy marriage.[42] Nor do they clarify the role of class and cultural influences in leading people to choose one or the other of these alternatives. Waller once suggested that nondivorce had become an anachronism in its own right, a form of "cultural lag" found chiefly in backward and provincial sectors of society.[43] The literature on marital adjustment might be taken to lend a certain support for his view. Instead of taking the correlation between conventionality and marital success as a criticism of the findings, we might better take it as a criticism of marital "success." But the findings are too inconclusive, too contradictory, too open to methodological objections, too heavily influenced by the underlying assumption that "interpersonal relations" can be studied in a cultural and historical vacuum, to lend themselves to this or any other interpretation.

Studies of marital "adjustment" are less interesting than the hope on which they were based: that predicting adjustment would lead, in Mowrer's words, to "control of what happens by changing the conditions in such a way as to modify the results."[44] If "unbiased" scientific study showed that romantic illusions often gave rise to domestic discord, the conditions under which people prepared for marriage could be changed so as to discourage romantic illusions. Although the studies themselves did not always support the view that the "romantic love complex" was at fault, most of the authors had a strong predisposition to accept such a conclusion. One student of courtship, having noted a positive correlation between length of engagement—as well as late marriage—and marital success, attributed these findings not to the possibility that a long courtship helped to prepare the basis for a solid marriage, but rather to the probability that impulsive, unstructured individuals were more likely to marry early in the first place, having fallen in love at first sight.[45] In repudiating the more obvious inference, he wished, to be sure, to alert people to the danger of confusing causes with correlations. But he was also influenced by the new stress on "maturity," which became so pronounced in the forties and fifties in both sociological and popular writing on marriage.

Like much else that is mistakenly attributed to the postwar reaction against the liberalism of the thirties, the theme of maturity, though it rose to a crashing crescendo in the Age of Eisenhower, originated in the twenties and thirties. It was implicit in the thesis that marriage had evolved through three stages—from arranged marriage through marriage based on romantic love and finally to "companionship"—while popular attitudes unfortunately remained arrested in the second.[46] By coupling such an explanation of the "marriage crisis" with a defense of their discipline as a "nomothetic science" that could predict and control, sociologists enlisted in the war against cultural lag. Backed up by a proliferating apparatus of practical therapy—family casework, courts of domestic relations, marital guidance clinics, psychiatry, courses in marriage and sex— sociology, it appeared, could help to adjust expectations to reality. What is surprising is not that scientific work was so often colored by ideology (this surprises only the "scientists" themselves) but that a discipline concerned with the study of society so systematically ex-cluded social influences on marriage and the family, preferring in-stead to lay almost its entire stress on the individual's "attitudes," on "unrealistic expectations," and on "cultural lag." Sociologists were not altogether unaware that these attitudes themselves had social roots, but they spoke of their origins only in passing, in a curiously offhand manner. Thus Folsom explained that the "romantic love complex" persisted largely because the "increasing monotony of work combined with shorter hours of work" led people to seek es-cape from boredom in "love behavior."[47] His insight might have served as the starting point for an analysis of the family's position in modern society and of the influence of society on the family. Such ideas, however, languished on the periphery of sociological study.

3

Roads Not Taken: Challenges to Sociological Orthodoxy

CARLE ZIMMERMAN AND THE CONSERVATIVE CRITIQUE OF THE "COMPANIONATE" FAMILY

Although sociologists in the twenties and thirties argued about whether people choose marriage partners like themselves or opposites, whether success in marriage depends more on age at marriage than on the choice of a partner, and whether children tend to promote family solidarity and inhibit divorce, they agreed on essentials. The very questions they chose to debate reflected the underlying assumption that marital solidarity lay at the heart of the subject and that sociology ought to concern itself with the influences tending to promote or destroy it.[1] The "interactional" approach to the study of the family dominated the field; it influenced even the few sociologists who attempted to subvert the conventional explanations of the family's evolution "from institution to companionship."

Of this handful, only two—Carle Zimmerman and Willard Waller—need to be discussed in any detail. It should be stated at the outset, however, that although the writings of these two sociologists differed in important ways from those of others, they did not attack the prevailing assumptions in a sustained or effective manner. Much of Waller's work could be absorbed into existing theories. Zimmerman stated his disagreement with the reigning orthodoxy more explicitly, but his own arguments lacked coherence and often dealt more with policy and ideology than with theory. Both writers nevertheless raised issues of fundamental importance—in Waller's case, with a sharpness and clarity unmatched in the whole field of family sociology.

Whereas most American sociologists approached the study of the family through study of urbanization, Zimmerman specialized in rural sociology. The work of urban sociologists did not help him to understand the Ozark families he studied empirically; looking elsewhere for theoretical guidance, he rediscovered the neglected work of Frédéric Le Play, who had distinguished three types of the family, allegedly corresponding to three stages of historical development. An evolutionist in spite of himself, Le Play, who deplored Darwinian materialism, nevertheless argued that "all the ages of the social world live again in the present time."[2] In Eastern Europe, society rested on the patriarchal family and a "permanent forced organization of labor"—that is, patronage or lordship.[3] Remnants of this patriarchal organization survived in selected backwaters of Western Europe in altered or intermediate form. In these isolated "oases of social peace"—the mountainous districts, the forests of Scandinavia, the Saxon plains, the Basque provinces—patronage, though no longer associated with forced labor, was upheld by custom. The pure form of the patriarchal family had given way to a modified version (the "stem family") whereby family holdings were passed on intact to a designated heir; he maintained any of his unmarried siblings who stayed at home, while the remaining brothers emigrated to the city or the colonies to seek their fortunes. This *famille-souche* no longer took the form of an extended family or clan, but it supported and perpetuated itself without assistance from the state and handed on traditional mores from one generation to the next. The "shoots" that it sent out invigorated the rest of the social order, providing the periodic infusions of vigorous peasant stock without which advanced societies fall into degeneracy and decay.[4]

The collapse of patronage, the Industrial Revolution, and the false

doctrines of 1789—equality, liberty, and the right of revolution—brought about the third stage, in which contractual labor succeeded permanent labor and families became unstable, no longer
able to support themselves without governmental assistance or to
transmit traditional learning from one generation to the next. The
spread of modernist ideas undermined religion and respect for paternal authority, leaving behind a vast moral devastation. Two
classes in particular both reflected this disorder and ceaselessly promoted it through political agitation—the industrial workers and the
intellectuals. Unfortunately, the dogmas purveyed by the intellectuals had an irresistible attraction for the workers. Ideas derived
from Rousseau promised material progress and flattered the masses
by teaching them that they, not the union of church and state, were
the source of all authority. It was hardly any wonder that the new
ideas were penetrating even Russia, seat of patriarchal authority.
"Since 1830 each error has followed an unvarying course: first
worked out in an intellectual's study, it is brought to public light in a
salon and twenty years later reigns supreme in the workers' huts."[5]
The only hope of restoring social peace lay in reforms based on social
science, itself no more than the rediscovery of folk wisdom.

Claiming to stand aloof from the "political passions" that were agitat-
ing his countrymen, Le Play invoked the impartiality of science on
behalf of a passionate indictment of modernism. His organic idea of
society and his geographical determinism have appealed to region-
alists like Patrick Geddes in Scotland and Lewis Mumford in the
United States. Mumford referred to Le Play as a forerunner of
regionalism and a "valiant exception" to the tendency of social
theory to reduce so many issues to abstractions like the individual,
the folk, or the proletariat.[6] In the twenties and thirties, regionalism
enjoyed a minor revival in the United States, especially among
Southerners or intellectuals sympathetic to the South as a last
stronghold of preindustrial values. The manifesto of the Southern
agrarians, *I'll Take My Stand,* condemned industrial civilization and
spoke eloquently but vaguely of an "agrarian restoration."[7] A distinguished group of intellectuals, including the historian Frank L.
Owsley and the sociologists Howard Odum and Rupert Vance, made
loving studies of Southern regional culture and the life of the "plain

folk."[8] Carle Zimmerman's studies of rural sociology and the rural family should be considered as part of this regional revival.

In *Family and Society*, published in 1935, Zimmerman argued that the homogeneous structure of the Ozark family—a type of family that he found "strikingly similar" to the stem-families described by Le Play—"gives a greater peace of mind, and effects a more excellent adaptation to environment than is found in many other areas." Even the poverty-stricken families of this region were "socially prosperous although not economically prosperous," preserving and transmitting the "moral and religious sentiments" that held the community together. By sending out "branches" to the city, the Ozark family helped to populate urban communities unable to reproduce themselves, and thereby preserved "the naïve provincialisms necessary to a strong society." Zimmerman warned reformers who proposed to eliminate rural poverty either by bringing industry to the hills (TVA) or by relocating the hill people in cities (as the Resettlement Administration was attempting to do) that such programs would destroy a healthy if hard-pressed rural culture without putting anything in its place. A family system that functioned under conditions of rural backwardness would collapse under industry. Reforms intended to diminish poverty would defeat their own purpose if they weakened the family, the basis of country life. It followed, therefore, that "if we wish to preserve this familism and still give the Highlander some of those things which we believe are the benefits of 'urbanization,' it probably could be done best of all through the agricultural development of the Highlander where he is."[9]

Like Pitirim A. Sorokin, the "master of sociology" to whom *Family and Society* is dedicated, Zimmerman refused to treat the family in isolation from other institutions. Zimmerman's quarrel with other sociologists of the family turned on this issue. He dismissed the "interaction" theory as a study of the "mechanics of marriage," not family sociology at all.[10] He insisted on the interconnections between the decay of the family, the growth of the welfare state (which takes over the work of the family without doing it any better), and social mobility, which "makes behavior more plastic and versatile" but also increases mental strain, anomie, and a sense of homelessness, thereby throwing people on the mercy of the state. Assimilating the

social typologies of Ferdinand Tönnies and Durkheim to those of Le
Play and Sorokin, Zimmerman argued that the Ozark highlanders
lived in a society of the *Gemeinschaft* type or, in Sorokin's terms, in
a "cumulative social group" held together by strong community and
familial ties. Selected components of the highland culture could not
be altered without disturbing all the others—a point ignored by "advocates of the 'new family,' " who "believe that personality reaches
its greatest development when the family concentrates its entire
strength on 'affection,' leaving education to the schools, religious
teaching to the church, protection to the state, and support to industry or the state."[11]

Besides criticizing the study of the family in isolation, Zimmerman attacked the theory of cultural lag, exposing its ideological basis
in naïve illusions of historical progress. Instead of dismissing irrational beliefs, violence, war, and other unprogressive phenomena as
survivals from the unenlightened past, Zimmerman argued that the
spread of "enlightenment" produced its own forms of superstition.
In his view, the modern world was witnessing a large-scale revival of
irrationality. New secular religions, far more pernicious in their psychological effects than the old theistic ones, had appeared in the
form of "strongly integrated and violent movements toward historical dogmatism"—a characterization that presumably included both
fascism and Bolshevism.[12]

Zimmerman recognized that the notion of cultural lag played an
important part in what he called the companionate theory of the
family, although he did not explain the connection clearly. At one
point he seemed to argue that advocates of the companionate hypothesis, equipped with an all-purpose theory of social change,
could brush aside any unwelcome evidence as evidence merely of
cultural lag. If it was objected, for example, that the family continued to perform other functions besides "affectional" ones, the objection itself was treated as an archaic survival—another case of ideas'
imperfectly adapting themselves to changing realities.[13] Unfortunately, Zimmerman wanted to combat individualistic ideologies
more than he wanted to understand the family and its relation to society. Recognizing the normative implications of the companionate
theory, he replied with a normative argument of his own. "If we
adapt the family to the individual," he complained, "we no longer
have the institution. . . . Either there is a family with institutional

values, or society is a loosely formed aggregate of individuals, changing and structureless." [14] He did not so much deny the validity of the latter view as question its desirability. He quarreled with sociologists who argued that the family had evolved "from institution to companionship," not on the grounds that no such change was taking place, but on the grounds that it was taking place all too rapidly and was thereby undermining the foundations of social order. Zimmerman condemned the prevailing sociological interpretation of the family not because it provided an inaccurate picture of modern society but because it approved of that society and offered a scientific rationale for the transition from community to individualism.

Although Zimmerman's charge of ideological bias was valid, bias did not in itself invalidate the work of the sociological profession. Exposing the ideological underpinnings of the liberal sociology of the family was not the same thing as refuting it. For that matter, Zimmerman wavered even in his work of ideological exposure. He could not seem to make up his mind whether he wished to accuse liberals of deliberately weakening the family or whether he objected to their refusal to admit that it was being weakened at all. The second line of criticism carried more weight than the first. Whatever the shortcomings of conservative thought, at least it had no illusions about the decay of traditional forms and the difficulty of finding substitutes. Liberal sociologists, on the other hand, kept insisting that the family was stronger than ever. As long as conservatives made this pious illusion the main object of their attack, they had a certain advantage in sociological combats over the family; but they lost this advantage when they argued that liberals actively sought to bring into being a "changing and structureless" form of society. What began as an attack on their understanding degenerated into an attack on their motives.

WILLARD WALLER:

SOCIOLOGY AS SATIRE

If Zimmerman attacked the dominant school of family sociology from a conservative point of view, Willard Waller attacked it from a leftist position that harked back to Veblen and the best of populism. Waller had the populist's suspicion of appearances, the conviction that a pleasing exterior necessarily conceals something embarrassing, discreditable, or downright sinister, which it is the job of analysis to bring to light. Like Veblen, he was a provincial in revolt against provincialism, which in his view included not only the insularity of the American village but the higher provincialism of Bohemia and the ostentatious immorality of the recently divorced. His first book, a study of divorce, made the point in passing that the bohemian, with his pose of emotional detachment, his "addiction to jokes," and his low-level promiscuity, is at heart "a Philistine who has gone on an excursion into the land of the creative person" but "cannot really live there." [15] Here as elsewhere, Waller showed great insight into the way in which liberationist ideologies—in this case the ideology of moral enlightenment—often support pseudo-liberations.

From 1929 to 1931, Waller taught sociology at the University of Nebraska; from 1931 to 1937, at Pennsylvania State University. In 1937 he finally escaped from academic obscurity and joined the faculty of Barnard College, but even there he was treated as an outsider by his fellow sociologists at Columbia. He remained an associate professor at the time of his premature death in 1945. Some admirers of Waller think he compensated for the neglect of his colleagues by throwing himself into journalism and profitable publishing ventures, to the detriment of his scholarly work. [16] Whatever the reasons, he did little serious work after his textbook on the family appeared in 1938. Earlier he had published a study of the teaching profession and a well-known article on the social life of college students. His reputation rested mainly on these three studies, *The Family: A Dynamic Interpretation*, *The Sociology of Teaching* (1932), and "The Rating and Dating Complex" (1937).

Waller was at his best as a critic of provincial customs and small-town university life. The removal from his native habitat probably explains why he found so little to say after 1938. He relished the iconoclast's role cultivated by so many American intellectuals. In a society lacking institutionalized mediation between social criticism and political action, the critic tends to express himself in personal and idiosyncratic judgments, rather than seeking to elaborate and revise a cumulative body of criticism.[17] "Our ancestral faith in the individual and what he is able to accomplish," as Van Wyck Brooks once pointed out, ". . . has despoiled us of that instinctive human reverence for those divine reservoirs of collective experience, religion, science, art, philosophy, the self-subordinated service of which is almost the measure of the highest happiness." In the absence of intellectual traditions against which to define his work, the American critic easily becomes a crank, according to Brooks—a man who "rides some hobby of his own invention until it falls to pieces from sheer craziness."[18] Thus Veblen deliberately placed himself outside all traditions of thought and then ransacked them indiscriminately as it suited his purpose, to deflate pomposity and unmask appearances. Veblen's work, undeniably brilliant, remained too eclectic, idiosyncratic, and intentionally obscure to be absorbed into a theoretical tradition. It could only be ransacked in turn by other "cranks," who paid more attention to Veblen's celebrated scorn for his colleagues and students, his heavy-handed irony, and his satire on manners than to whatever theoretical substance could be extracted from his writings.

The same can be said of Willard Waller, a lesser Veblen and admirer of Veblen. Waller's studies can be used only as he used the studies of others: by abstracting isolated insights and observations from the context in which they appear. The observations themselves, however, are of high quality. In the vast dreariness of sociological writing on the family, Waller's studies bristle with indignation and scorn, emotions rigorously repressed in the rest of the literature. Instead of eschewing "value judgments," Waller made no effort to conceal his opinion that marriage often becomes a private hell to which otherwise well-meaning people consign themselves out of inertia, illusions about themselves, and a strong taste for self-inflicted punishment. Instead of treating "interpersonal relations" as a convenient formula for banishing from sociological study precisely everything that is personal and idiosyncratic, Waller wrote case studies rich in narrative detail, in which "interpersonal relations" appear as a form of warfare. Rather than trying to keep himself out of his writ-

ing, he drew freely on his own experience of marital discord, making
only the most perfunctory gestures toward what usually passes for
sociological objectivity. The long section in *The Family* entitled
"Forty Years of Marriage Conflict" is a barely disguised account of
his parents' marriage. The many brilliant vignettes of marital combat, with which this "textbook" bristles, undoubtedly derive in large
part from Waller's first marriage, which ended in an acrimonious
divorce. "I did not exactly *learn* from my experience with you," he
wrote to his first wife long after the marriage was over, "but I was
sensitized and excited and thrown into a maelstrom from which I
emerged as a different person."[19] The vitality of Waller's work on
marriage and divorce testifies again and again to the accuracy of this
assessment.

The following passage can stand as an example of Waller's sociological method and especially of his ability to draw on his own experience of the struggle for moral advantage, which plays such an important part in most marriages. First he presents an imaginary
dialogue, seemingly an exchange of banalities devoid of any larger
significance.

He: Shall we go to the movies tonight?
She: What's there?
He: Babe Darling in "Hearts Aflame."
She: Oh, no, let's don't and say we did.
He: All right, then to hell with it!
She: If that's the way you feel about it, let's go.
He: I don't want to go now.
She: Oh, come on now, let's go.
He: No, I only mentioned it because I thought you would like it.
She: Well, I would like it.
He: I doubt it.

Waller's gloss on this colloquy shows the hand of an accomplished
satirist.

The man begins by making a concession to the wife, hoping perhaps to
reap some benefit. The woman is suspicious and begins by attempting to
make light of the concession, and the man immediately shifts his ground
by assuming the role of one who has attempted to do a favor for another
and encountered a surly response. The woman now attempts to take the
pose of one who gives in to the other's wishes; it is well understood between them that this concession involves the right to criticize the program for the evening if anything goes wrong—and something probably

will. The man sturdily holds his ground and refuses to go to the movies under such circumstances. The pattern of antagonisms beneath the surface is often less complex—less complex but not necessarily easier to deal with.

The suggestion that the husband "perhaps" hopes to reap some advantage by asking his wife to go to the movies; the glee with which Waller predicts that if they do go, something will "probably" go wrong; his delight in exposing "the pattern of antagonisms" underlying a minor domestic disagreement; and his perception that these antagonisms obey unspoken rules, enforced by mutual agreement of the antagonists—all show a good ear, hard-won knowledge of the tactics of hand-to-hand conversational combat, and an ability to use understatement for ironic effect. But Waller can shift effortlessly into hyperbole: the whole exchange, he observes, reveals "a maneuvering and shifting of positions in accordance with principles of strategy which would not be more rapid or more sensitive if the antagonists were Frederick the Great and Napoleon Bonaparte."[20]

Like Veblen, Waller sometimes succumbed to the temptation to play his material for purely comic effects. In this instance, however, satire serves an important substantive point. It leads straight to the heart of Waller's thought: the recognition that romantic conventions conceal a fierce sexual struggle; or better, that the struggle expresses itself, in disguised form, in the very conventions that supposedly lead to the perfect union of the sexes. "Beneath the soft words and euphemisms of 'the line,' there is a resounding clash of one human will upon another. Each is determined not to be caught by the sugared words of the other."[21] As he observed the dating practices of his students at Nebraska and Penn State, Waller was struck by the importance both sexes attached to what they called a good line—the smooth flow of talk by means of which a young man hopes to convince a woman that his affection is deeper than it really is. The woman understands very well the uses of the line, and she tries not to be taken in by it; but at the same time she knows that a good line is one of the indispensable attributes of popularity. Meanwhile, she employs a line of her own: she pretends to be taken in by the man's blandishments, while in fact she remains "wary"—a word to which Waller's informants constantly resort. The man is wary too, but women, Waller thinks, play this game better than men.

At a deeper level, both partners instinctively understand the validity of what Waller calls the principle of least interest, according to which "that person is able to dictate the conditions of association whose interest in the continuation of the affair is least." Falling in love carries with it the risk of emotional dependency and disappointment, as we are constantly reminded by the popular songs that provide both the seductive background for the dating ritual and a commentary on it. Therefore one tries to remain detached while feigning the opposite, meanwhile attempting to lure the other into making wholehearted emotional commitments. Waller takes us so far but leaves it to his readers to ask the obvious question: Is it any wonder that modern men and women complain of being "unable to love"?[22]

Although the principle of least interest plays a central part in his analysis, Waller states it in a somewhat confusing way. As he himself recognizes at the level of empirical description, the reason women are more adept than men at dating, courtship, and marriage is not that they have less "interest in the continuation of the affair." Precisely because they have so much more at stake, in a practical sense, women must take care to have less at stake emotionally. E. A. Ross, from whom Waller borrowed the principle of least interest, stated it more clearly: "In any sentimental relation the one who cares less can exploit the one who cares more."[23] Women have a special stake in caring less. As Waller himself puts it in a characteristic passage:

> Exploitation of some sort usually follows the realization that the other person is more deeply involved than oneself. So much almost any reasonably sophisticated person understands. The clever person, in my observation usually a woman, knows how to go on from that point. A girl may pretend to be extremely involved, to be the person wholly dominated by the relationship; this she does in order to lead the young man to fasten his emotions and to prepare for the conventional dénouement of marriage, for, in the end, while protesting her love, she makes herself unavailable except in marriage; this is certainly not an unusual feminine tactic and is executed with a subtlety which makes the man's crude attempts at guile seem sophomoric. . . . There seems no doubt that women understand the intricacies of courtship better than men. If such a book as this were written by a woman, what secrets might she not reveal![24]

Woman's economic interest in marriage, according to Waller, gives her a greater stake in fighting clear of emotional entanglement. She learns to withhold her sexual favors in exchange for concessions, and this pattern, established in courtship, continues in marriage. Although Waller does not press the point, his analysis of the woman's use of her body as an instrument of sexual warfare provides an explanation of the much-discussed problem of female frigidity, which absorbed so much medical and psychiatric attention in the first half of the twentieth century: she finds that she can no longer let go even when she wants to. Waller's analysis also helps to clarify some of the secondary characteristics of frigidity, which interest him more than frigidity itself: the woman's bodily prudery and fastidiousness, her narcissism, her identification with "culture," her fear of "lowering herself." The story of his parents' marriage (and probably of his own first marriage as well) recalls the story told by D. H. Lawrence in *Sons and Lovers*—the history of a marriage in which the wife feels acutely her husband's lack of refinement and tries to give her son the advantages associated with art and learning, meanwhile seeking to enlist him as an ally in the struggle against her husband. A great many upwardly mobile intellectuals probably grew up under such conditions, but Waller characteristically ignored the influence of such marriages on children and concentrated his attention on the dynamics of the marital relationship. "The modern woman cannot help trying to dominate her husband and cannot help hating him if she succeeds"—this paradox fascinated Waller (as it fascinated Lawrence), and he devoted his best efforts to unraveling its implications. In the end, like Veblen, he subscribed to an economic interpretation of morality. It is woman's "parasitic role" that forces her to become a "beautiful object" and to "pay more attention than men to bodily morality and relatively less to general social morality." "The tendency to use the woman as a symbol of the husband's success"—an instrument of vicarious leisure, in Veblenian terms— "is apparently at the basis of the whole social complex under discussion."[25]

THE RATING AND DATING COMPLEX:

WALLER'S CRITIQUE OF PURE PLEASURE

Convention requires women to marry men older and taller than themselves. It forbids them to marry their social inferiors—another sense in which women must not marry "beneath themselves." These requirements not only restrict the supply of eligible men, they set limits to the exercise of free choice, for men and women alike. The much-discussed transition from arranged marriage to "free choice" is an illusion, according to Waller. "When we think of marriage choices concretely, we see that in many cases there has been no choice at all." In small towns, "the situation . . . probably does not differ enormously from preferential marriage (often enforced in a lax manner) in primitive groups."[26] Elsewhere—for example, in cities or large universities—the pool of eligible partners appears to be larger. But if we look more closely, Waller insisted, we find that restrictions surrounding courtship set strict limits to whatever choice exists. These restrictions may not always be the same ones that prevailed when parents and elders controlled courtship, but they have scarcely less rigid effects.[27]

I speak of "courtship," but Waller's famous essay on dating takes the position—one side in a lively dispute among sociologists of the family—that dating is not a form of courtship at all. Courtship leads to marriage; dating is undertaken purely for amusement. Like a number of other sociologists, notably Talcott Parsons in his earliest writings on the subject, Waller saw American youth culture not as a medium that initiates young people into adult life (or even prepares them for it), but as a quasi-autonomous culture organized around the pursuit of fun and "thrills." At first sight, his own account of dating appears to contradict this characterization by revealing the deadly competition that underlies activities supposedly having no other purpose than amusement. The point is, however, that organized "amusement" is by no means amusing—a point already familiar to readers of the fourth chapter in Waller's book on divorce, "Why the Bohemian Adjustment Is Unsatisfactory," in which he satirized the joyless hedonism of the newly emancipated. Among other things, Waller's sociology sets forth a critique of pure pleasure—a survey of the moral and emotional havoc that results from the organization of free time as commercialized "leisure." Both gropingly in "The Bohemian Adjustment" and with a surer touch in "The Rating and Dating Complex," Waller attempted to deal with a new phenomenon in modern life, the pursuit of love and sexual pleasure without any stated aims beyond themselves, such as the reproduction of the species or the rational provision for the future.

Both bohemians and those engaged in the rating-and-dating complex, according to Waller, seek to avoid emotional entaglements while encouraging them in others. The bohemian is "not ready to answer with his whole personality for the consequences of the affair, nor to give any assurance of its continuance." He thereby forfeits the right to be jealous; "to show jealousy is nothing short of a crime." If he gets hurt, he can expect no sympathy and must suffer in silence. "So if one falls in love in Bohemia, he conceals it from his friends as best he can." The same rules apply to dating. But Waller failed to explore the possibility that increasingly they applied to marriage itself, although he did remark that "in its very highest form," the bohemian's promiscuity "approximates a marriage terminable at will."[28] His own work on divorce, which suggested that marriage terminable at will was becoming the standard form of marriage, should have raised the possibility that a low-level promiscuity was emerging as the norm of sexual relations not just for adolescents and young divorcés—people at either end of the marital cycle—but for the adult population as a whole. Waller's isolation of dating from courtship enabled him to study what happens when sex becomes an end in itself, but it deprived him of a perspective from which to study the effects of this change on marriage, or even to examine the destructive effects on marriage of the sexual antagonism generated by the dating system that precedes it. Waller not only mounted no attack on the tendency of sociological study to isolate the family from the rest of society, he carried this tendency even further by isolating dating from courtship.

Within this narrow compass, however, his analysis is enormously useful, precisely because it has so many applications beyond the immediate subject of dating. Ostensibly undertaken on behalf of excitement and fun—sex for the man, free admission to amusements and other financial rewards for the woman—dating really aims at prestige, according to Waller. The dating complex is also a rating complex. The men and women who take part in the system discuss

among themselves the relative merits of the candidates of the other
sex, ranking them in order of desirability and excluding those who
fail the relevant tests. They also rank themselves, and it is highly sig-
nificant that this ranking depends on an ability to exploit the opposite sex while avoiding emotional entanglement:

> Status in the one-sex group depends upon avoiding exploitation by the
> opposite sex. Verbatim records of a number of fraternity "bull sessions"
> were obtained a few years ago. In these sessions members are repeatedly
> warned that they are slipping, those who have fallen are teased without
> mercy, and others are warned not to be soft. And almost all of the partici-
> pants pretend a ruthlessness toward the opposite sex which they do not
> feel.

It is no surprise that, as one of Waller's student informants wrote,
"Wary is the only word that I can apply to the attitude of men and
women students toward each other."[29] In the words of another
student, "A fundamental antagonism exists on this campus between
the men and women students." According to this informant, the
women cultivate a defensive cynicism against the cynicism of men.

> They're out for what they can get? That's fine. So are we. Everything is
> just one grand, big joke. Many of the girls really fight against liking a boy
> and try very hard to maintain this cynical attitude. One way in which
> they do this is the use of ridicule [i.e., among themselves]. . . . Often
> the less a girl feels like doing this, the worse she will make it.[30]

Two conclusions follow. Not only is individual choice an illusion,
but the peer group exercises its control of matchmaking on behalf of
objectives that have nothing to do with "romantic love." On the contrary, the dating system repudiates those who make the mistake of
falling in love and awards its highest prizes to the cynical. In addition to controlling the choice of partners, the rating and dating complex puts a high premium on the control of one's own emotions. The
best that can be said for it, according to Waller, is that "the ganging
experience and its equivalent in the life of women . . . give to each
sex a sort of in-group morality which enforces a high standard of behavior with regard to one's own sex," even as it encourages exploitation of the other.[31] Sexual solidarity constitutes the other side of sexual antagonism and exploitation. Yet this solidarity rests on
deception—on the deliberate and systematic misrepresentation of
the emotions.

ATTEMPTED REFUTATIONS OF WALLER

If Waller was right, behavior that other sociologists mistook for a "romantic love complex" disguised an effort to create a counterfeit atmosphere of glamor and seductiveness—an effort in which a substantial part of the entertainment industry took part, to its profit. Commercial recreation provided an indispensable accompaniment of the "line" by creating a seductive illusion of romance that most sociologists, confusing it with romance itself, proceeded to blame for the increase in marital breakdowns. Waller's account, on the other hand, suggests that marital tensions derive from the emotional deformities imposed by dating and courtship, especially from the patterns of sexual antagonism to which the dating system gives rise.

The work of a scholar who challenged so many conventional pieties could be dealt with in either of two ways. Most sociologists chose simply to ignore it.[32] Burgess and Locke used some of Waller's material but discussed it under the heading of courtship and paid no attention to the competition and exploitation generated by dating.[33] John Cuber, like Burgess and Locke, saw dating and courtship as "one continuous process." Yet the questionnaire on which he based his conclusions, in which students were asked to give reasons for dating, listed as the first reason that dating was enjoyable, an end in itself. The second reason was that it conferred status; the third, that it provided access to forms of recreation otherwise inaccessible; and only the fourth, that it provided a means of finding a marriage partner and of testing the desirability of a contemplated marriage. Cuber himself noted that "preference seems to be for the 'no-strings-attached' type of relationship," and he made the further suggestion that the significance of the so-called sexual revolution lay not so much in the increased incidence of premarital intercourse as in "the casual nature of the man-woman relationship in course of which the act was performed." This analysis left the relation of dating to courtship and marriage as ambiguous as before. Although presented as a refutation of Waller, Cuber's evidence—for what it was worth—actually supported Waller's argument in several respects.[34]

Conclusions based on questionnaires do not mean much, however. The questionnaires used by Waller's opponents measure attitudes and values rather than practice, which often conflicts with stated beliefs. In any case, interested parties are not the best judges of their own beliefs and actions. Several writers, troubled by the implication of Waller's study—as one of them put it, that "college dating appeared to be dysfunctional as a prelude to marriage since it distracted students from the kinds of personality appraisal and interaction which pay off in the marriage relationship"—tried to refute his findings by showing that students valued neatness, cheerfulness, and good manners, according to their own reports, more highly than money, clothes, and cars. The failure of these last items to "receive majority support," in the words of Robert O. Blood, disproved Waller's analysis; a similar study, published in 1952, claimed that Waller's account did "not represent current campus values," whatever it may have revealed about the thirties.[35] But Waller's account described actions, not beliefs—except insofar as action implies beliefs—and what he found in the ritual of courtship suggested that money is often the most important ingredient in a pleasing personality, whatever people like to think about their own immunity to material considerations.

Another group of studies attacked Waller for relying on his own observations instead of on those of the participants. According to this line of argument, dating, like any other social arrangement, has to be seen as it appears to those directly concerned with it, not as it appears to an outsider. The participants themselves, it seems, do not see dating as Waller sees it. They do not see themselves, when asked, as engaged in a form of controlled competition, status-seeking, and exploitation. Instead, their answers to certain leading questions place "small emphasis on reasons which are . . . of the competitive-prestige type."[36] It is not difficult to see that this type of reasoning can be used to refute almost any critical judgment on human actions. Only if the participants themselves agree that they are engaged in exploitation can the sociologist describe their actions as such![37] But in any case, Waller did make use of student informants, and the charge that he was indifferent to student perceptions of the rating and dating complex is absurd on its face. Some of the most scathing commentaries on the dating system came not from Waller but from his students. Here, as in his other work, Waller showed that he understood the value of carefully conducted interviews in probing beneath the bland surface of American sociability.

He had no confidence, however, in statistical surveys, believing that "intensive study of a few cases" usually proves more enlightening than "collecting facts about many," and that "no generalization can be so clearly buttressed by facts as one which is definitely supported by one or two well understood cases."[38] When Waller's critics accused him of ignoring student opinion, what they really found unforgivable was his refusal to submit the whole question of rating and dating to a majority vote.

In many ways, the most interesting feature of the literature on dating is what it says about the issue of free choice. In itself, Waller's attack on the illusion of individual choice was not unacceptable to other sociologists. Sociology, after all, contains a built-in determinism; it hesitates to regard any social phenomenon as arbitrary. Most sociologists did not object to a search for the hidden determinants underlying the "choice" of marriage partners, but they never advanced beyond the most generalized and banal characterization of those determinants: racial, religious, ethnic, and class endogamy; homogamy in general (similarity of habits and temperaments); and psychological determinants such as "the influence of parent-images upon marital choice."[39] The commonplace criticism of sociology—that it tells us in bad English things we knew already—applies with particular force to the study of mate selection. Waller's studies, on the other hand, laid bare the specific mechanisms through which abstract determinants like class, race, and ethnicity translate themselves into social action, in a system that has banished the direct intervention of parents. They showed that activities ostensibly undertaken for pure pleasure had been invaded by the same machinery of organized domination from which pleasure and "fun" were intended to provide relief.

A similar critique could have been made of marriage itself, an institution that supposedly provides a refuge from the competitive free-for-all but increasingly submits to pressures from without. Such a critique could not be formulated, however, except by calling into question not merely the empirical work done by sociologists of the family but the theoretical premises of that work—an act of negation that even Waller was unwilling or unable to undertake.

4

Culture and Personality

By the mid-thirties, American sociology had worked out an interpretation of the contemporary family and its functions that effectively answered those who deplored the family's decline. As a "unit of interacting personalities," the family made up in emotional services, according to this interpretation, for the other functions it had lost. Later scholars made no important modifications in this view, but they restated it with far greater subtlety and conviction. They added, moreover, what was so notably missing from the work of Burgess, Folsom, Waller, and their contemporaries—an analysis of the family's role in socialization. In doing so, they corrected the most obvious weakness of the earlier work, its almost exclusive preoccupation with marriage.

These developments, however, had to wait for theoretical improvements in the related field of psychology and anthropology. Anthropology, having split off from sociology after the collapse of evolutionary theories, entered a fruitful period of reexamination. Although it showed some inclination, like sociology, to substitute a narrow empiricism for the grand theories it now repudiated, anthropology in the twenties and thirties invested even empirical problems with theoretical significance, in part because it could not fall back so easily on the threadbare rationale that empirical work contributed to the formation of social policy and therefore needed no other excuse.

At this time, the field attracted more daring and original scholars than did sociology. It demanded field work in distant places. Under the influence of George Boas, moreover, anthropology had made its mission the criticism of cultural complacency, ethnocentricity, and racism. With its implicit promise of intellectual liberation, anthropology appealed to scholars who belonged to the generation for whom Randolph Bourne had been the principal spokesman— "young intelligentsia," as Margaret Mead wrote to Ruth Benedict, who admired Bourne's conquest of his own "provincialism" and his "sense of what a real national culture might mean," and who "calmly accept[ed] the fruits" of his victories.[1]

New work in psychology provided anthropologists with important ideas, which they eagerly put to use.[2] Gestalt psychology, developed in opposition to behavioral theories of perception, held that the mind perceives structures of experience instead of isolated sensations, and it stimulated anthropologists to speculate about cultural "patterns" or "configurations." Jung's character types suggested the possibility, in the words of Edward Sapir, "that certain recognized pathologies, associated with Jung's types, were given more scope in one culture than in another."[3] Ruth Benedict applied this idea to the study of particular cultures in a paper published in 1928, "Psychological Types in the Cultures of the Southwest."[4] Her famous book *Patterns of Culture* substituted Nietzschean for Jungian terminology, exploring various combinations of "Appollonian" and "Dionysian" elements in three cultures. Margaret Mead used a similar methodology in her studies of Samoa and New Guinea. But it was the work of Freud, simultaneously attractive and repugnant, that most deeply influenced American anthropology in its formative years.

THE CONCEPT OF PERSONALITY

Psychoanalysis commended itself to anthropologists, particularly in contrast to behaviorism, as a dynamic psychology, one that sought not merely to classify mental phenomena but to explain their origin and development.[5] It dealt with daily life in its fullness and complexity, instead of abstracting fragments of experience that could be re-capitulated as experiments in a laboratory. When Ralph Linton argued that the study of personality, because it lay at the "meeting point" of psychology, anthropology, and sociology, would bring these disciplines together, he added that behaviorism, being abstract and undynamic, had nothing to contribute to this reconciliation. Psychoanalytic theorists, on the other hand, understood that "personalities are dynamic continuums" and therefore directed their attention to the growth and development of personality in a complicated human environment. The most important problem confronting students of personality, according to Linton, was the degree to which it was "conditioned" by this environment; and the problem, he insisted, "cannot be solved by laboratory techniques."[6]

Edward Sapir, like Linton, deplored the fragmentation of the "sciences of man" and looked to the study of personality as the best hope of unifying them. Psychiatry had much more to say to the anthropologist than behavioral psychology, according to Sapir, because it dealt with the "total personality," and of the various forms of psychiatry, psychoanalysis stood out as the most promising, having traveled the furthest distance from its medical origins.[7] In throwing off their "largely useless medical training," Freud and his followers had become students of interpersonal relations.[8] Whatever crudities still remained in their approach to interpersonal dynamics could be attributed to the unseemly origins of psychoanalysis, traces of which unfortunately survived in spite of heroic attempts to overcome them. In company with "revisionists" within the psychoanalytic movement itself, cultural anthropologists claimed to have completed the work, begun by Freud himself, of eliminating whatever traces of "biological determinism" clung to a science that had allegedly become clear, cogent, and academically respectable (it might be added) only when it turned from biology to the analysis of personal "interaction."

The validity of psychoanalysis, on this view, by no means depended on Freud's "one-sided" interpretation of sex.[9] Acknowledging the concept of the "unconscious mind" to be the "invaluable kernel" of Freudian thought, Sapir nevertheless identified the unconscious mind purely with intuition and habits, socially "patterned" activities that could be performed without reflection. Whereas Freud's unconscious referred to the unknown (that is, the fiercely repressed), Sapir's referred, on the contrary, to "patterns" that are so well known or at least so familiar that they can be reproduced automatically. Psychoanalysis, he thought, could help anthropologists to understand how social habits are learned, by exposing the influence of "the special pattern of family relationships into which the individual has had to fit himself in the earliest years of his life."[10] Sapir thus reinterpreted psychoanalysis as a contribution to learning theory. Although "nearly everything that is specific in Freudian theory, such as the 'Oedipus-complex,'" might prove to be invalid, he thought Freud's contribution to "pure psychology" would nevertheless survive.[11] Sapir upheld psychoanalysis over behavioral psychology only to redefine psychoanalysis itself as a theory of behavior.

In his later writings, Sapir dissociated himself even further from Freud, whose "haunting imagery of society as censor and of culture as a beautiful extortion from the sinister depths of desire" was already "beginning to take on a certain character of quaintness."[12] At the same time, he drew closer to Harry Stack Sullivan, founder of the psychiatry of interpersonal relations—the most useful form of psychiatric theory, it now seemed to Sapir, for anthropologists who tried to think "not of culture in the abstract nor of society as a hypothetically integrating concept in human relations, but rather of the actual day-to-day relations of specific individuals in a network of highly personalized needs."

Sapir now complained of "the violence with which Freud and his followers have torn many of the facts of primitive behavior out of their natural cultural setting."[13] He relegated not just psychoanalysis but all the social sciences, including anthropology itself, to the realm of "preliminary disciplines" engaged in collecting and classifying data and incapable of going further. Their practice of wrenching out of context only what could be subsumed under their respective disciplines violated the complexity of human experience, according to Sapir, and contributed to the fragmentation of knowledge. They dealt not with the whole personality but with bits and pieces of it, with abstractions like "economic man" or "sociological man." Their "obscure opposition of spirit" would have to give way to a higher form of objectivity, one that tried "to bring every cultural pattern back to the living context from which it has been abstracted in the first place."[14] Repeatedly Sapir spoke of the need to rehumanize anthropology, to put man back into the study of man.

In one of his last essays, he let fall a revealing observation about
the "unconscious motivations" of scholars. Those who study culture,
he wrote, have a deep and unacknowledged desire to lose themselves in historically determined patterns of behavior, while the
study of personality "proceeds from the necessity which the ego
feels to assert itself significantly."[15] But the growing concern with
personality in our society originates in the ego's need to assert itself
not for the sheer joy of self-expression, as Sapir seems to imply, but
in order to counter the forces that seem bent on its annihilation. This
defensive "assertion" of the ego takes many forms, among them the
demand for study and understanding of the "whole personality."
The divided self insists on its own wholeness. The theory of interpersonal relations bases itself on the premise that personality constitutes not a battleground (Freud's more accurate perception) but an
integrated, harmonious whole. Yet this same "science" occasionally
betrays the uneasiness that brought it into being. When he condemns scholars who abstract fragments of the personality from its
"natural" context, Sapir resorts to images of violence and violation
that seem to express the ego's sense of being invaded by enemies
which it feels increasingly powerless to resist. The "unity of the individual," it appears, is precisely what science can no longer take for
granted, and the demand that science address itself to that unity assumes what most needs to be proved.

Attracted to psychoanalysis in the first place because it seemed to
encompass every facet of human experience, Sapir misinterpreted
this inclusiveness as an announcement that personality had to be
studied as a unified whole, a notion completely at odds with the intention of psychoanalysis. Thus he found safety of sorts in the heart
of danger, but only by sacrificing Freud's essential insights into the
divided self, as well as his own hope of a social science without abstractions. Seeking to banish abstractions like "economic man," he
ended by hypostatizing the integrated personality, an abstraction to
end abstractions.

PSYCHOANALYSIS AS A THEORY OF FAMILY DYNAMICS: MALINOWSKI'S "REFUTATION" OF FREUD

Cultural anthropology grew up as part of a humanistic, reformist, and vaguely radical protest. It first invoked the principle of cultural relativism against racist interpretations of cultural differences. Throughout the twenties, thirties, and forties, students of culture and personality continued to battle against racism, made more menacing than ever by the rise of fascism. Not only did they employ cultural explanations to undermine racial ones, but they also provided a cultural explanation of racial prejudice itself, linking it to a psychological pattern of authoritarianism allegedly created by special patterns of culture. Kardiner and Ovesey's sociopsychoanalytic study of American blacks, *The Mark of Oppression;* the famous Myrdal study of race and racism, *An American Dilemma;* the studies of prejudice conducted by Allport, Bettelheim and Janowitz, and others; Adorno's *Authoritarian Personality,* and other landmarks of American social science originated in the need to provide a scientific basis for the new tolerance that grew out of the New Deal, the Popular Front, and the struggle against fascism. Although it signaled a genuine shift in popular thinking, the new tolerance of racial and ethnic diversity never enjoyed such acceptance that it was not in danger of repudiation. All these works came from liberals or socialists, and all of them, except perhaps *The Authoritarian Personality,* reflected a reformist, integrationist, and pluralistic outlook.

It was the war against racism that predisposed social scientists in the United States not only to reject evolutionary theories, which often had racist overtones, but also to disallow anything that looked like "biological determinism," including Freud's insistence on the primacy of libidinal drives. Yet Bronislaw Malinowski's "refutation" of Freud opened the way, curiously enough, for the reconciliation of psychoanalysis and anthropology. In a series of controversial articles published in the early twenties and brought together in 1927 under the title *Sex and Repression in Savage Society,* Malinowski argued, among other things, that "psycho-analytic doctrine is essentially a theory of the influence of family life on the human mind." Having subtly perverted the Freudian view, he could now protest that "if family life is so fateful for human mentality its character deserves

more attention" than Freud gave it. Closer study of the family revealed that it "is not the same in all societies." In Melanesia, for example, where descent is matrilineal and the father's status in the
family is correspondingly diminished, the mother's brother plays the
paternal role; but since he lives in a household of his own and exercises his authority only at a distance, Malinowski argued, he never
appears in the child's eyes as a rival for the sexual favors of the child's
mother. More easygoing in their sexual practices than the Europeans, the Trobriand Islanders allow "the sensuous clinging of the
child to his mother . . . to take its natural course till it plays itself
out." Under these conditions, according to Malinowski, the "typical
configuration of sentiments" associated with the Oedipus complex
never takes shape. If anything, the Trobriand Islander wishes to
marry his sister and to kill the maternal uncle. Instead of assuming
the universality of the Oedipus complex, then, we need to study
"every type of civilization, to establish the special complex which
pertains to it." [16]

Far from refuting Freud, Malinowski simply shifted the discussion from unconscious mental life to the study of "attitudes" and
"sentiments." For the study of unconscious mental processes, as
revealed in dreams, fantasies, and neurosis, he substituted the study
of family structure, child rearing, and the formation of "sentiments."
In place of analysis of symbolism and of ideas produced in free association, he substituted simple observation, thereby restricting anthropological study to conscious, overt, and explicitly acknowledged
"attitudes." The Oedipus complex became a family psychodrama, a
"typical configuration of sentiments." Claiming to have made a theoretical advance over Freud, Malinowski retreated to earlier ways of
looking both at the mind and at society. He referred his readers to
A. D. Shand, whose theory of "sentiments" showed how some of
Freud's ideas could be put "on a sound theoretical basis," while
others—for example, the "nuclear [family] complex"—were to be
rejected in favor of the study of "the family sentiments, of kinship
ties typical of a given society." [17]

As a theory of society no less than of the psyche, Malinowski's
work represented a backward step. It reverted to the tradition of
Comte, Spencer, Durkheim, and Cooley, just when it appeared to
have received a blow from Freud as damaging as the one it had earlier received from Marx—just at the point, in other words, when the

theory of society as an evolving body of ideas and attitudes, an essentially harmonious equilibrium, encountered the challenge of a theory that placed renewed emphasis on the conflict of material interests. The tradition of "sympathy" now became one of the chief props of cultural anthropology and structural-functionalist sociology. In the same way that Comte and Durkheim had banished from sociology the Marxian conflict of class against class, Malinowski tried to banish the conflict of culture against nature. Whereas Freud saw instinct as a mass of insatiable appetites on which culture is superimposed only with great difficulty and never with more than partial success, Malinowski treated culture and nature as a harmonious continuum. Building on the natural sympathy between parents and their offspring, culture cooperates with nature to develop familial "sentiments," while prohibiting the incestuous relationships that would be their undoing. "Culture emphasizes rather than overrides the natural tendencies," in Malinowski's bland formulation.[18] Thus marriage and the family originate in "strong mutual attachment," without which, indeed, marital institutions would have a poor chance of survival. Culture "modifies" instincts, which as a matter of fact are eminently adaptable and "plastic," but it has no occasion to deny them altogether, since instincts complement culture rather than subvert it.[19]

In arguing that marriage rests on the maternal "instinct," Malinowski followed Westermarck, whom he defended against advocates of the matriarchal theory of the family's origin. In debates with Robert Briffault, he argued that marriage "is everywhere based on love and affection" and that mutual dependence between husband and wife is "universal."[20] Although he disputed the universality of the Oedipus complex, Malinowski by no means questioned the universality of the nuclear family, and it is ironic, therefore, that his lyrical description of the matrilineal society of the Trobriand Islands helped to revive the matriarchal theories he sought to refute. Himself a traditionalist, more conservative in his sexual attitudes than Freud himself, Malinowski gave unwitting aid and comfort to the "misbehaviorists" he liked to berate, who criticized the modern nuclear family because it thwarted individuality and sexual freedom. Such ideas in his opinion were "rubbish"; yet his tropical paradise, where nubile maidens and their lovers disported themselves under the benevolent eye of their elders, proved to be a sexual liberationist's dream. It gratified the progressive's need to believe that alternatives to the nuclear family—alternatives less oppressive to women and children and more open to sexual experimentation—existed not only in the socialist utopia but in historical experience. Even Boas, though he complained that Malinowski was "much too influenced" by Freud, took a lively interest in "the problem he had in mind": the possible existence of societies without sexual guilt and stormy adolescent rebellion. When Margaret Mead sailed for Samoa, Boas urged her to find out whether adolescents in the South Seas went through a period of rebellion comparable to that of American adolescents, or whether "the desire for independence," as he clearly preferred to think, "may be simply due to our modern conditions and to a more strongly developed individualism."[21] Judging from the results of her work in the South Pacific, his encouragement was superfluous. Studies that painted such a glowing picture of the sexual life of savages, throwing so many doubts over civilized practices by contrast, could only have grown out of an inner predisposition to find among primitives an alternative to modern disorder and neurosis. Ironically it was Malinowski, however, whose studies must clearly pointed the way to such conclusions.

ANTHROPOLOGY IN THE SERVICE

OF PSYCHOSEXUAL REFORM

Following Malinowski's example, Margaret Mead analyzed the "organization of the household" and domestic sentiments—not unconscious mental life—and then concluded that Freud's interpretation of mental life exaggerated the importance of biology and minimized the role of culture. The Samoans, she believed, grew up untroubled by the "conflicts," "philosophical queries," or "remote ambitions" of adolescents in the West. The Oedipus complex was unknown and psychic development "painless," "normal," and "unneurotic." The study of Samoa confirmed what anthropologists had already suspected, that psychoanalysis erred in regarding childhood and adolescence as "unavoidable periods of adjustment through which every one has to pass." On the contrary, "much of what we ascribe to human nature," according to Mead, "is no more than a reaction to the restraints put upon us by our civilization."[22]

The rise in juvenile delinquency, together with the increasingly open and visible rebellion of the young, prompted the question: "If it is proved that adolescence is not necessarily a specially difficult period in a girl's life—and proved it is if we can find any society in which that is so—then what accounts for the presence of storm and stress in American adolescents?"[23] Mead, Benedict, Geoffrey Gorer, and other students of personality and culture returned many times to this question, to which they provided a variety of answers. In 1938, Ruth Benedict published an essay exploring "discontinuities" in the life cycle of the average American. As children, she argued, Americans are segregated from the adult world, especially from work and sex, in a world organized around play, strong taboos on sexual expression, and submission to adult authority. As adults, however, these same Americans are expected to work, to give and receive sexual satisfaction, and to assert themselves as autonomous individuals. "Adult activity demands traits that are interdicted in children." The disjunction between the child's role and the one he is expected to perform as an adult makes the transition between them awkward and painful; hence the *Sturm und Drang* of adolescence. Many "maladjusted persons" never manage the transition at all. Instead of helping to ease it, however, adults make matters worse by punishing those who fail to negotiate it smoothly, thereby reinforcing the very habits of passive obedience they expect the adolescent to overcome.[24]

In an essay written eleven years later, Benedict took a more genial view of the American family. Passing over the "youth question" in silence, she argued that "the family in the United States is an institution remarkably adapted to our treasured way of life." In a society based on "free choice and privacy," the family naturally reflected those values. Both the rising divorce rate and the increasing use of contraceptives, according to Benedict, had to be seen not as signs of decay but merely as extensions of the individual's freedom of choice. Traditionalists might deplore these developments, but to an anthropologist with a professional awareness of the variety and diversity of familial institutions, the outcry signified nothing more serious than the natural tendency to make the family "a convenient whipping boy among many peoples who disapprove of the way their world is going."[25]

Margaret Mead's ideas about adolescence and the American family developed in a different direction. In her book on Samoa, Mead blamed the plight of American adolescents on romantic love and unhealthy attitudes toward sex. Whereas Americans regarded sex with a mixture of prudery and prurience, the Samoans, according to Mead, showed a healthy "acceptance of sex."[26] Whereas Americans stigmatized homosexuality and other perversions, Samoans tolerated them as forms of play and thereby "legislated a whole field of neurotic possibility out of existence."[27] Americans are jealous and possessive in love; Samoa happily lacks the idea of romantic love, with its associated "ideas of monogamy, exclusiveness, jealousy, and undeviating fidelity." As for the nuclear family, "it cripples the emotional life" and produces "maladjusted individuals," whereas in Samoa the "large family community" "diffuses" affection and prevents the formation of the "crippling attitudes which have been labelled Oedipus complexes, Electra complexes, and so on."[28]

In her next book, *Growing Up in New Guinea*, Mead shifted her ground, largely because the Manus of New Guinea presented such a different kind of contrast to the United States. Unlike the Samoans, they regarded sexuality with what Mead described as "puritanical" misgivings. Instead of raising their children in the "mild warmth" of the extended family, they bound them closely to their fathers in the hope of imbuing them with patriarchal values. Yet here too, adolescence in the Western sense was unknown. The trouble with the American system, Mead decided, was that it combined the worst features of the Samoan and Manuan "systems of education" without achieving the advantages of either. It provided neither the diffused warmth of the extended family nor the close paternal companionship of the Manus. Like the Manus, Americans imposed little effective discipline on their children, giving them "years of cultural non-participation in which they are permitted to live in a world of their own"; but then American parents perversely insisted on the importance of family ties and made it hard for their children to break away. The erosion of patriarchal authority, it now appeared to Mead, underlay both these incompatible practices. "The degeneration of the father's role into that of a tired, often dreaded, nightly visitor has done much to make his son's happy identification with him impossible." The growing dominance of women over child rearing, including much of the daily discipline, weakened this identification even further. American girls, Mead thought, "often get a better time of it," since their initial identification with the mother offered "a workable pattern of life." "Our boys," on the other hand, "are condemned to approximate to a dull generic idea of *manhood,* rather than to a number of interesting, known *men.*"[29]

In books and articles written during the forties, Mead restated and amplified this indictment of the American family. Like Geoffrey Gorer in his study of American national character, she traced the decline of paternal authority to rapid social change, which allegedly rendered the values of one generation useless to the next. Children and adolescents, sensing the incompetence of the older generation—carried to an extreme in the first-generation immigrants' helplessness in dealing with conditions their children took for granted—turned to their peers for guidance. But the substitution of youth culture for parental authority did not solve the problem, according to Mead, since individuals who are "striving hard to meet the standards of persons who inspire no great respect," such as their adolescent peers, tend to devalue themselves, unlike those who are "attempting to meet standards represented by remote and highly respected persons."[30] Nor did the peer group free American adolescents from the cloying ties of maternal dependence. The mother, thanks to her role in providing care and love, still commanded a degree of respect long since denied to the father, becoming in Gorer's words "the dominant parent in the American family, almost, as it were, by default."[31] But she used her power not to help her sons grow up, as a father would, but to keep them tied to her apron strings. In the eyes of Gorer and Mead, the erosion of patriarchal authority thus gave rise to the twin evils of the American family system, the tyranny of the adolescent peer group and the condition popularly decried as "Momism."

This analysis of the American family contained a great deal of truth, but it remained imprisoned in the reformist outlook of the twenties and thirties. Margaret Mead, like other progressives, wanted Americans to cultivate the idea that "sex is a natural, pleasurable thing."[32]

She shared the social pathologists' suspicion of romantic love and the emotional excesses of adolescence. Societies like Samoa appealed to advocates of sexual "realism" and "health" because of their matter-of-factness about sex, which had the desirable effect, in their eyes, of eliminating passion, jealousy, and what Mead called "violent preferences." Her criticism of the American family originated in a belief that the "mild warmth" of comradeship was healthier than attachments modeled on family ties and therefore vested—as is inevitably the case with passionate attachments—with neurotic anxiety and desire. If she condemned Momism, it was because she wished in general "to mitigate . . . the strong role which parents play in children's lives." Her reservations about the adolescent peer group rested on reservations about adolescence itself, which in her mind epitomized the neurotic anxieties of modern civilization. She saw adolescence as a disease, a prolonged fever, a tumult of overheated infatuations, self-absorption, and psychic conflict.[33]

By centering her criticism of the American family on Momism and adolescence, Mead singled out familiar features of domestic life that were already passing from the scene. The mother's influence in the middle-class American family has increased only in relation to that of the father. The decline of paternal authority has weakened the influence of both parents and undermined the affective identification of the younger generation with the older. Recent evidence suggests that American children, far from becoming overly dependent on their mothers, form strong attachments to neither parent, acquiring instead, at an early stage in their lives, a cool, detached, and realistic outlook on the world. Adolescence, formerly the tumultuous transition from childhood dependence to the responsibilities of adulthood, has become almost obsolete.

The growing importance of the peer group, which at first sight appears to reflect the growing importance of adolescence—the "prolongation of adolescence" in a society that requires more and more training for most adult roles—actually coincides with the decline of adolescence. "Development has ceased to exist," wrote Max Horkheimer as early as 1941. "The child is grown up as soon as he can walk. During the heyday of the family the father represented the authority of society to the child, and puberty was the inevitable conflict between these two. Today, however, the child stands face to face with society at once, and the conflict is decided even before it arises."[34] As Mead herself noted two years later, "the child's eyes are focused upon the outside world."[35] He masters that world more easily than his parents and learns to survive by getting along with his peers. He rejects the family not as the intermediary through which social demands are transmitted but, on the contrary, as an institution itself out of step with those demands. He throws off the older generation not because it upholds the reality principle but because it appears out-of-date, old-fashioned, ineffectual, superfluous. In Horkheimer's striking phrase, "The child, not the father, stands for reality."[36]

Under these conditions, the traditional turmoil of adolescence subsides. Instead of withdrawing into himself or trying to overcome his loneliness through passionate friendships and love affairs, the adolescent now prefers the casual, easygoing sociability of his peers. Confronted from early childhood with demands for adaptability, flexibility, and "considered acquiescence in the demands of group living," the adolescent, historically the quintessential rebel, "abandons the task of defining himself in dialectical combat with society and becomes its captive and its emissary."[37]

Margaret Mead's analysis of the American family belongs to the category of social criticism which attacks arrangements already on the wane, disguising as independent, somewhat cantankerous and unpopular judgments what in many ways amounts to an apology for the emerging order. Such criticism boldly defends views that have already become acceptable to everyone except the most hardened reactionaries. Mead's attack on jealousy and passion gave support to one of the strongest currents in modern society. Her plea for sexual realism—for what has recently been referred to as "cool sex"—represented not so much a demand for change as the description of a change in attitudes that had already come into being. As for her indictment of Momism and of the excessive influence of parents, the collapse of parental influence has rendered such "criticism" innocuous—indeed, has created a considerable demand for it in a country where defense of an emerging status quo usually takes the form of urgent calls for sweeping reform.

CULTURE AGAINST "BIOLOGICAL DETERMINISM":
THE CONTROVERSY ABOUT
FREUD'S PSYCHOLOGY OF WOMEN

The revisionist movement in psychoanalytic theory, which shaped
culture and personality studies in so many ways, sprang from the
same reformist, humanitarian spirit that gave rise to cultural anthropology.[38] In particular, revisionism was shaped by feminism. We are
only beginning to understand—thanks to renewed criticism of
Freud by neofeminists today—that debates about the psychology
of women played a crucial part in the controversies over revisions of Freud in the twenties and thirties, among anthropologists
but especially among psychoanalysts themselves (many of whom
were women). From the start, revisionism in psychoanalysis was informed by feminist criticism of Freud and by a social democratic
outlook, which objected to the "pessimism" of Freud's theories and
sought to recast them in a form more congenial to reformist and
pseudo-revolutionary hopes of social improvement. The revisionist
strategy was to argue that Freud had stressed biology at the expense
of culture and that in his psychology of women, for example, he had
attributed to biology (the lack of a penis, leading to penis envy) a
sense of inferiority that was in fact rooted in social reality—the objectively inferior position of women in Western society. It is easy to
see why the psychology of women became an issue seemingly made
to order for the purpose of a "cultural" refutation of Freud.

The continuing criticism of Freud both by feminists and by
writers claiming to work in the psychoanalytic tradition makes it important to be clear about what Freud actually said about women,
especially since his critics cannot be trusted to represent his ideas
correctly. Much more is at stake in this dispute than the psychology
of women. The revisionist critique of Freud profoundly influenced
the study of culture and personality in the twenties and thirties, and
the sociology of the family that later grew out of it. Anyone who
believes that Freud's ideas remain indispensable to an understanding of the contemporary family—in particular, of the psychological effects of the socialization of reproduction—has to show how
the revisionists, in the very attempt to incorporate psychoanalysis

into the study of culture, lost its most important insight: the irreconcilable antagonism between culture and instinct. Without this insight, it becomes impossible to understand how the family mediates between the two or to understand what happens, psychologically, when the socialization of reproduction weakens or abolishes this mediation.

The revisionist interpretation of Freud not only found its way into social science, it pervaded the thought and practice of social pathology. Colored by feminism, by enlightened ideas about child rearing and sex education, and by the "prophylactic" version of Freudian theory that seized on psychoanalysis as a major instrument of social reform in its own right, revisionism ideally suited the needs of social workers, child development specialists, marriage counselors, and other experts bent on replacing the "authoritarian" family with a democratic or "developmental" style of domestic life.[39] Revisionist ideas thus contributed indirectly to the family's development, at the same time that they made the psychological consequences of that development so difficult to understand.

Freud did not pay much attention to the psychology of women, as such, until the 1920s. Although his first patients were women, who furnished much of the material on which he based his interpretation of dreams and hysteria, the theory of the Oedipus complex—the culmination of this early work and the core of psychoanalytic theory— attempted to explain the psychology of the male on the assumption that "with little girls," as Freud later put it, "things must be similar, though in some way or other they must nevertheless be different."[40]

The vague sense that things must be different made Freud reject the concept of the "Electra complex" when it was proposed by Jung in 1913 to describe the female equivalent of the Oedipus complex— an experience more or less exactly paralleling that of the male, it was thought, with the sexual roles reversed. But it was not until 1925, with the publication of a short paper entitled "Some Psychical Consequences of the Anatomical Distinction Between the Sexes," that Freud decisively repudiated the supposition that the psychic history of men and women runs along parallel lines. He now began to realize that "what we have said about the Oedipus complex applies with complete strictness to the male child only."[41] Two further essays— "Female Sexuality" (1931) and "Femininity" (1933)—explored the implications of this statement and provided for the first time the outlines of a psychoanalytic theory of womanhood.[42]

As Juliet Mitchell explains in her recent account of Freudian theory, Freud rejected theories of parallel development only when he had attained a clearer understanding of the pre-Oedipal phase in women.[43] Clinical analysis showed that the little girl, like the boy, is first drawn to her mother; nor is this a passive attraction, any more than the boy's. Children of both sexes, according to Freud, tend to convert passive impressions into an active desire to master and possess the object that aroused those impressions. "This is part of the work imposed [on the child] of mastering the external world." Accordingly, the girl wishes to possess and to penetrate her mother. ("No doubt this sounds quite absurd, but perhaps that is only because it sounds so unfamiliar.") Freud himself found it difficult, he says, to credit the little girl's wishes, until his experience with patients "removed all doubts on the matter."[44]

It is only the subsequent discovery of her own "castration" that causes the little girl to relinquish the hope of "giving her mother a baby," not without a prolonged struggle in which the girl reproaches her mother for not providing her with a proper penis and ends by repudiating the mother in favor of the father. This shift also requires that the girl translate her sexuality from an active to a passive mode. The wish to possess is transformed into a wish to be possessed.[45] The longing for a penis is transformed into the longing for a baby.[46]

The pre-Oedipal phase, Freud concluded, has "a far greater importance in women than it can have in men," and it is dissolved only through "an especially inexorable repression." Whereas a boy has only to translate the wish for his mother into the deferred reward of a future wife, the girl has to go from a "phallic" phase to a passive one, a process "to which there is nothing analogous in the male." The little boy resolves or at least represses the Oedipus complex through the fear of castration, which causes him to repudiate the wish to possess his mother, to introject his father's authority, and thus also to accept the authority of society itself, internalized through the paternal intermediary. The dissolution of the Oedipus complex in the male "leads to the creation of his super-ego and thus initiates all the processes that are designed to make the individual find a place in the cultural community."[47]

Whereas in the boy the fear of castration dissolves the Oedipus complex, the *fact* of "castration" initiates it in the little girl. In women, therefore, the Oedipus complex amounts to "a secondary formation," according to Freud, not only because it is preceded rather than followed by the "castration complex" but, more important, because the "motive for the demolition of the Oedipus complex is lacking." The little boy not only abandons the wish for the mother but represses it out of recognition, and this "catastrophe to the Oedipus complex (the abandonment of incest and the institution of conscience and morality) may be regarded as a victory of the race over the individual." The girl has no comparable motive for the ruthless repression of her father-fixation. The father was second-best to begin with. Renunciation of the mother already entailed acceptance of "castration." The girl therefore does not so much resolve the Oedipus complex as take refuge in it. In doing so she already becomes "a little woman," in Freud's words; and although it will later be necessary to renounce her father in favor of another man, this act does not involve, as did the earlier renunciation of the mother, a fundamental shift in the girl's sexuality. Nor does the dissolution of the Oedipus complex entail, as it does in the boy, the internalization of the father's authority and with it the prevailing culture and morality. For this reason, Freud thought, women's "superego is never so inexorable, so impersonal, so independent of its emotional origins as we require it to be in men"—a conclusion, he insisted, from which "we must not allow ourselves to be deflected . . . by the denials of the feminists, who are anxious to force us to regard the two sexes as completely equal in position and worth."[48]

Freudian theory, wrongly accused of biological determinism, attempts to explain how the cultural heritage is acquired and internalized by each generation; it analyzes the psychic consequences of this process, showing, among other things, how these consequences differ in men and women. If women are typically more emotional than men, more dependent on the approval of others, less strongly committed to abstract standards of honor and justice, less fiercely competitive, more loving and "maternal," psychoanalysis ascribes these differences neither to women's nature nor, on the other hand, to the sexual division of labor that assigns child rearing to women. "Femininity" is not innate, but neither is it the product of "cultural conditioning." For psychoanalysis the important point is not that women are victimized (as they are) by sexual stereotypes

perpetrated by men in their own self-interest, but that in any culture the process of becoming a woman requires the repression of the
active and phallic side of woman's sexuality, a repression so thorough, and so little accessible to conscious understanding or control,
that passivity comes to resemble a fact of nature, an inherent attribute of womanhood.

Without conceding anything to those who wished to see the psychic history of women as parallel to that of men, Freud nevertheless
qualified his remarks on the special psychology of women by
upholding a theory of bisexuality. The feminine psyche, he argued,
contains active as well as passive traits (as ought to be abundantly
clear from the foregoing analysis). Likewise, men are partly "feminine." Strictly speaking, the concepts of masculinity and femininity
are without meaning: in the first place because empirically any individual will show a combination of "masculine" and "feminine" characteristics, and in the second, because masculinity and femininity
are merely synonyms for activity and passivity and nothing is
gained—as Freud argued on many occasions—by sexualizing these
terms. "Psychoanalysis does not try to describe what a woman is—
that would be a task it could scarcely perform—but sets about
enquiring how she comes into being, how a woman develops out
of a child with a bisexual disposition."[49] This distinction, essential to the psychoanalytic theory of womanhood, was soon forgotten
by those who began to dissent from Freud's findings.

THE ALLIANCE OF REVISIONISM
AND FEMINISM

Revisionism was full of ironies. Attempting to radicalize Freud, the
revisionists eliminated what was radical from his thought, the articu-
lation of contradictions without any attempt to resolve them: the
contradiction between the bourgeois myth of the autonomous individual and the evidence of unconscious determinism uncovered by
the analysis of dreams and neurosis; the contradiction between "civilized sexual morality" and the rampant, insatiable sexuality underly-

ing it; above all, the conflict between nature and culture. In attempting to rid psychoanalysis of its "biological reductionism" in favor of an emphasis on culture, the revisionists forgot that psychoanalysis offers precisely a theory about the ways in which culture is assimilated and handed on. As a result, they often fell into a biological reductionism of their own. Finally, the feminist version of this social democratic critique of Freud accused Freud of an uncritical masculine bias at the very moment Freud repudiated the male bias that saw the psychology of women as parallel to that of men.

In 1926, Karen Horney published her essay "The Flight from Womanhood," in which she argued on the one hand that woman's cultural subordination explains more about the psychology of women than penis envy does, and on the other hand that the concept of penis envy is in any case unnecessary in explaining the girl's shift from father to mother. That shift, Horney contended, merely reflects an "elementary principle of nature"—the "mutual attraction of the sexes."[50] The founder of the so-called cultural school of psychoanalysis thus upheld the theoretical primacy of culture only to fall back into biological mystification—"a solution of ideal simplicity," as Freud wrote in 1933,[51] but a solution that had the unfortunate effect of blotting out the pre-Oedipal phase of the girl's development, of burying still further her buried desire for her mother, and of obscuring all the ways in which this primal attraction later enters into her relations with fathers and husbands. Already the insights of psychoanalysis were giving way to "common sense."[52] In her eagerness to argue that "femininity" establishes itself in earliest infancy, moreover, Horney showed no awareness of the problem to which Freud referred when he warned that psychoanalysis could not hope to define the essence of femininity but could only explain how the girl becomes a woman.

Horney's arguments were elaborated in subsequent papers by herself, Alfred Adler, Clara Thompson, Frieda Fromm-Reichman, Gregory Zilboorg, and others. "The belief in her inferiority is forced upon a girl by her environment," wrote Adler—by the objective fact of her inequality and by "the prejudice concerning the inferiority of women."[53] Clara Thompson argued that penis envy, which in her opinion had "little to do with sexual life," was the symbolic expression of a wish for equality with men. Women "envied" the masculine power and prestige symbolized by the penis, not the penis itself.[54]

In any case, it appeared that men envied the womb as ardently as women the penis. "Men are envious of women's ability to bear children," wrote Erich Fromm in 1949. ". . . Somewhere in the man exists an awe of woman for this capacity which he lacks."[55] Zilboorg, reviving the matriarchal theory in order to explain men's "fundamental hostility" to women, argued that "birth envy" preceded penis envy and was therefore "more fundamental."[56] In a word, these writers either qualified the concept of penis envy by proposing an equivalent "womb envy" in the male or dismissed the idea altogether as an expression of Freud's "androcentric" bias. In both cases—as this inconsistency suggests—they seemed to wish not so much to understand what is distinctive about women's psychic development as to exonerate women from what the revisionists, with their tendency to substitute normative judgments for critical analysis, mistook as an ethical indictment.[57]

The revisionists invoked the fact of women's cultural subjection only to deny it. They argued that this subjection tells us all we need to know about women, but they refused to concede that it has any important psychic effects. Their program of exonerating women led some of these writers so far as to argue that women are biologically the superior sex—in which case it becomes impossible to account for their historical subjection, on which, nevertheless, the "cultural" argument has to rest.

In their writings on women, as in the rest of their work, the revisionists preferred to deal with conscious rather than unconscious mental processes and—what comes to the same thing—to downplay the importance of sex. They saw the lack of a penis merely as a "badge" of women's cultural inferiority in a patriarchal society, just as they saw a black skin as a symbol of inferiority in a racist society.[58] Then they advanced elaborate theories of sexual antagonism in order to explain the "battle of the sexes." The study of "interpersonal relations" replaced analysis of the unconscious. Politically, the revisionist argument implied a reformist strategy. Just as an attack on racial prejudice was the practical outcome of comparable psychoanalytic studies of racism, so the reduction of penis envy to the status of an incident in the sex war dictated an attempt to change sexual attitudes: to abolish male chauvinism and to raise the consciousness of women.

The concept of bisexuality suffered a fate similar to that of penis envy. Uncomfortable with the implications of bisexuality, Freud's interpreters explained away the phallic phase in women as a reaction, essentially "regressive" in character (according to Ernest Jones), to the fact of woman's subordination.[59] Accurately perceiving her fate as a woman, the little girl may seek to deny her femininity—Karen Horney's "flight from womanhood"—in acts and fantasies that must not be misinterpreted as evidence of a primary identification with the phallus. The validity of Freud's phallic theory—and therefore, by extension, of the theory of bisexuality—is further undermined, we are told, by empirical evidence showing that girls discover the vagina and its pleasurable feelings at an early age. In asserting the contrary, Freud supposedly gave scientific currency to popular slanders designed to keep women in their place. Accordingly, the business of eradicating these "prejudices" and "ideologies" begins with an attack on psychoanalysis itself, their pseudoscientific rationale.

In devoting so much of their attention to the role of ideology, the feminist critics of Freud drew on a theory of what Karen Horney called "cultural contradictions," according to which neuroses and other sociopsychological problems originate in the conflict between ideals and reality and are cured by bringing ideals and reality into closer agreement. An all-purpose explanatory principle which explains nothing, this idea runs all through modern social science. Sociologists of the family attributed marital unhappiness to the disparity between romantic illusions and the reality of marriage. Students of culture and personality made much of the "contradiction" between the ideal of brotherly love and the reality of economic competition. In the same vein, Myrdal analyzed American race relations as a conflict between the ideal of equality and the reality of discrimination. Robert Merton attributed anomie to the disparity between the myth of success and the fact of economic inequality. Parsons's theory of social "strains" rests on the same kind of thinking, which appeals to liberals and social democrats because it leads to the conclusion that most issues can be resolved by a judicious combination of "education" and social reform. In practice, this usually means adjusting expectations to reality rather than the reverse. Thus the revisionists, both as theorists and as therapists, hoped that by refuting popular and scientific prejudices against women they could upgrade women's self-esteem and give them a more positive conception of femininity. Through attacks on penis envy, on the notion that women are incapable of sharing fully in the pleasure of sex, on conventions that equate menstruation with a "curse," and on a great variety of other stereotypes, the revisionists intended to make it possible for women to "accept" womanhood instead of blindly submitting or blindly seeking to escape it.[60]

When the revisionists attempted to dig somewhat deeper into the sources of woman's subjection, it was only to explore another level of interpersonal relations: the play of feelings and sentiments within the family. Horney, for example, reinterpreted the Oedipus complex as a series of "destructive and lasting jealousy relations" and argued that anthropological studies showed these relations to be not "so common as Freud assumes." Citing Fromm, Reich, and Malinowski, she insisted that the Oedipus complex is "culturally conditioned." In our own culture, it derives from "lack of harmony in marriage . . . ; unlimited authoritative power of the parents; taboos on every sexual outlet for a child; [and] tendencies to keep a child infantile and emotionally dependent on the parents."[61] This indictment of jealousy, possessiveness, and excessive parental influence resembles that of Margaret Mead, as does the program of social reform or social therapy to which such observations give rise. If the Oedipus complex is only a special form of jealousy, the task of psychoanalysis is not to analyze dreams and fantasies in the hope of uncovering their unconscious roots but to overcome jealousy, which originates, according to Horney, in the "neurotic need for affection" that afflicts modern society like a scourge:

> Competitiveness and its potential hostilities between fellow-beings, fears, diminished self-esteem, result psychologically in the individual feeling that he is isolated. . . . It is this situation which provokes . . . an intensified need for affection as a remedy.[62]

We are back to the need for "community." Reform psychoanalysis proposed to combat the loneliness of modern life not by eliminating its sources but by instituting prophylactic measures designed to improve the mental health of the public: better education, adjustment of attitudes to reality, general enlightenment.

THE AUTHORITARIAN PERSONALITY:
REICH, FROMM, AND THE FRANKFURT SCHOOL

The study of culture and personality in the United States—the joint undertaking of cultural anthropologists and psychoanalysts seeking to humanize Freudian theory and to overcome its "biologism"— grew up side by side with a new school of social theory led by Wilhelm Reich, Erich Fromm, and the so-called Frankfurt school, which in its attempt to make use of both psychology and sociology, psychoanalysis and Marxism, raised many of the same issues.[63] Both movements—psychoanalytic revisionism and cultural anthropology on the one hand, neo-Marxism on the other—drew on the German tradition of philosophical idealism, and both had adherents in the German refugee community in the United States. They shared, moreover, a commitment to social change, which made them critical of the authoritarian family, sexual repression, and "puritanical" morality. The critique of bourgeois repression, a dominant theme in the early work of the German neo-Marxists, became more and more pronounced in the writings of Reich, Fromm, and often in those of Herbert Marcuse, whose call for "cultural revolution" made him a spokesman of the American left in the 1960s. From the beginning, however, these ideas coexisted, especially in the work of Max Horkheimer and T. W. Adorno, with a growing awareness that changes in personality organization, which all these theorists saw as having laid the psychological basis for fascism and other forms of political repression, derived not from the power of familial authority but from its collapse.

Like the students of culture and personality in the United States, the German radicals often took contradictory views of the contemporary family. According to a critic of the Frankfurt school, this contradiction betrays the fatal influence of the "Hegelian legacy." It shows that both sets of conclusions are "rationalistically derived from prior premises rather than the result of empirical inquiry."[64] Empirical research, however, cannot in itself dissipate theoretical confusion and uncertainty, which in this case arises not so much from "prior premises" as from the intrinsic obscurity of the problem under investigation: the rise of a new type of despotism that does not depend on the authoritarian family but precisely on its dissolution.

The German radicals became interested in the study of culture and personality for political, not purely theoretical, reasons. As Marxists, they wished to explain why bourgeois society had survived the revolutionary crisis of 1914–1919—why the revolutionary movement had failed, although the objective conditions for the collapse of capitalism had been present for decades. After Hitler's seizure of power in 1933, this question merged with another: Why had German workers failed to put up any effective resistance to fascism, even though they opposed it at the polls and could see that fascism did not represent their material interests? To put the question more broadly: By what means do the few tyrannize over the many? As they pondered these issues, many Marxists in the twenties and thirties (not merely those associated with the Frankfurt school) came to understand the limits of a purely mechanical and objective Marxism. It was the subjective conditions of social revolution, it appeared, that were missing from European society; hence only a Marxism capable of analyzing subjectivity (instead of simply deducing it from economic "laws") was capable of analyzing the crisis of bourgeois society. This insight gave rise in turn to an interest in culture and ideology, the rediscovery of the early Marx, and the revival of the dialectical element in a Marxist tradition that had succumbed to positivism.

"Man is above all else mind, consciousness," wrote Antonio Gramsci in 1916—"that is, he is a product of history, not of nature. There is no other way of explaining why socialism has not come into existence already, [for] there have always been exploiters and exploited, creators of wealth and selfish consumers of wealth." The real strength of exploitive systems of class rule, he reasoned, lay not in force or violence but in the success with which the ruling class imposed its own "conception of the world" on the masses.[65] Gramsci, soon followed by Georg Lukács and Karl Korsch, hereby launched a powerful attack on the crude Marxism which held that thought merely reflects economic interests. His formulation of the problem, however, still retained a crudity of its own, evident in the equation of mind with "consciousness." Without the help of psychoanalysis, it was impossible to see that the cultural "hegemony" of the ruling class rested on something besides ideology and that resistance to the ruling class, accordingly, had to involve more than "intelligent reasoning," "social criticism," and "cultural penetration and diffusion"—the tactics Gramsci proposed to employ in the struggle on the "cultural front."[66] Without psychoanalysis, Marxism can explain the dynamics of cultural domination only where ideology is the direct and unmediated expression of economic interests. It cannot explain how coercion is interiorized in the psyche, how this internalization of authority reconciles the lowly man to "the idea of a necessary domination of some men over others," and how it affects not only "his mind, his ideas, his basic concepts and judgments, but also his inmost life, his preferences and desires."[67] In order to explore these issues, Marxists had to turn to Freud.[68]

Every society, the neo-Marxists argued, reproduces in its members the type of character structure it needs in order to achieve its objectives. Society does this not only by means of explicit instruction and discipline but also by implanting in the psyche certain characteristic patterns of thought and response, patterns of which the individual is not even aware. Not merely the school and other educational agencies but the entire cultural apparatus participates in this work, which ought to be thought of, accordingly, not simply as cultural "transmission" but as the reproduction of society (to use Reich's term) in the broadest sense. The most important reproductive agency is the family, the structure of which enables or rather forces the child to interiorize culture in the form of unconscious parental images and the powerful emotions they evoke. By repressing sexuality or channeling it into socially acceptable outlets, the family shapes not only the superego but the ego and the instincts as well.[69] Thanks to this early repression, the individual experiences suffering as guilt rather than injustice, according to Fromm.[70] By cultivating the "capacity to suffer," the family serves as the "psychic agency" of class society, the "medium through which the society or the social class stamps its specific structure on the child." In bourgeois or patriarchal society—terms the German neo-Marxists tended to use interchangeably—the family reproduces the characteristic "patricentric" or "authoritarian" type, the individual with "a strict superego, guilt feelings, docile love for paternal authority, desire and pleasure at dominating weaker people, acceptance of suffering as a punishment for one's own guilt, and a damaged capacity for happiness."[71] The patriarchal family is the seat of what Fromm calls the "authoritarian character"; in Reich's terms, it represents "the authoritarian state in miniature."[72]

In order to clarify the political questions that gave these theories such urgency, the Institute for Social Research undertook an empirical study of the German working class. Using a combination of psychological tests, questionnaires, and interviews—techniques later used in a similar study conducted in the United States, *The Authoritarian Personality*—the investigators found that about 10 percent of those studied had what could be called an authoritarian character structure, 15 percent a "democratic" or "revolutionary" structure, and the rest a mixture of the two. Subsequent events in German political history, according to Fromm, bore out the assumption that "the authoritarians would be ardent Nazis, the 'democratic' ones militant anti-Nazis, and the majority neither one or the other."[73] But this was too complacent an assessment of what the study had accomplished. It threw little light on the questions that had given rise to the concept of the authoritarian character in the first place: Why had the German working class failed to carry out a socialist revolution, and why had it submitted so meekly to fascism? If anything, the study seemed to suggest that indifference, not authoritarianism, best characterized the political attitudes of the German working class; yet neither empirical research nor the theory guiding it explained or even attempted to explain the psychological foundations of that indifference.

The same thing was true of *The Authoritarian Personality*, the empirical study of anti-Semitism conducted under Adorno's supervision in the forties. At best, this second study demonstrated how authoritarian family structures reproduce an authoritarian personality. It left unexplored, however, the suggestion contained both in Horkheimer's earlier essay on authority and the family (1936) and, in considerably different form, in Fromm's *Escape from Freedom* (1941)—that bourgeois society had moved steadily away from authoritarian family systems toward a system of social discipline founded on reason and what Horkheimer called "education to realism, the goal of every good pedagogy in the more developed phases of bourgeois society."[74]

"As in the economy of recent centuries," Horkheimer wrote in his contribution to *Authority and the Family*, "direct force has played an increasingly smaller role in coercing men into accepting a work situation, so too in the family rational considerations and free obedience have replaced slavery and subjection."[75] Fromm's *Escape from Freedom* can be taken in part as a theoretical analysis of the content of this "free obedience"—an analysis, even if it was not entirely successful, that should have helped to guide the empirical investigations later undertaken by Adorno and his colleagues at the University of California. According to Fromm, authoritarianism is only one of two psychic mechanisms through which men seek to escape the loneliness and sense of helplessness engendered by the modern world. The other escape from the burdens of individuality is what Fromm called compulsive conformity—and it is the "conformist," not the authoritarian, that Fromm found to be so well suited to the needs of advanced industrial society. Based on large-scale bureaucratic organization but still giving lip service to individualism, free consent, and freedom of conscience, late bourgeois society needs men and women who feel free but act as the information apparatus prompts them to—men and women who can be "guided without force and led without leaders." "In recent decades," according to Fromm, "'conscience' has lost much of its significance," while authority has become "anonymous." The result is that "modern man lives under the illusion that he knows what he wants, while he actually wants what he is *supposed* to want."[76] Having freed himself from external authorities, he has achieved the illusion of individuality without its substance. His "free choice" is the consumer's choice of brands, his freedom of conscience the freedom to disbelieve everything—a pervasive cynicism that merely exposes him all the more easily to fraud. In a world where nothing is true (and where the very idea of truth gives way to the idea of credibility), everything is "true." Skepticism thus coexists with a naïve trust in "experts."[77]

The trouble with Fromm's analysis of the mass man is that it does not explain his psychological origins. It throws out a few hints. Returning, for example, to the historical problem of how to account for the collapse of the revolutionary movement and of resistance to fascism, Fromm noted that political defeats suffered by the German working class after 1919 gave rise to "a deep feeling of resignation, of disbelief in their leaders."[78] Presumably this "disbelief" did not derive, however, merely from political failures; it must also have been rooted in the decline of familial authority and of other kinds of authority as well. Such a conclusion seems to be implicit in Fromm's own observations about the decline of conscience and the spread of cynicism (a phenomenon recently referred to by Philip Rieff as "the democratization of contempt").[79] Yet Fromm alluded only in passing to the decline of the family, and he confusingly invoked it as an explanation not of "conformity" but of authoritarianism itself.[80] For the most part, he avoided analysis of the family altogether, preferring to dwell on "existential" aspects of the human condition like isolation, the feeling of impotence, and alienation. By the time he wrote *Escape from Freedom,* Fromm had rejected most of psychoanalysis, on the grounds that it reflected "the spirit of nineteenth-century physiological materialism."[81] He had also severed his ties with the Institute for Social Research. Although in the "conformist" character he may have identified the key to the problem to which the concept of authoritarianism provided no answer, he treated the problem with much less theoretical insight than he had brought to his earlier work on the integration of Marxism and psychoanalysis.

This earlier work in any case contained important conceptual flaws. Not only Fromm but Reich and Horkheimer were heavily influenced by the "socialistic theory of the family," which they absorbed, rather uncritically, as a kind of political inheritance from the left. Especially in the work of Reich and Fromm, who absorbed it most eagerly and clung to it longest, the matriarchal theory served to obscure important issues. Morgan, Engels, Bachofen, and more recently Robert Briffault taught these writers to regard the overthrow of "mother-right" as an essential precondition of the rise of private property and the state. Patriarchy—more specifically, authoritarianism—furnished the psychological supports of class rule. The social theorists associated with the Frankfurt school, having understood the importance of supplementing the Marxian sociology of the family with psychology, provided for the first time a coherent account of the dynamics of that support; but in doing so, they gave insufficient attention, especially in their empirical work, to the possibility that advanced capitalist society had outgrown its dependence on authoritarian character structures and that the concept of the authoritarian personality no longer shed light even on the rise of fascism. Reich, Fromm, and the Frankfurt school analyzed the authoritarian family at the moment of its demise. They showed how the family instills the "capacity for suffering"—for experiencing injustice as religious guilt—at the historical moment when guilt, as a means of social control, became obsolete. Once again, Minerva's owl flew out at dusk.

The bourgeois family, Horkheimer wrote in 1936, had the "indispensable function of producing specific, authority-oriented types of character." For this reason, totalitarian regimes stressed the sanctity of the family in their propaganda and tried to shore it up by relieving it of some of its educational functions.[82] In fact, the dependence of fascism on the family is purely rhetorical and sentimental. Itself the product, in part, of the decay of patriarchal authority, fascism rules not through conscience and guilt but through terror, psychological manipulation, and a primitive loyalty to the blood brotherhood.[83] As for the industrial state in the Western democracies, it does not rest on the authoritarian family at all. Here too, the individual's emancipation from the family makes it impossible but also unnecessary to appeal to his guilty conscience; instead, society appeals to shame, self-interest, and his duty to enjoy himself.

The gradual erosion of authoritarianism and the authoritarian family, which went on throughout the liberal phase of bourgeois society, has had an unexpected outcome: the reestablishment of political despotism in a form based not on the family but on its dissolution. Instead of liberating the individual from external coercion, the decay of family life subjects him to new forms of domination, while at the same time weakening his ability to resist them. The reasons for this result were best stated by Horkheimer himself when he noted that the bourgeois family is related to society "in an antagonistic no less than a promotive way" and that it "not only educates for authority in bourgeois society; it also cultivates the dream of a better condition for mankind." The "complicated historical process in which coercion was partially interiorized" gave rise to a crippling sense of guilt, according to Horkheimer, but it also gave rise to ideals by which bourgeois society itself stood condemned. The restriction of sexual intercourse to marriage required "frightful coercion," but "the romantic love which arose in the course of such regulation is a social phenomenon which can drive the individual into opposition to or even a break with society."[84]

Today the relaxation of sexual controls, on the other hand, blurs the antagonism "between sex and social utility," in Marcuse's words, and assimilates "sexual relations to social relations," pleasure to consumption.[85] The decline of the family brings with it the decline of romantic love, the decline of transcendent ideals in general, and the undisputed triumph of the reality principle. That reality has triumphed over pleasure in the name of pleasure itself—a debased and commercialized leisure organized by the same forces that have debased work—completes the irony that the individual's subjection to new forms of coercion rests on his "emancipation."

These ideas never received any systematic exploration in the work of the Frankfurt school; nor did they play any part in *The Authoritarian Personality*, unfortunately the only work of the Frankfurt school that influenced American social science. The authors of that study argued, in the one chapter devoted to the family, that authoritarian individuals submit to their parents more out of fear and material self-interest than love, but they avoided the question of whether certain types of family structure are more likely than others to produce this pattern of submission. The study did not bear out the assumption with which the authors obviously began, that authoritarian personalities are rooted in authoritarian family structures; yet the authors never confronted the discrepancy between their expectations and the results of their research. As Horkheimer wrote elsewhere, the research seemed to show that although authoritarian types professed great respect for their parents, "on a deeper level" they showed "no genuine attachments to the parents, whom they accept in a thoroughly conventionalized and externalized way." Abstract glorification of the family concealed a lack of emotional ties, positive or negative, to the parents. "What they seem to suffer from is probably not too strong and sound a family but rather a lack of family."[86]

These conclusions can be derived from *The Authoritarian Personality*, however, only by reading between the lines. That work says nothing to the effect that authoritarian types suffer less from a strong family than from a lack of family; and although the authors noted the contrast between overt admiration for the parents and "underlying hostility," in itself this observation merely repeated a point made in earlier studies of the authoritarian family—that authoritarian individuals have ambivalent feelings about authority.[87] Adorno repeatedly denied that the contributors intended to substitute psychological for sociological analysis, but they gave exactly that impression by leaving the sociological aspects of the problem implicit. It was no answer to argue that the book merely added "something new and complementary," in the form of psychological research, to a sociological theory that "was already known."[88] The trouble was that the authors' psychological analysis of the authoritarian personality simultaneously "complemented" two incompatible theories about the sociology of the family: that strong families were more than ever the basis of authoritarian social and political structures, and that on the contrary, authoritarian regimes had outgrown their dependence on the family. Given this underlying ambiguity, *The Authoritarian Personality* contributed very little to an understanding of the family and its future.

If "critical theory" made little impression on American social science—partly because of its foreignness and inaccessibility, partly because of defects in the empirical work through which it tried to overcome this inaccessibility—the work of Fromm and Reich, on the other hand, proved all too easily adaptable to the American scene. They themselves contributed to the assimilation of their ideas by modifying them in a way that brought them into closer harmony with the ideas of the culture and personality school. Initially, their work shared with American anthropology only a common concern with character and the dynamics of cultural transmission. Even here there were major disagreements. The transmission of culture is not the same thing theoretically as its reproduction, nor is the concept of character as used by Fromm and Reich the same thing as "personality" in the work of Sapir, Mead, and Benedict. The term "reproduction" clarifies the connection between culture and society in a way that "transmission" does not. It reveals the subjection of culture to society, exposing culture, in Horkheimer's words, as "a dependent but nevertheless special sphere within the social process as a whole."[89] In speaking of cultural transmission, on the other hand, American anthropologists inflated the idea of culture to the point where it swallowed up the social order, becoming synonymous with a people's "total way of life," the entire man-made environment, the "totality of products of social men."[90] By making it impossible to distinguish culture from society, they made it equally impossible to study the relations between them; while by defining culture as the totality of learned behavior, they obscured the importance of unconscious processes and of repression.

The concept of personality, in the work of the culture and personality theorists, implies its wholeness and integration—the very qualities the absence of which Reich's and Fromm's concept of "character" was designed to expose. In the early writings of these German theorists, character appeared precisely as the psychic manifestation of disintegration—of the demands imposed on the individual by society, as a result of which the integrated personality remains merely an ideal, impossible of attainment under existing forms of social organization. In Reichian terms, character is a kind of psychic "armor"; with it, the individual resists not just psychoanalysis but any other influence threatening to bring unconscious thoughts and wishes to light. Such "armor" constitutes the chronic or characteristic form of the defenses by means of which unconscious mental life is rigorously repressed.[91]

From a position close to that of Horkheimer, Adorno, and Marcuse—a position, indeed, to which the latter were much indebted in their own work—Fromm and Reich moved to a position close to the one already outlined by students of culture and personality. Increasingly they attached positive value to "health," "maturity," "genitality," and the capacity for "growth." By playing off the healthy personality against the neurotic one, they implied that neurosis originated in specific social conditions instead of in culture itself. In his later books, Reich, for all his insistence on the conflict between instinctual life and the social order, took a simplified view of this conflict, conceiving of the unconscious as pure libido and of socialization as the restriction of sexuality by the growth of conscious moral prohibitions. He now saw the Oedipus complex merely as the "result" (rather than the prototype) of "the sexual restrictions imposed upon the child by society"—restrictions deliberately designed to make the child neurotically dependent on his mother and thus incapable of functioning as a fully sexed adult.[92] In a society where sexuality is allowed free play—as among the Trobriand Islanders— the Oedipus complex, Reich thought, is unknown. After postulating a clear-cut conflict between capitalist morality and sexuality, consciousness and unconsciousness, Reich envisioned its resolution as a return to matriarchy, in which the underlying unity of nature and culture would be reestablished.

In Freud's writings, the battle between nature and culture inheres in the very fact of culture and is irreconcilable. The struggle between them takes place largely within the unconscious, which is formed out of the warfare between the pleasure principle and the cultural heritage internalized in the form of identification with parents and other upholders of authority. For Reich, on the other hand, sexual repression is overt and explicit. Phenomena that were treated by Freud as psychic events—for instance, the threat of castration, which as Juliet Mitchell notes "was not necessarily, as he had once thought, the real threat of nursemaids or parents, but a more tenuous amalgam of this and of the child's phantasy fears"— became in Reich's hands real social events connected with what he called "the imposition of sexual morality."[93] The conclusion follows more or less automatically that a more enlightened morality, even if it takes a "revolution" to bring it about, will overcome repression and allow the reemergence of "orgonic" energy. At the heart of Reich's radical psychoanalysis, at least in its later phase, lies an essentially reformist view of social change, one that relies on diffusion of a new and supposedly less repressive sexual morality.

In Fromm's case, the rapprochement with American social science became even closer. As he himself pointed out, his idea of "social character had essential points in common" with Ralph Linton's concept of "basic personality," and his increasing emphasis on "interpersonal relations" blended in with the ideas of Sullivan, Sapir, and other advocates of the "cultural approach to personality."[94] Others noticed the resemblance between Fromm's writings on cultural patterns and the attempt of American anthropologists to trace cultural "configurations" that allegedly revealed "the general patterns of behavior and culture and their influence on what Fromm would call 'social character.'"[95]

Given these resemblances and the direct encouragement they received from Fromm himself, students of culture and personality did not find it difficult to incorporate his work and to process it for domestic consumption. In doing so, they discarded whatever was negative and critical in it. Notwithstanding Fromm's unwarranted faith in human nature, his tendency to exhort rather than analyze, and the damage that was inflicted on clarity of thought and expression by his "revision" of Freud, his view of advanced industrial society remained uncompromisingly critical and bleak; yet his work en-

joyed a considerable vogue in the forties and fifties—just at the time
when American intellectuals were eager to affirm the virtues of capitalism, at least in comparison with communism—because that work
was so easily assimilated to the outcry about totalitarianism that
served simultaneously as propaganda for the free world. Fromm's
work, in spite of its underlying optimism about the reconciliation of
man and nature, could also be assimilated to the superficial pessimism so fashionable in this period—pessimism about "conformity," "alienation," the existential absurdity of the human condition, and the decline of "humane values" in the modern world.

In the humanities, this pessimism often served to justify a retreat
from politics into religion, art for its own sake, and the "tragic sense
of life." In the social sciences, on the other hand, it issued in a rousing call to action. The forties and fifties were years when American
social science came into its own, winning students away from the
humanities, building new departments and programs, attracting
generous grants from government and private foundations, and
turning loose on the world a flood of publications. The sense that
things were falling apart merely persuaded spokesmen for the profession that they had an obligation to put their expert knowledge at
the disposal of social reconstruction and reintegration. With undiminished confidence in their own powers of healing, social scientists and social pathologists set out to make the world safe for democracy—to solve what one of them called "World Problem No. 1, the
harmonization of conflicting ideologies." [96] The study of culture and
personality had taught them that authoritarian families produced authoritarian personalities, thereby providing them with both the incentive and the theoretical armaments to renew their campaign to
democratize the family and spread the gospel of psychological enlightenment. The golden age of "social relations"—the science of
social hygiene—was about to unfold.

5

Doctors to a Sick Society

SOCIETY AS THE PATIENT

American psychiatry, always more confident than European psychiatry of its power to change the world, in the forties and fifties reformulated its claims with imperial immodesty. Psychiatrists now demanded nothing less than "a world-wide mobilization of psychiatry," in the words of Harry Stack Sullivan, against war, class conflict, personal anxiety, and what Henry A. Murray called "the present ominous epidemic of antagonisms." Social scientists needed to "invade . . . the realm of values," according to Murray, and become "physicians to society."[1]

Closely associated from the beginning with "New Thought," mind cure, positive thinking, and "practical idealism," American psychiatry disentangled itself from these unsavory associations without renouncing the spirit of uplift, the missionary fervor these earlier movements had called up.[2] Having attained the status of a full-fledged social science, as the bolder members of the profession now insisted, psychiatry simultaneously claimed, as the modern successor to religion, to represent a comprehensive world view—in the words of John Money, a scientific "philosophy of life" that replaced discredited beliefs, superstitions, "absolutist" orthodoxies, "ready-made philosophies." Psychiatrists now proposed not merely to treat patients but to change "cultural patterns," as Money put it—to spread the new gospel of relativism, tolerance, personal growth, and psychic maturity.[3] A critic of the profession noted that the mental health movement increasingly pronounced on moral and cultural issues and thus sought "to occupy the heartland of the old territory." The "cure of souls" had given way to "mental hygiene," the search for salvation to the search for peace of mind, the "attack upon evil to the war against anxiety."[4] The psychiatrist had translated "everything human" into "medical terms of illness," according to Leslie Farber, and thereby assumed "a heavy burden of responsibility. . . . Morality itself has been turned over to him, along with philosophy and religion."[5]

The medicalization of religion facilitated the rapprochement between religion and psychiatry. Advocates of existential and humanistic therapies pointed out that Martin Heidegger, Martin Buber, and Paul Tillich had redefined religion as a form of psychotherapy. Neurosis, in the view of these existentialist theologians, reflected a pervasive modern anxiety, and religion, like psychiatry, had to enlist in the organized effort to undo modern society's dehumanizing effects: to equip men to tolerate anxiety and thus to make them whole again, self-accepting, authentic, and capable of achieving a state of "being." Acceptance of existential points of view among psychiatrists had the effect of making the therapist less of a catalyst and more of a priest, willing to risk "nonmoralistic judgments," to love the patient in spite of his faults, and to provide "the warmth of understanding and sympathy—a we-feeling between the participants—which makes it possible for both to look at the patient's self-condemnation, to judge, and to accept in spite of the judgment."[6]

The new psychiatric imperialism not only expanded the doctor's authority over the patient, it ministered to all of "society as the patient," in Lawrence Frank's memorable phrase.[7] A sick society, according to Frank, needed the same therapy a doctor gave to his patient, "enabling him to revise his 'past' . . . and escape from its coercion."[8] The establishment of the World Health Organization provided the mental health profession with a forum from which to preach the new gospel of "complete physical, mental and social well-being." The expansive definition of health adopted by this organization, as one expert pointed out, enlarged the health profession's constituency to include "the home, the church, the school, the prison, industrial firms," and almost any other institution one could name.[9] One of the guiding spirits of the World Health Organization, the Canadian psychiatrist and former army officer C. B. Chisholm, provided a magisterial restatement of the psychiatric mission in his William Alanson White lectures of 1946.[10] Repeatedly drawing analogies between psychiatry and preventive medicine, Chisholm urged his colleagues not to confine their attention to individual patients but to "go into the preventive field where the big job needs to be done." Bad social conditions, bad schools, and bad families produced psychiatric patients faster than doctors could cure them. "The training of children is making a thousand neurotics for every one that psychiatrists can hope to help with psychotherapy." A progressive in the tradition of John Dewey, Chisholm demanded that education, informed by psychiatric principles, become the highest social priority. "To produce a generation of mature citizens is the biggest and most necessary job any country could undertake, and the reward in saving of misery and suffering would be colossal."

In an age of total war, Chisholm argued, the prevention of war had to be approached as a psychiatric problem. Men's compulsion to fight, a "pathological psychiatric symptom," arose from "authoritarian dogma," "inculcated loyalty," "guilt and fear." The mature person, independent, flexible, and tolerant, experienced no inner need to make war. Like Erich Fromm, Erik Erikson, and the humanistic psychologists, Chisholm hoped to break down local and national loyalties and to create more inclusive identities. "Would it not be sensible to stop imposing our local prejudices and faiths on children and give them all sides of every question so that in their own good time they may have the ability to size things up, and make their own decisions?" Critical intelligence, according to Chisholm, had been "crippled by local certainties, by gods of local moralities, of local loyalty, and personal salvation, and prejudice and hate and intolerance." He pleaded for the substitution of therapeutic for religious outlooks. "The re-interpretation and eventual eradication of the concept of right and wrong which has been the basis of child training, the substitution of intelligent and rational thinking for faith in the certainties of the old people"—these ought to become the goals of psychotherapy and of a psychiatrically oriented program of education. Only in this way could mental hygiene free "the race . . . from its crippling burden of good and evil."

Not only psychiatrists and educators but liberal lawyers and politicians acclaimed these lectures as the beginning of a great crusade for world peace and health. Harry Stack Sullivan, Abe Fortas, and Henry A. Wallace, among others, endorsed the goals of what another psychiatrist called "mass preventive psychiatry." [11] Sullivan described Chisholm's program as a "cultural revolution to end war." Educators and psychiatrists, he wrote, had to assume the burdens of parenthood, so wretchedly performed by most parents. "Parents must be made to see that children are in no sense their chattels but instead their wards, held in trust as future members of the community." [12] The "helping professions" had long demanded greater control over socialization, but they had never before won such widespread approval for their program. Nor had they drawn such explicit analogies between social engineering and preventive medicine. The prestige of the psychiatric profession, the growing domination of psychiatric points of view in social work and marriage counseling, and the growing belief among liberals that war and class conflict originated in the "authoritarian personality" created a cultural climate highly receptive to medical modes of thought. [13] Enlightened opinion now identified itself with the medicalization of society: the substitution of medical and psychiatric authority for the authority of parents, priests, and lawgivers, now condemned as representatives of discredited authoritarian modes of discipline.

FRIENDSHIP, THE "NEW RELIGION"

While the social pathologists expanded their jurisdiction over both the individual and society, dissident scholars tried to deflate their pretensions by exposing the ideological roots of their thought. In an essay provocatively entitled "Mental Hygiene and the Class Structure" (1938), Kingsley Davis, a sociologist, attacked the mental hygiene movement as a "panacea" for industrial unrest. Increasingly the movement concerned itself with objectives "beyond the goal of medical health," according to Davis, disguising its "implicit ethical system" as "rational advice based on science." "Psychologism," because it ignored the social determinants of mental life, provided a "scientific rationalization" for the "philosophy of private initiative, personal responsibility, and individual achievement." In his capacity of "practising moralist," the psychiatrist imposed an individualistic ethic on a complex, interdependent society that had long since outgrown it.[14]

In "The Professional Ideology of Social Pathologists" (1943), C. Wright Mills argued that the profession conceived of social change as "adjustment" and sought to adapt the individual to institutions rather than changing institutions to fit the needs of men. Social pathologists' penchant for "situational" analysis encouraged them "to slip past social structure to focus on isolated situations." Most of the social pathologists, Mills claimed, came from small towns or farms and adhered to "rural principles of stability, cultural lag, and social change." Their work represented "a propaganda for conformity to those norms and traits ideally associated with small-town, middle-class milieux."[15]

Two critics of "Value Congeries and Marital Counseling" (1953) mounted a similar attack. Like Mills, they accused marriage counselors of trying to preserve outmoded small-town values. Marriage experts measured "emotional maturity" against "middle-class morality." They upheld an obsolescent model of the family as the norm of marital success. Incapable of distinguishing between the "institutional" family and the "companionate" family that had replaced it, marriage counselors devoted their energies to keeping the family together instead of dealing with "conflicts in the area of strong interpersonal relations." It never occurred to them that "the good family might conceivably be something quite different from the middle-class conventional family."[16]

These criticisms of the mental hygiene movement anticipated later attacks on the psychiatric profession by "radical therapists" and later criticism of the nuclear family, often presented in the sixties and seventies with a breathless air of original discovery. When they showed that social pathologists had developed a professional ideology and that it served as an agency of social control, these earlier critics performed an important service. Their criticisms, however, did not challenge the basic assumptions of American social science. Davis attacked psychologism in the name of sociologism, hoping by discrediting psychiatry as an objective science merely to clear the way for sociology, which holds that man is wholly the product of society. Mills too berated psychiatrists merely for reducing social problems to individual problems. When these critics accused the ideology of mental hygiene of providing a scientific rationale for "Protestant individualism," of shoring up small-town, middle-class values, and of upholding an obsolete, patriarchal model of the family, they went far off the mark. On the contrary, social pathologists played a leading role in undermining Protestant individualism, rural values, and the old-style family. They promoted a "democratic" conception of domestic life, advocated permissive child rearing, defended the rights of women, attacked sexual repression and censorship, and sought to make the members of the family more responsive to each others' emotional needs, more skilled at communicating their own, and more adept, in short, in the art of interpersonal relations. John R. Seeley and his collaborators got closer to the truth, in their study of "Crestwood Heights," when they caught the implicit feminism of the social relations experts and their alliance with women against patriarchal values.[17] Indeed, the mental health movement, and more broadly the "helping professions," positioned themselves in the vanguard of the revolt against old-fashioned middle-class morality. Their ideology, rather than harking back to the past, anticipated the needs of a society based not on hard work but on consumption, the search for personal fulfillment, and the management of interpersonal relations.

Social pathologists wanted to replace the old morality of "right and wrong," "guilt and sin," with the new morality of "human relations." They themselves had already "escaped from these moral chains," according to General Chisholm, and they now had a mission to spread the new gospel among the unenlightened.[18] "What the social scientists have learned," declared the president of the National Conference on Family Relations, "must now be made available to larger and larger circles of men and women, through educational institutions, through churches and synagogues, community centers, . . . press, . . . radio."[19] The authors of *Mental Health in Modern Society* pointed out that society spent "sixteen to twenty billion dollars a year on police departments, courts, and prisons without getting at the sources of social pathology. People keep on getting married, but the only preparation we provide is a civil contract."[20] Only a vast

program of "preventive psychiatry," it appeared, could produce better parents and "mature" individuals with the capacity, in the words
of two army psychiatrists, "to work with others, to work in an organization and under authority, . . . to show tolerance, . . . to adapt and
compromise."[21] Lawrence K. Frank, drawing on the studies of
Margaret Mead, Ruth Benedict, Gregory Bateson, and Erik Erikson, compared the "affection, tenderness, and benevolent patience"
shown to children in primitive cultures with child-rearing practices
in the West, where the child was "terrorized, humiliated, and often
brutalized." Such practices, he maintained, produced the "aggressive, destructive, exploitive individuals from whom Western European culture has suffered for so many centuries."[22]

Having long since set up the juvenile court to protect the child
from his parents, social pathologists in the forties and fifties sought
to extend the principles of medical jurisprudence to other branches
of the law—in their eyes, one of the last strongholds of the old ethic
of crime and punishment. Whereas the doctor sided with the patient
against his illness, the lawyer sided with the law against its violators,
according to Gregory Zilboorg; "even a lawyer for the defense is
tinged with this social hostility, which the criminal law teaches him
as apparently it must."[23]

Enlightened members of the legal profession took up the battle
against retributive justice. Historically, the courts had regarded the
actions of adults as deliberate and calculating, but modern psychiatry, in the words of Judge David L. Bazelon, "now recognizes that a
man is an integrated personality and that reason, which is only one
element in that personality, is not the sole determinant of his conduct." On these grounds, Bazelon overturned an old rule under
which the courts allowed a plea of insanity only if the defendant
showed no ability to distinguish right from wrong. Relying heavily
on a brief submitted by Abe Fortas, he ruled that "an accused is not
criminally responsible if his unlawful act was the product of mental
disease or mental defect."[24] Five years earlier, Justice Hugo Black
had declared: "Retribution is no longer the dominant objective of
criminal law. Reformation and rehabilitation of offenders have become the important goals of criminal jurisprudence."[25] Another lawyer wrote in the same year, still more sweepingly: "The concept of
'treatment' has replaced the concept of 'punishment.' "[26]

Margaret Lantis, an anthropologist, attempted one of the most ambitious statements of the new psychiatric morality in an article of 1950, "The Symbol of a New Religion."[27] Her formulation, more clearly than any other, shows the links between medical jurisprudence, the cult of "maturity," the psychiatric attack on parochialism and prejudice, and criticism of the nuclear family. Society needed a new religion, Lantis argued—one that promised mastery not over nature, as the old one did, but over social organizations and human relations. Earlier religious symbolism, with its emphasis on submission to patriarchal authority, on the mediating influence of maternal love, and on the brotherhood of believers, derived from the "family configuration." In the modern world, the reality of family life contradicted its religious idealization, and men searched for new gods in the form of liberators, emancipators, and leaders—symbols of authority based on the father-son relationship but going "far beyond it." In place of these hierarchical symbols, which had recently done so much social damage, Lantis proposed to exalt the "coordinate" symbolism of friendship, which might serve as the basis of a "world community."

The patriarchal family, according to Lantis, had served as the model of a society of "superordinates and subordinates," and even the stripped-down companionate family still bred narrow, particularistic loyalties which had to give way, in an age of interdependence, to global loyalties. The companionate family gave rise to the religion of romantic love, the nineteenth-century secular religion that replaced Christianity but retained much of its neurotic intensity. In the twentieth century, romantic love had given way to "a more mature and wider love, not based solely on physical attraction or even marriage." Formerly, lovers clung together in a "heartless world," irresponsibly lost in each other's arms; today men and women needed the "emotional support" of mature friendship "without the strain of competition," the neurotic jealousy, or the glorification of youth associated with the cult of love. Friendship raised love to a higher plane and dispensed with its possessiveness, rejected standards of fidelity "set impossibly high," made no claim to abiding permanence, and thus relieved those who failed at friendship of responsibility or guilt. "The appeal of friendship is that it is freely entered into and withdrawn from, that there are alternative, coterminous, and successive friendships, *not* that all one's happiness is contained in one relationship." Yet friendships often proved more durable than marriage itself, precisely because they lacked compulsion.

Friendship provided a sounder basis than love not only for the relations between men and women but for child rearing. "Today it requires more than mere enveloping love to prepare a person for a specifically challenging world. The child must learn practical social techniques of affiliating himself to others outside the family, neighborhood, and parish." The child needed also to develop "realistic self-esteem and self-respect," validated by friendship. Thus the ideal of "reciprocity" served as a healthy substitute both for romantic love and for parental love. It served, in short, as a "new religion" based on a new type of family—more accurately, on its supersession.

Here again, the psychiatric thought of the forties and fifties foreshadowed ideas popularized in the sixties and seventies. The call to replace love with friendship, the nuclear family with a wider circle of "coordinates," anticipated the counterculture, with its idealization of the commune as an extended family of equals. If the fifties glorified domestic life, it was a type of domesticity already reorganized on the principle of "friendship." This point has been lost in the superficial commentary on the postwar "cult of domesticity" that has become so fashionable in recent years. It is true that many people in the forties and fifties felt a strong impulse to recoil into the satisfactions of family life, and that the rapid growth of suburbs in this period—the retreat from the job and the city—rested on a conscious attempt to revive domestic virtues. The economic disasters of the thirties, followed in rapid succession by World War II and the cold war, had strengthened the belief that history and politics could be neither understood nor controlled. Meanwhile, dissatisfaction with work had grown more intense than ever. Bureaucracy reduced even business and the professions to a dull routine, while the academic training required for bureaucratic careers encouraged intellectual and artistic aspirations that actual conditions of work inevitably thwarted. Writers of advertising copy dreaming of the novels they would never write, commercial artists trying to do serious work on the side populated the suburbs. But "those of us who wrote off the 9-to-5 portion of our lives," as one member of the so-called silent generation later explained, "pinned most of our hopes on creating a comfortable and comforting family life which embodied the ideals we had picked up in our own childhoods."[28]

Yet the dream of domestic bliss implied no repudiation of the "new morality" that had grown up in the twenties. Those who married young and raised large families cultivated a low-keyed, easygoing style of personal intercourse, undemanding and nonpossessive. Parents attempted to "relate" to their children instead of imposing their authority. Husbands and wives agreed to regard fidelity as an unattainable ideal. They had no wish to revive the discredited doctrine of romantic love or to recreate the emotional intensity of the inward-turning bourgeois family of the nineteenth century. Married couples sought out the company of other couples and took satisfaction in the intermingling of their offspring. Their ideal of domestic happiness already implied the styles of cultural revolt later adopted by those who wished to dramatize their emancipation from the "conformity" of the fifties—exchange of partners, attempts to simulate "extended families," a vague communalism. John Updike's *Couples*, hailed by critics with short memories as an expression of the sixties' sexual "breakthrough," captured, at the point it was beginning to turn sour, an ideal of domesticity that flourished widely in the fifties—an ideal based not on romantic love but on companionship.

The fifties did not even fully repudiate feminism. College-educated women shunned graduate and professional schools and renounced careers in favor of marriage, admitting without embarrassment that they went to college in the first place only to find husbands. Yet these same women asserted their sexual rights without reserve, and refused to consider themselves bound by older canons of respectability. They no more wished to revive the nineteenth-century ideal of the lady than their husbands wished to pose as patriarchs. Both sexes, repudiating the mystical exaltation of womanhood formerly associated with the cult of romantic love, tried to ground marriage in what Randolph Bourne once called "charm." Their program, in effect, represented a domesticated version of Bourne's "salon," where "masculine brutalities and egotisms and feminine prettinesses and stupidities have been purged away so that there is left stuff for a genuine comradeship and healthy frank regard and understanding."[29]

THE NEW GOSPEL OF
MARRIAGE AND PARENTHOOD

The practical advice offered to husbands and wives in this period indicates that the experts who gave it had absorbed the "new religion" of friendship and assumed, moreover, that their clients were increasingly familiar with its tenets. Marriage counselors agreed that success could no longer be equated with holding the marriage together. One of them wrote: "I now hold the view that [marriage counseling] should be designed to help people to work out their own solutions to problems centering around marriage and to work them out in terms of their own values." The marriage counselor should regard himself not as "a mechanic for broken-down marital machinery [but as] a psychotherapist who specializes in helping persons with problems which center in the marriage relationship."[30] Educators, marriage counselors, and therapists all rejected the "problem" approach that remained fixated on the prevention of divorce. They saw the object of their efforts as "raising the level of happiness in marriage, improving mental health, raising the quality of parenthood, and providing a climate for healthier personality growth."[31] Social workers agreed that their intervention should seek "to foster psychological growth."[32] Many studies showed that couples often found more happiness in their second marriages than in their first; such evidence confirmed the helping professions in the belief that personal growth should take precedence over marital stability. According to Albert Ellis, everyone agreed that people caught up in marital troubles needed psychotherapy in order to solve their personal problems, even at the expense of the marriage; the only question was what kind of therapy they needed, psychoanalysis or his own "reality therapy."[33]

Experts agreed that marriage and "growth" had to be based on equality between men and women. A sociologist, congratulating his colleagues on breaking down "patriarchal, sacramental, romantic" prejudices, insisted that college courses in marriage and the family had to teach men to accept women as equals and to challenge sexual prejudices such as the cult of virginity and the double standard.[34] Sociological studies of the family, according to an expert in human relations, had shown "that the movement from a simple agrarian society to a modern urban society has [broken] up the closer knit cohesion of the patriarchal type of family, and [replaced] it with the more fragmented and individualized democratic pattern," in which men and women faced each other as equals.[35] In an article entitled "The Institutionalization of Equalitarian Family Norms," two family sociologists repeated the same point.[36] Harvey Locke's studies of marital adjustment, according to another report, confirmed "the assumptions of students in this field," that modern marriage rested on "intimate communication; sympathetic understanding; [and] mutual respect on the basis of equality."[37] Summing up this line of sociological thought, a writer in *Marriage and Family Living* declared:

> The traditional conception of the family holds that the father is head of the house, that the mother is entrusted with the care of the house and of the children, and that in return for the unselfish devotion of the parents to their duties, the children owe their parents honor and obedience. Today, these values are being discarded by those who are creating developmental families, based on inter-personal relations of mutual affection, companionship, and understanding, with a recognition of individual capabilities, desires and needs for the development of each member of the family, be he father, mother or child.[38]

These sociological truisms, now widely diffused among the health and welfare professions and among their clients, dictated a new style of child rearing. According to a social worker, parents and children alike had to "receive training in at least the elementary foundations of mental hygiene," the "subtle arts of human relationships."[39] The director of the Association for Family Living, Evelyn Millis Duvall, complained that "only one profession remains untutored and untrained—the bearing and rearing of our children." Parenthood, in her view, remained "the last stand of the amateur." The health industry had an obligation to teach parents not only the principles of sexual hygiene but, more important, a "democratic acceptance of difference."[40] The editor of *Psychiatry,* in a discussion of child rearing, endorsed Erik Erikson's definition of the mature person as someone "tolerant of differences, cautious and methodical in evaluation, just in judgment, circumspect in action, and . . . capable of faith and indignation."[41]

By the fifties, experts in the family had reached a consensus about the condition most likely to produce healthy, well-adjusted, cooperative, achievement-oriented, and upwardly mobile offspring: parents who had absorbed the ideology of mental health. Again and again, they condemned unenlightened sexual attitudes and the damage inflicted on children by parental attempts to suppress masturbation.[42] They condemned religious dogmas and the danger of imposing them on children. Above all, they condemned possessiveness, which imperiled the relations between parents and children in the same way it imperiled marital relations. "Maternal overprotection," allegedly the most common form of parental possessiveness, kept the child in a state of arrested development, prevented him from "meeting his own problems," and made it difficult for him to form "normal friendly relationships."[43]

While documenting the awful effects of parental incompetence, the social pathologists incongruously urged parents not to assume the entire moral responsibility for their children's development or to blame themselves if things went wrong. It was a mistake, according to one expert, "to allow the responsibilities of parenthood to rest too heavily on our shoulders."[44] Hilde Bruch argued that psychiatrists and child development specialists often intensified parental anxiety rather than allaying it.[45] Another expert agreed that the "problem approach" to family education made parents feel needlessly guilty and therefore "hostile toward family experts and counsellors."[46] Still another argued that the "deepest roots" of parental failure "lie not in the mistakes of parents but in cultural attitudes of which the parents are merely the purveyors."[47] Such claims enlarged the scope of therapeutic authority, which now set out to "eradicate certain basic contradictions in our cultural attitudes," while doing nothing to reassure parents about the limits of their own responsibility.[48] Modern psychiatry's insistence on the harm parents unwittingly inflict on their children appeared to relieve them of direct responsibility, but merely intensified the irrational sense of guilt and failure which so many psychiatrists complained of in their clients. The health industry assumed most of the responsibility for child rearing, while leaving parents with most of the guilt. This growing sense of guilt in turn increased the demand for psychiatric services.

The health industry's ministrations to the family benefited the "helping professions" far more than they helped the family. In the long run, however, the popularization of the psychiatric gospel not only undermined parental authority but weakened the unchallenged authority of the psychiatric profession. In the act of bringing psychiatric enlightenment to the masses, social pathologists lost their monopoly of medical wisdom and inadvertently encouraged programs of psychiatric self-help. The triumph of the therapeutic paradoxically ended the undisputed reign of the therapeutic professions, while lodging therapeutic modes of thought more deeply than ever in the popular mind. Before analyzing these developments, however, we must examine the contribution of Talcott Parsons's sociological synthesis to the legitimation of therapeutic authority and its extension over the family. In Parsons, the social pathologists found their most eminent apologist—one who restated the principles of the "new religion" in the guise of social theory, at a suitably exalted level of abstraction.

6

The Social Theory of
the Therapeutic:
Parsons and the Parsonians

THE TRIUMPH OF
"SOCIAL RELATIONS"

When Talcott Parsons and his colleagues set up the Department of Social Relations at Harvard in 1950, they institutionalized the dominant drives in American social science: its ambition to displace the humanities as the center of the academic curriculum, its heady sense of itself as an important component (and beneficiary) of the welfare state, its crusading zeal to harmonize the world. The founders of the Department of Social Relations hoped to subordinate facts to theory and to unify sociology, anthropology, and psychology, in the words of the psychologist Henry A. Murray, under "a new discipline, basic social science."[1]

Murray insisted that research in the social sciences had to begin with something more definite than the thought that "it would be 'interesting' to study this or that." It had to begin with a clearly formulated hypothesis, which if empirically verified would "stand as a basic proposition or constitute the logically next step in the systematic development or validation of a theoretical system." In order to facilitate this kind of work, Murray urged his colleagues to build "a comprehensive system of concepts" on the definition and meaning of which everyone could agree. Nor did he neglect to point out the practical applications of such an approach. A "strategic hypothesis," he argued, not only advanced theory but promoted "fellowship, social integration, and ideological synthesis." The collapse of "social morality" threatened to tear the world apart. "Hence, the crucial task today is the formulation and pragmatic validation of a regenerated system of morality and the discovery of the means by which the system can be represented to the growing child so that it becomes exemplified in action."[2]

Edward Shils of the University of Chicago, Parsons's friend and collaborator, complained that American sociology "feels" problems rather than conceptualizing them clearly. Under these conditions, the results of sociological research

> are only with difficulty applicable, i.e., translatable into another concrete situation by an investigator who seeks to confirm, revise, or disconfirm the previously 'established' proposition. As a result of the vagueness of the categories . . . the material gathered by costly and meticulous methods of observation and recording cannot be classified.[3]

Unlike Murray, Shils made no explicit claim for the therapeutic value of theory, but he shared Murray's belief—common to most social scientists in this or any period—that social organisms, large and small, are held together principally by shared beliefs, or as Murray put it, by "mutual affection and moral conduct."[4] Shils argued that industrial studies by Elton Mayo and others had shown productivity to be a "function of morale, which in turn was the function of small group solidarity." He went on to claim that Mayo—almost alone among American sociologists to appreciate the value of Émile Durkheim's theories for "concrete research"—had vindicated Durkheim's interpretation of the sources of social solidarity. Writing in 1948, he added: "We may expect that Parsons's reinterpretation of Durkheim . . . will remind American sociologists of what they never should have allowed themselves to forget."[5]

Talcott Parsons had a similar grasp of the connection between social theory and the practice of social therapy. He turned his back on empiricism not because he did not care about practical results but because he wanted to approach practical problems more systematically. American sociologists, in his view, held the mistaken belief that the progress of science consisted merely of the accumulation of empirical data, as if knowledge were an "entirely quantitative affair." Empirical discoveries, on the contrary, had no interest unless they forced modifications in theory. "Theory not only formulates what we know but also tells us what we want to know, that is, the questions to which an answer is needed."[6] The question that troubled Parsons, more than any other, was the same question that troubled Murray, Shils, and before them Durkheim. What holds society together, especially in a time of moral and cultural crisis?

Like Shils, Parsons hoped to "translate" the work of various thinkers into a common system of concepts. In his first book, *The Structure of Social Action*, he emphasized the "convergence" between thinkers as dissimilar as Alfred Marshall, Vilfredo Pareto, Durkheim, and Max Weber, just as he later insisted on the convergence between Durkheim and Freud. According to Parsons's account of his own intellectual development, "I came to attribute great importance to the convergence of Durkheim and Freud in the understanding of the internalization of cultural norms and social objects as part of personality."[7] Having decided that sociology needed to work out what Shils called a general theory of behavior, Parsons in the 1940s "came to terms" with psychoanalysis and cultural anthropology, hoping to find in those fields a comprehensive theory of culture and personality. He then grafted Freud onto Durkheim— translated psychoanalytic ideas into the language of Durkheim's sociological synthesis.

Durkheim had demonstrated that belief systems played a major role in social integration, according to Parsons; Freud showed how the growing child internalized those systems. Freud's work made it clear, moreover, that personal interaction, in Parsons's words, constituted "the crucial element in socialization." Meanwhile, the small-group studies conducted by industrial sociologists, such as the classic study of the Western Electric plant at Hawthorne, Illinois, had made it clear that the quality of personal interaction or "social relations" constituted an equally crucial element in the morale of industrial workers. The next step in the development of a sociological theory of socialization, obviously, lay in the application of small-group theory—together with its practical contribution to the prevention of social conflict—to the family itself.

THE FAMILY AS

A SMALL GROUP

When Shils called for the "generalization and reformulation of psychoanalysis and its incorporation into a systematic theory of human behavior," he predicted that research into the dynamics of small groups would play a central part in this work, bridging the gap between fact and theory, providing empirical verification for the stronger psychoanalytic concepts, and forcing the weaker ones to be abandoned.[8] The study of small groups promised to provide detailed accounts of the mechanisms through which the "common culture" is internalized in the form of roles.

According to Robert Bales and Philip Slater, the "association of particular members [of the small group] with particular extensions of the common culture is the beginning of role differentiation."[9] Even in groups unlike the family in other respects, the same kind of role differentiation took place. Experimental problem-solving groups, set up for the purpose of observation, never assigned intellectual and emotional leadership to the same person. Every group, it appeared, required both instrumental and emotional specialists, both problem-solvers and "sociometric stars"—people who reduce tensions, provide positive emotional support, or through negative reactions "give indirect gratification to suppressed negative feelings."[10] According to Morris Zelditch, who extended the findings of Bales and Slater to the family—"a special case of a small group"—any system lacking these differentiated roles would find itself "under great strain."[11] It followed that the sexual division of labor in the family, which distinguished so clearly between expressive and instrumental roles, arose not from biology or even from cultural needs and requirements peculiar to the family but from the dynamics intrinsic to small groups in general.

The division of roles in the family, according to this analysis, serves to facilitate the emotional development of the child: the father plays the leading role in prying the child loose from excessive dependence on the mother. From the Parsonian point of view, Freud's Oedipus complex merely describes the psychic mechanism through which this feat is accomplished; and if the family constitutes a special type of small group, the incest taboo, which gives rise to the Oedipus complex, also has analogues in groups otherwise very different from the family. In every group, instrumental and emotional leaders potentially compete for leadership, even though their roles complement each other. Either may try to cultivate a following so as to undercut the other. One way to forestall such a "status struggle," according to Bales, is for the instrumental leader and the "sociometric star" to make a tacit agreement "not to be 'seduced' into attempting to form a coalition with lower status members in order to displace each other." Such an agreement makes it "quite difficult for lower status members to revolt." Similarly, the incest taboo prevents the child from "seducing" his mother and forces his socialization

> by putting him in a position where he must accept the authority and values of the father in order to obtain gratification, rather than allowing him to retain and overdevelop an affectively gratifying relation to the mother which would leave him insufficient incentive to acquire the skills, values, and other characteristics of the adult role. It may well be . . . that the ubiquity of the incest taboo . . . as it applies in the nuclear family is simply another case of the much more general equilibrium problem. [12]

The Parsonians, with considerable ingenuity, thus devised a logical proof of the universality of the nuclear family. Their work appeared to give scientific support to the "cult of domesticity" in the fifties; and it is on these grounds that their work has been recently attacked by those pseudo-radicals who confuse the individual's emancipation from the family with social and cultural progress. [13] As usual, spokesmen for the "cultural revolution" challenge forms of authority, such as the "patriarchal family," which already lie in ruins. This keeps them from understanding the real significance of the Parsonian theory of the family: that it upholds the family's indispens-

ability while at the same time providing a rationale for the continued
invasion of the family by experts in the art of social and psychic
healing.

On the one hand, Parsons argued that the "isolation" of the nuclear
family from other kinship units, together with the loss of many of its
functions, enables it to serve more effectively as an agency of "pat-
tern-maintenance" and "tension-management." Specialization of
functions always increases efficiency, according to Parsons. The
"transfer of functions," or in Parsonian terminology the process of
structural and functional differentiation, relieves the family of its
educative, economic, and protective functions in order that it may
specialize in child rearing and emotional solace. The conjugal family
becomes a haven of intense feeling in a world where competition
rules other relations. In Parsons's terms, the family stands preemi-
nently as the institution in which relations are determined by "ascription" rather than by achievement. The child receives love and
admiration simply because he is the child of particular parents; elsewhere, he has to earn respect and affection by means of his objective
achievements.[14] To state the point less abstractly, the occupational
system demands patterns of behavior that "run counter to many of
the most deep-seated of human needs," such as loyalty, love ("sentimental attachment to persons as such"), and security. These needs
can be satisfied only in the family.[15]

Having provided the usual sociological justification of the family's
importance, Parsons undercut it with another line of argument
about the rationalization of human relations and the "professionalization" of parenthood. In the book on the family that he wrote
with Bales, Slater, and Zelditch, Parsons referred to "the enormous
vogue of treating 'human' problems from the point of view of mental
health and in various respects of psychology." In American society,
he noted, "technological-organizational developments closely related to science have taken over on a very wide front." It is "the
American method" to solve problems "by calling in scientifically expert aid."

> In industry we take this for granted. In human relations it is just coming
> to the fore. The immense vogue of psychiatry, of clinical psychology and
> such phenomena are, we suggest, an index of the importance of strain in
> the area of personality and the human relations in which persons are

placed. In the nature of our society much of this strain relates to family and marriage relations. [16]

In plain English, psychiatrists and other experts in human relations have begun to apply to the family techniques already perfected in industrial management. The isolation of the nuclear family intensifies the emotional climate of the family and creates "strains" that only experts know how to ease. Because parents depend more and more heavily on expert advice, the care of children has become a profession, especially for women, who take chief responsibility for it. The "'professionalization' of the mother role" implicates women "in the attempt to rationalize these areas of human relations." Women represent the principal constituency to which the psychiatric profession offers advice and spiritual consolation; and "women do not act only in the role of patient of the psychiatrist, but often the psychiatrist also is a woman." [17]

We now see more clearly why the Parsonians drew so heavily on small-group theory when they turned to the study of the family. Not only did it imply a functional explanation of the sexual division of labor and a method by which psychoanalytic concepts could be operationalized, in the jargon of the social sciences; it also showed how experts could rationalize the management of domestic relations along industrial lines. The first studies of small groups had the practical objective of organizing personnel management on a scientific basis. When they took industrial sociology as the model for study of the family, the Parsonians attempted, in effect, to bring sociological theory into line with the historical development which had extended managerial control from the factory into every other area of the worker's life. Scientific study of the family thus ratified the social process which simultaneously brought the family and other forms of private life under public, scientific control.

SOCIALIZATION AS THERAPY

The affinity between Parsonian sociology and therapeutic modes of social control appears even more clearly in another line of argument, in which Parsons draws an analogy between socialization and therapy, the family and the psychiatric clinic. "Each phase of the socialization process," he argues, "is analogous to a therapeutic process." In both cases, the socializing agent plays a dual role, at once instrumental and expressive, and his attitude toward the patient/child combines tolerance of expression, support in spite of failure, manipulation of rewards, and "denial of reciprocity." Although the doctor rewards his patient with emotional support, ideally he can no more allow himself to be "seduced" by the patient than the mother allows herself to be seduced by the child. Parsons refers to these analogies as "our social control or therapy paradigm." [18]

As a therapy, psychoanalysis attempts to model the doctor-patient relationship on the family, recapitulating, this time consciously, the patient's childhood relations with his parents. Parsonian theory reverses Freud, modeling the family on the doctor-patient relationship—in many ways, the type of "small group" that interests Parsons most. [19] Elsewhere Parsons argues that the similarity between the doctor's role and the parent's arises out of an underlying identity "between illness and the status of the child in the family." Neither the child nor the sick person can function fully as an adult. Sickness, moreover, no matter whether it takes somatic or psychic form, often represents a deliberate withdrawal from adult responsibilities and therefore amounts to a mild form of deviance in a society that "enforces an unusually high level of activity." Sickness "connects so closely with the residua of childhood dependency" that it generates psychological difficulties even when it is not deliberately chosen as an escape from unbearable burdens—especially in a society where childhood dependence is so pronounced. For these reasons, all doctors, and not only psychotherapists, practice a form of psychotherapy. Sickness unavoidably gives rise to "problems of personality adjustment," which demand from doctors some of the same skills that raising children demands from parents. [20]

In Parsons's sociology of medicine, the doctor legitimizes the patient's withdrawal from everyday life by calling it sickness. He certifies the patient into the "sick role," thereby absolving him of moral responsibility for his actions. The patient, in return, promises to follow the doctor's orders in the interest of his recovery.[21] Therapy shares with child rearing a disciplinary aspect, an element of social control. Life must not be made too comfortable for the patient; otherwise he will lose his incentive to recover. Just as the incest taboo serves to "propel" the child out of the family, so the hospital—ultimate embodiment of medical authority—subjects the patient to a regimen deliberately made harsher than home. In both cases, medical intervention protects the welfare not only of the "deviant" but of the family itself. Both sickness and prolonged emotional dependence in the young threaten the family's "equilibrium."[22] If the father gets sick, the wife has to withdraw attention from the children. If a child gets sick, she has to neglect her husband. Her own sickness threatens everybody. The family is too fragile, in short, to cope with sickness—too "precariously balanced," in Parsons's words; too "highly-charged" emotionally.[23] Even under normal conditions, emotional tensions overburden the family and strain it to the breaking point; the outbreak of sickness threatens to disrupt it completely.

In any case, according to Parsons, doctors give better treatment for the sick than families can provide—and perhaps by implication, better treatment for the young. The family finds it difficult to strike the right balance between the supportive and disciplinary aspects of cure. "Therapy is more easily effected in a professional milieu, where there is not the same order of intensive emotional involvement so characteristic of family relationships."[24]

"Although the American family is well adapted to the exigencies of a modern industrial society," according to Parsons, "it is also highly susceptible to many grave strains."[25] Indeed sickness often arises in the first place, Parsons argues, precisely out of the tensions of family life. If sickness provides a refuge from pressures at school or work, it also serves as an escape from family pressures—a haven from home. "It is easy to see . . . how the wife-mother, for example, might 'choose' the sick role as an institutionalized way out of her heavy 'human relations management' responsibilities in the family; or how she might seize upon illness as a compulsively feministic way of reacting to her exclusion from the life open to a man."[26] In the same way, children, Parsons explains, might choose sickness as an alternative to the painful process of growing up. The family causes many forms of sickness, without being able to cure them. Thus Parsons defines family life as analogous to therapy, only to conclude that professionals do a better job of treating diseases that arose in the first place, moreover, in the very bosom of the family. The Parsonian praise of the nuclear family already implies a Laingian critique of the family.

The modern family provides indispensable emotional services, according to Parsons, yet it performs them so badly, on his own account, that its efforts have to be supplemented by an army of healers who attempt to repair the emotional ravages inflicted, in the last analysis, by the family itself. Only a short step brings us to the conclusion that trained therapists ought to take charge of socialization in the first place, in order to attack sickness at its source. Parsonian analysis of the family as a small group seems to point to the same conclusion, by attempting to show that the functional differentiation of instrumental and expressive roles, not the biological and emotional connection between parents and children, provides the decisive element in socialization. In his eagerness to establish this point, so important to his functional analysis of social relations, Parsons concedes the possibility of replacing the family with some other agency of socialization. "Even if the socialization function could be cut loose from the biologically constituted family, . . . it could *not* be performed without placing the child in a small group the structure of which was generically the same as that of the family."[27]

Parsons's translation of Freudian concepts into role and learning theory provides added support for the contention that the "professionalization" of parenthood logically culminates in the supersession of the family and the assignment of child rearing to trained experts. Like so many others who seek to "improve" on psychoanalysis by giving it a cultural dimension, Parsons tries to correct Freud's "overemphasis" on biology. Although Freud in his opinion "was clearly very much on the right track," psychoanalysis attributed too much importance to instincts and too little to "the structure of social relationships as systems in which the process of socialization takes place."[28] According to Parsonian theory, the child learns to play appropriate roles by "interacting" with his parents and siblings, in the course of which he progresses from what Parsons calls a mother-centered system of solidarity to a family-centered system. The Oedipus complex, originating in the cultural demand that the child outgrow dependence on its mother, appears as the climax of this progress, and its resolution results in the full integration of the child into the family—itself the first stage in his integration into the larger society beyond the family.

As learning becomes the focus of socialization theory, fantasy, the unconscious, and sexuality slip back into the darkness from which psychoanalysis tried to bring them to light. Parsonian theory relegates sex to an incident of the learning process. "Erotic gratification is a peculiarly sensitive source of conditioning in the 'classical' Pavlovian sense."[29] In Parsons's reinterpretation of Freud, sexuality is purely passive—a sensation mildly pleasurable, not an active, overpowering desire. The overwhelming fact in the mother-child relation, according to Parsons, is the child's dependence on the mother's care. That the case appears very different in the child's fantasies does not interest him in the slightest. Neither does the possibility that these fantasies figure more prominently in the child's subsequent development than the child's dependence on maternal care.

In his long discussion of the "transition from oral to love-dependency," Parsons takes note of Freud's well-known argument that feces, penis, and baby are closely linked in the child's unconscious thoughts. Then he proceeds to distort the argument out of all resemblance to the original. He misrepresents the symbolism by which feces, penis, and baby are equated, in a way that allows him to maintain that in the phallic phase, as in the pre-Oedipal phase generally, the child "internalizes" the mother's role rather than the father's. "The famous symbolic equation of 'feces-child' seems very plausible," Parsons says, "in view of the reciprocity of role pattern between mother and child. Just as mother gives birth to child, so the child also 'gives birth' to an object, he hereby in some sense is able to identify himself with his mother, symbolically to take her role." The suspicion that we are reading a heavily censored version of Freud's thought deepens when we note that Parsons has neglected to mention the third component, the third "member" in Freud's equation. But only the equation of feces with a penis as well as a baby makes the equation intelligible: it is not that the child wishes to

imitate the mother in "giving birth to an object," but that he wishes
to present the mother with a baby—her own baby—through the in-
strumentality of his penis, associated in turn with feces because both
are associated with gifts presented by the child to his parents. According to Freud's interpretation of the symbolism in question, it is
not the mother's role the child plans to "assume"—usurp—but the
father's.[30]

Parsons's bowdlerization of this material, which is so crucial to an
understanding of the psychoanalytic theory of sex, not only renders
sex passive but identifies it exclusively with the "expressive" role—
not, as in Freud, with the child's need to master his environment.
These distortions in turn lead to the conclusion, elaborated in Parsons's later work, that parents serve their offspring best when they
provide each child with undemanding emotional security in his early
years and then give him a high degree of independence: the personal freedom, designed to ease the child's break with the family,
that strikes many foreigners as an "incredible leeway."[31] Parents
serve their children best, in other words, when they seek consciously to diminish the emotional intensity of family life.

Repeatedly in his writings on socialization, Parsons struggles to
explain why the child's emotional involvement with his parents does
not incapacitate him for the harsh realities of adult life, for a career of
"achievement." Having rejected the psychoanalytic explanation—that sexuality itself is closely bound up with the urge to master
the world, and that repression or sublimation of sexuality forces this
urge for mastery to seek objects beyond the family—Parsons finds it
impossible to explain why the family, which keeps the child in a
state of prolonged dependency, simultaneously fosters an "achievement orientation." The main features of his analysis—an analysis
which stresses the professionalization of parenthood, refers to the father as "chairman of the board" and the mother as "personnel manager," repeatedly warns of the danger that the child may "seduce"
his mother, and returns again and again to the importance of parental solidarity in the face of the child's emotional demands—all seem
to suggest, though Parsons himself does not draw this conclusion,
that most problems of family life could easily be avoided by substituting professional experts for parents. The "rationalization" of child
rearing in the home, which greatly diminishes the intensity of the

parent-child relationship, already represents an important step in this direction. On the strength of Parsons's own reasoning, the rise of the "helping professions" has already made most of the traditional functions of parenthood obsolete; all that remains is to "transfer" the remaining functions to those best qualified to carry them out.

By renouncing Freud's "biological determinism," Parsons deprived himself of the best argument for the indispensability of the family: that children grow up best under the very conditions of "intense emotional involvement" which Parsons thought it wise to avoid in therapy and, by implication, in the family itself. Without struggling with the ambivalent emotions aroused by the union of love and discipline in his parents, the child never masters his inner rage or his fear of authority. It is for this reason that children need parents, not professional nurses and counselors.

The confusion of parents dependent on professional theories of child rearing, their reluctance to exercise authority or to assume responsibility for the child's development, and the delegation of discipline to various outside agencies, have already diluted the quality of child care, but Parsons's censorship of psychoanalysis makes it impossible to understand the most important element in this process— the weakening of the psychic mechanism whereby the young internalize their parents. The father's withdrawal into the world of work has not only deprived his sons of a "role model"; it has also deprived them of a superego, or to speak more precisely, it has transformed the contents of the superego so that archaic, instinctual, death-seeking elements increasingly predominate. In societies where the family still serves as a center of production or at least hands down useful knowledge to its offspring, sons learn from their fathers more than techniques and "roles." The deeper psychological significance of paternal training lies in its capacity to temper the child's fantasies with practical experience, softening the early impression of an omnipotent, wrathful, and punitive father. If the son is to overcome his jealous hatred of the father, the terrifying figure of the father has to be reduced by daily contact, in the course of which the father establishes himself in his son's affections by his mastery of the skills and techniques the son also needs to master. The modern father finds it difficult to provide this information. Such skills as he possesses become technologically obsolete in his own lifetime, and there would be little point in transmitting them to his children even if he had a chance to do so.

The weakening of paternal care makes it easier than it used to be for sons to break away from their fathers, but precisely because it has eliminated overt conflict between fathers and sons, it has made it more difficult than ever for the child to become an autonomous adult. Such autonomy as we manage to attain, according to Freud, comes after terrific struggles to overcome inferiority and dependence, and lapses into infantilism remain an ever-present possibility. Autonomy, in the Freudian view, rests on intense emotional identification with parents, not on literal imitation of them, as Parsonian sociology would have it.[32] The essence of the Oedipus complex and its resolution is that the son transforms the wish to get rid of the father into the wish to succeed him. Without by any means overcoming his original longing for the mother and hatred of the father, he transfers the maternal longing to another woman, while redirecting many of his aggressive impulses against himself—against his own failures to live up to his father's example and standards. The decline of the father's participation in family life makes this identification difficult or impossible. The child no longer wishes to succeed the father. Instead, he wishes merely to enjoy life without his interference—without the interference of any authorities at all.

At the same time, his desire to get rid of authority, starting with the father, has grown stronger than ever, not only because authorities interfere with his pleasure (as always) but also because he has formed an exaggerated idea of their power. The absence, remoteness, or inaccessibility of the father does not mean that the child forms no ideas about him; it only means that those ideas will seldom be tested against everyday experience. The child imagines a remote, vindictive father and comes to see the world as starkly divided between power and impotence. He reduces all questions of justice and morality to questions of strength.

Under these conditions, the child remains a slave to pre-Oedipal impulses and external stimuli, with which he is bombarded by a culture devoted to consumption and immediate gratification. He resorts to violence in order to satisfy his desires, or else represses his violence and anger at a high psychic cost. Wishing to get rid of his father instead of taking the father's place, he has little incentive to grow up. Psychologically he remains in important ways a child, surrounded by authorities with whom he does not identify and whose authority he does not regard as legitimate. Their only importance to him is that they represent raw superior force which is capable of thwarting his wishes. If he bows to those authorities—if, for example, he stoically accepts a punishment he regards as unjust or unfair—it is only because he fears retribution. Meanwhile, he may harbor dreams of revenge, the most prevalent form of which, perhaps, is the fantasy of a general uprising of the young.[33]

THE "PRODUCTION OF PERSONALITY"

Talcott Parsons and his colleagues cannot be regarded as propagandists for the nuclear family. They are liberals, not traditionalists, and their work on the family incorporates the progressive ideology of the social pathologists. According to Parsons, an impersonal process beyond human control—the process of structural and functional differentiation—has created a new kind of democratic, egalitarian family structure. This new type of family, by a remarkable coincidence, closely resembles the ideal of the social pathologists. It has proved to be an ideal instrument for training achievement, emotional independence, critical judgment, tolerance of ambiguity, and "maturity"— the very qualities, according to spokesmen for the health and welfare professions, on which the peace of the world has come to depend. Parsons restated the prescriptions of these experts as descriptions of modern society, thereby giving them an aura of sociological inevitability.

Never a polemicist, Parsons nevertheless defended his view of the family with considerable vehemence when it was challenged by other sociologists—for example, by David Riesman in *The Lonely Crowd*. Riesman argued that American culture has entered a new phase. As the focus of economic activity shifts from production to consumption, and social life comes to rest on highly organized forms of cooperation instead of on individual exertion, "the world of interpersonal relations," according to Riesman, "almost obscures from view the world of physical nature and the supernatural as the setting for the human drama."[34] The family's importance in socialization declines; the "other-directed" child, who must learn at an early age how to get along with the group, grows up under the influence of the media, the school, and his peers. "The family is no longer a closely knit unit to which he belongs but merely part of a wider social environment to which he early becomes attentive."[35] The child learns from radio, comics, and movies how parents are expected to act and holds this ideal over his parents' heads. He develops a precocious mastery of the external world and a certain self-righteousness, as the conduct of his parents falls short of the ideal. Formerly it was parents who were self-righteous. Now they are unsure of themselves, defensive, hesitant to impose their own standards on the young. Forced at every turn to defend their authority by abstract standards of justice and legitimacy, they fall back on argumentation, negotiation, and covert manipulation—"stage-managing." The same thing happens at school. The distance between teacher and students narrows, the teacher becomes an "opinion leader," and the curriculum stresses "realism"—how to get along with others, not how to think for oneself. Imagination "withers in most of the children by adolescence."

Both parents and teachers, according to Riesman, have abdicated most of their authority to the adolescent peer group; and although the culture of children and adolescents in some ways mirrors the older ideology of competitive individualism and achievement, it subtly transforms those values into new forms.

> The peer-group becomes the measure of all things: the individual has no defenses the group cannot batter down. In this situation the competitive drives for achievement sponsored in children by the remnants of inner-direction in their parents come into conflict with the cooperative demands sponsored by the peer-group. The child therefore is forced to rechannel the competitive drive for achievement, as demanded by the parents, into his drive for approval from the peers. Neither parent, child, nor the peer-group itself is particularly conscious of this process. As a result all three participants in the process may remain unaware of the degree to which the force of older individualistic ideology provides the energies for filling out the forms of a newer, group-oriented characterology.[36]

Parsons begins his rebuttal of Riesman by announcing two propositions, characteristically adding that he does not intend to defend them empirically: American society long ago developed a "well integrated and fully institutionalized system of values," and this value system has remained essentially unchanged in recent years.[37] American culture continues to attach great importance to "instrumental activism," individualism, and achievement. Meanwhile, changes in the social structure, most of which can be considered under the general heading of structural differentiation, bring society into closer correspondence with the dominant ideology. In the occupational system, the white-collar and managerial sectors grow at the expense of unskilled labor, standards of competence for white-collar jobs constantly rise, and for both reasons educational credentials become more and more important in determining access to the best jobs. The demand for trained manpower and the geographical mobility of the labor force undermine the traditional bastions of family-based privilege. More than ever before, the ideology of equal opportunity accurately characterizes American society, even though competition for the best places remains fierce, and heavy emotional demands are made on those who compete.

In a society in which personality, in effect, has become an important industrial resource, the family specializes in the "production of personality"—a trend that is reflected, according to Parsons, in the new interest in education and child rearing, the shifting emphasis in psychoanalysis from depth psychology to ego psychology, and the growing concern with mental health. The family trains the "capacity for role-performance"; but this "mastery of personal relationships," he adds nervously, should by no means be confused with " 'domination' of other people."[38] By providing the child with emotional security in his early years and then by giving him a high degree of independence, the isolated nuclear family trains a type of personality ideally equipped to face the rigors of the modern world. Permissiveness, which many observers mistake for an abdication of parental responsibility, actually amounts to a new way of training achievement. It prepares the child to deal with an unpredictable world in which he will constantly find himself faced with unstructured situations. In dealing with such exigencies, he has little use for hard-and-fast principles of duty and conduct learned from his parents. He needs the ability to take care of himself, to make quick decisions, and to adapt quickly to many types of contingencies. In a slower world, parents could act as role models for their children, but the modern parent, according to Parsons, can hope only to provide his children with the resources he needs to survive on his own. We should not be deceived by the "leeway" granted to their children by American parents. "What Riesman interprets as the abdication of the parents from their socializing responsibility can . . . be interpreted in exactly the opposite way." Modern parents fulfill their obligations to the young precisely by refraining from the attempt to inculcate precepts and standards that would prove useless in a world where nothing is fixed. What looks like "abdication" is simply realism.[39]

Drawing on S. N. Eisenstadt's study of youth culture—itself inspired by Parsons's earlier work—Parsons treats youth culture as a differentiated part of the socialization system, which eases the adolescent's transition from particularism to universality, ascription to achievement. According to Eisenstadt, the adolescent needs the emotional security of relationships that are "largely ascriptive" yet take him outside his own family.[40] By providing this kind of "emotional support," the subculture of American adolescents fulfills "one set of needs," in Parsons's words. It complements the family on the one hand and the school on the other. Riesman exaggerates its importance in socialization, however, and he errs again, according to Parsons, by treating youth culture as merely a reflection of American culture as a whole. In fact, youth culture is semiautonomous, "more definitely structured about a normative culture of its own than Riesman's formulations imply."[41] Not that youth culture is in conflict with adult culture. Certain values may be specialized in a given institution without creating conflicts with other institutions. "In universalistic societies," according to Eisenstadt, "there is an inherent tendency for instrumental, solidary and expressive roles to be segregated in different sectors and groups." Far from creating conflicts, this compartmentalization ensures that each set of values will be "supreme" in its own sphere.[42] Adolescent culture, in the Parsonian view, specializes in "expression" while at the same time integrating young people into the roles they will occupy as adults.

By arguing that youth culture eases the transition from the family to full participation in adult roles, Parsons finally disposed of a difficulty that troubled his work on the family from the beginning. His own insistence on the highly specialized "expressive" functions of the family raised the possibility that the family might be in conflict with a society increasingly organized around "instrumentalism." It raised the further possibility that this conflict might appear in its most acute form in contradictory demands made on young people—that they establish unusually strong ties to their parents in childhood, which adulthood then requires them to repudiate. The Parsonian resolution of this problem, in its final version, argued that early dependence itself provides the basis of later autonomy. More generally, "heightened expressiveness" complements a rise in demands for achievement; the dependence of childhood itself nourishes the capacity for achievement.

The trouble with this solution, which is a model of elegance and simplicity, is first of all that it has no capacity to explain empirical events, as any theory must. Far from explaining events, Parsonian theory has been overtaken by them. Writing in 1962, on the eve of an unprecedented upheaval of youth, Parsons thought young people were becoming more serious and "progressive," but his theory hardly anticipated the emergence of a youth culture that condemned American society in the most sweeping terms, repudiated the desirability of growing up in the usual way, and sometimes appeared to repudiate the desirability of growing up at all. It would be the height of perversity to interpret the youth culture of the sixties and seventies as a culture that eases the transition from childhood to maturity, when that culture sees the attainment of adult status and responsibilities as a betrayal of its ideals, by definition a "sellout," and therefore as something to be accepted only with deep feelings of guilt. As for the argument that a heightened dependence in childhood furnishes the basis of increased autonomy in adulthood, it does not explain why personal autonomy seems more difficult than ever to achieve or sustain. Nor does it explain why so many signs of cultural and psychological regression should appear just at the historical moment when, according to Parsons, the family has emerged from a period of "crisis" and has "now begun at least to be stabilized."[43] It is precisely the instability of the family that strikes us wherever we turn. Youth culture itself has made the family a prime target—not just something to "rebel" against but a corrupt and decadent institution to be overthrown. That the new youth culture represents more than adolescent rebellion is suggested by the way its attack on the family reverberates, appealing to a great variety of other groups—

feminists, advocates of the rights of homosexuals, cultural and political reformers of all kinds. Hostility to the family has survived the demise of the political radicalism of the sixties and flourishes amid the conservatism of the seventies. Even the pillars of society show no great inclination to defend the family, historically regarded as the basis of their whole way of life. Meanwhile, the divorce rate continues to rise, young people avoid or at least postpone marriage, and social life organizes itself around "swinging singles." None of these developments bears out the thesis that "loss of functions" made the family stronger than ever by allowing it to specialize in the work it does best. On the contrary, no other institution seems to work so badly, to judge from the volume of abuse directed against it and the growing wish to experiment with other forms.

When a theory is open to so many empirical objections, we begin to suspect that there is something wrong with the theory itself. Parsons's theory of the family rests on an unwarranted assumption which he took from his immediate predecessors and never subjected to critical analysis: that some of the family's functions can be surrendered without weakening the others. In fact, the so-called functions of the family form an integrated system. It is inaccurate to speak of a variety of functions, some of which decline while others take on added importance. The only function of the family that matters is socialization; and when protection, work, and instruction in work have all been removed from the home, the child no longer identifies with his parents or internalizes their authority in the same way as before, if indeed he internalizes their authority at all. The father figures in the child's life merely as a disciplinarian and provider, and even these roles have lost much of their former content. Parsons himself has inadvertently provided a clue that helps to clarify the significance of these changes. In an essay not devoted to the family, he notes in passing that the American family, in contrast to that of China, tends to "accept a commitment to reward universalistically judged classificatory qualities . . . rather than blood ties." Even obligations to a parent, he notes, are based on "the extent to which the parent is considered 'worthy' in universalistic terms." Nor does Parsons flinch from the next step in this line of reasoning: "worthiness in universalistic terms" will depend on the degree to which the parent provides certain goods and services. For example, "the definition of a son's gratitude and hence his obligation toward his mother, is based less on the biological *fact* of the relationship than on her services and attitudes on his behalf."[44]

If the modern family rests on the parents' "services" to the child, however, it rests on a shaky footing, for recent events have drastically curtailed the parents' ability to provide those services. Unless uncommonly rich, they cannot provide even the basic necessities without assistance from the state. The family no longer protects the child or shields him from the encroachments of the outside world. Nor does it provide emotional security when marriages end so often in divorce and are conducted on the principles of business life, according to which "one leaves a position as soon as a better one offers itself."[45] For all these reasons, the family can no longer perform the functions assigned to it by sociological theory.

It is eminently characteristic of the quality of Parsons's thought that he does not so much repudiate this view of the family as put another alongside it, with seeming modesty, as "another view" of the matter in question. In itself it is no reproach to say that Parsons has a conciliatory rather than a combative temperament, but his refusal to engage in argumentation, except on rare occasions, has had the unfortunate effect—perhaps not entirely unintentional—of seeming to place his own work above controversy and to give it a quality of scientific detachment. What looks like modesty conceals vast claims to scientific objectivity.

A final example of this technique—one that also raises an important substantive issue—will conclude our discussion. In one of his many essays on psychoanalysis, Parsons noted that both Alfred Kazin and Lionel Trilling had argued that Freud brought psychology closer to biology than to the study of culture. But instead of admitting that this assertion carried implications opposed to those of his own work, Parsons presented his own culturized version of psychoanalysis as "another side" of the picture, not before remarking, as if in passing, that the other view was held predominantly "in literary circles."[46] It has long been a standard tactic of Freudian revisionism to pretend that only literary people resist its scientific correction of Freud, and Parsons, for all his disdain for polemics, was not above resorting to this sneer when it suited his purpose. The underlying dispute, however, cannot be brushed aside so easily, as if it were a disagreement between two types of sensibility, each valid in its own "sphere." On the contrary, it concerns an issue that no social theory can hope to avoid: the relative contributions of biology and culture to what is known as human nature. By insisting on the biological basis of mind, psychoanalysis undermines the belief that personality derives wholly from culture. It thereby challenges both the naïve optimism that sees human history as the steady subjugation of instinct by enlightenment and the sophisticated optimism of social science, according to which the primacy of culture inheres in the very fact of culture, the precondition of social life and thus of human life itself.

According to Trilling, the concept of culture in the nineteenth and early twentieth centuries emerged from a growing sense that the individual was "far more deeply implicated in society than ever before." Students of culture not only tried to explain this development but provided a justification for it, by making culture impervious to criticism. In the very act of relativizing culture, social science made it into a kind of absolute. Since every culture had to be judged on its own terms, no culture was "to be judged 'bad' or 'neurotic'; it was the individual who was to be judged by the criteria of the culture." Freud's biological determinism, Trilling argued, limits the determinism of culture and thus provides the individual with defenses against a culture that is becoming more and more integrated and demanding.[47] Trilling accepted the accuracy of the assertion (while deploring the fact) that modern man is almost wholly the product of social relations or culture, and he held up this condition against an idealized past when personal integrity was allegedly intact and a healthy strain of savagery made men resistant to total socialization.

A deeper criticism of Parsonian sociology—and of social science in general—is that this total socialization of instinct, the assumption on which so much of social science rests, is an illusion. Having confused socialization with conscious learning and the acquisition of habits, social science has lost sight of biological resistance to socialization and of the inner conflict to which it leads. "And it is this [conflict] that is central to Freud's view," as Dennis Wrong has written, "for in psychoanalytic terms to say that a norm has been internalized, or introjected to become part of the superego, is to say no more than that a person will suffer guilt-feelings if he fails to live up to it, not that he will in fact live up to it in his behavior."[48]

Outbreaks of mass violence in the twentieth century suggest that, if anything, civilized restraints are weakening—partly because of a general weakening in the care of the young. Modern society, Alexander Mitscherlich has observed, "counts too easily on the domestication of man. The great upheavals of history show us that no part of his cultural adaptation is so secure that it can be relied on as a permanent human possession."[49] Because it ignores the precariousness of socialization—not because it threatens to annihilate the last remnants of instinct—academic social science obscures the issues it pretends to unravel and contributes to the general confusion.

7

The Attack on the Nuclear

Family and the Search for

"Alternate Life-styles"

THE IDEOLOGY OF
"NONBINDING COMMITMENTS"

The American economy provides people with more skills and education than the available jobs require. Recently it has begun to turn out large numbers of highly educated people who cannot find employment at all. The demand for a more "relevant" education, so insistent in the sixties and early seventies, originated in the disparity between the training needed to qualify for work and the content of that work. In the forties and fifties, however, many people simply withdrew their energy from the job and tried to satisfy a wish to be "creative" by raising large families; they approached marriage, householding, and parenthood as a fine art. Such experiments usually failed. Educated women soon tired of undiluted domesticity.

Indeed, the educated housewife turned out to be the supreme example and victim of overtraining, and her growing resentment of her lowly status—so sharply at odds not only with her expectations but with the status to which academic training entitled her—helped to generate a full-scale revival of feminism at the end of the sixties. Meanwhile, the educated housewife and her husband gave a great deal of attention to their children; but child rearing too proved disappointing in the long run. The children of the forties and fifties became the rebels and dropouts of the sixties and seventies. Demanding and reproachful, they simultaneously condemned their parents' values and criticized their failure to live up to them.

Caught in the crossfire of generational revolt and the revolt of women, the domestic revival expired. Once again the family found itself under heavy criticism, this time as the symbol of a sentimental privatism universally repudiated in an equally sentimental search for "community." Feminists condemned domestic life more bitterly than before, drawing on the writings of Laing, Cooper, and other theorists of the revulsion against domesticity to buttress their increasingly comprehensive indictment.[1] Spokesmen for the counter-culture joined the attack, accusing the nuclear family of promoting neurotic individualism. Lesbians and homosexuals became politically militant. The news media—biased, as always, not in favor of any particular program or point of view but simply in favor of novelty—gave as much publicity to feminism, cultural radicalism, and denigration of the family as they had once given to "togetherness," the slogan put forward by *McCall's* in 1954 to evoke and apologize for the retreat to familial pleasures.

Recent criticism of the family often reflects the popularization of psychiatric clichés formerly associated, if only superficially, with the "cult of domesticity." As psychiatry takes on the characteristics of a new religion or antireligion, a "protestant" conception of the priestly function has grown up in opposition to the "catholic" conception. The "protestants" have translated psychiatric theory into the vernacular, in order to make it more accessible to their constituents. They have introduced innovations in psychiatric ritual, like Carl Rogers's "client-centered psychiatry," with the intention of diminishing the magisterial authority of the psychiatrist.[2] They have condemned the arrogance of the psychiatric priesthood, not because they object to

therapeutic conceptions of reality, but because they wish to diffuse
them more widely than ever, rooting them in popular understanding and daily practice. When they argue, for example, that psychiatry should be considered not as treatment but as education in interpersonal relations, the "protestants" demand not a restriction of
its scope but a further expansion.[3] Instead of confining therapy to
medical practice, they propose to import it into every activity. They
hope to model education, law enforcement, and spiritual salvation
on what has variously been called nondirective therapy, reality therapy, behavior therapy, or client-centered therapy, in which "no
strict demands are made on the patient, nor is he admonished in any
way."[4] Critics of the concept of "mental illness" would abolish the
hospital only to make the whole world a hospital.

Most of the ideas associated in the sixties and seventies with psychiatric radicalism have had a long history; nor is there anything new
about the criticism of the family to which they often give rise. Only
an increased popular awareness of this criticism gives the impression
of radicalism and novelty.[5] Criticism of the family, moreover, is easily absorbed into a defense of the existing social order. Demands for
what purport to be sweeping changes now issue not only from
feminists and cultural radicals but also from ministers, psychiatrists,
counselors, and other healers. A recent collection on that inexhaust-
ible topic, the future of the family, endorses the "sexual revolution"
as an adjustment to "an era characterized by abundance rather than
scarcity." The authors, a group of Catholic liberals, flatter the
young—who allegedly "prefer the risks of insecurity and uncertainty
to the risks of conventionality and security"—and insist that "parents
should stay together because they want to, not because they have
to." At the same time, they assure their readers that some form of
marriage will undoubtedly survive the exercise of this freedom,
since man "has ineradicable familial needs" (and "ineradicable religious needs" as well, luckily for the ministry). Twenty-five years
ago, liberal Catholics like Denis de Rougemont perceived that
unrestricted divorce, the movement for women's rights, and the
equation of marriage with sexual and spiritual fulfillment threatened
the family's stability. Catholic liberals today, having absorbed social
science and much of popular radicalism as well, speak soothingly of
movements toward more inclusive identities ("widening family cir-

cles") and the restoration of "community." In place of isolated families that "insulate ourselves and our loved ones against the encroachments of the world," they recommend a "transitional" form of the family that "would stem from a blood-tied nucleus of man, woman, and offspring, and include a number of non-related people of any ages who just happen at a given time to live in the same vicinity."[6]

Whereas many experts seek to rescue domesticity by reviving the extended family, others advance the opposite solution, a further shrinkage of the family. Recent debates on the family turn on a renewed insistence that companionship, not child rearing, is the essence of married life. Advocates of "open marriage," "creative divorce," and other panaceas have resurrected the argument that marriage can survive even the transfer of child-rearing functions to the state, simply because it meets the psychological need for "one-to-one relationships." The humanist psychology of Rogers, May, and Maslow, widely diffused by such best sellers as the O'Neills' *Open Marriage* and the Francoeurs' *Hot and Cool Sex*, converges with pop sociology in a defense of monogamy that ingeniously incorporates a bitter attack on the family. According to theorists of "future shock," the family can no longer transmit values in an age of accelerated change, impermanence, mobility, and expanding options ("overchoice"). If industrialism demanded that the family be stripped down from its extended to its nuclear form, then superindustrialism, as Toffler calls it, requires a further "streamlining"—a reduction of the family to marriage. Parenthood, too important to be left to amateurs and dilettantes, will be professionalized by assigning children to special clinics or, if that seems too cold and impersonal, to couples specially trained and certified for parenthood (a solution advanced by Margaret Mead), or even to communes or other kinds of extended families. The rest of the population, freed from the burdens of child rearing, will find spiritual enrichment in the intensive exploration of one-to-one relationships.[7]

Monogamy can survive, however, only if it is detached not from child rearing alone but from the "unrealistic expectations" formerly associated with marriage: such is the emerging consensus of professional healers and their popularizers. "Privatization" and the "togetherness syndrome," according to this view, produce unhealthy marriages as well as unhealthy children. The future of marriage, it appears, depends on "kicking the togetherness habit." Husbands and wives should respect each other's need for individuality, "self-awareness," and "personal growth." They should reject "enforced role-playing" and accept each other "as people, not as actors in a family drama." "In today's world, when change is so rapid and so constant, flexibility is an absolute necessity," according to the O'Neills, and flexibility means among other things shaking off rigid sex roles and the expectations that go with them.[8] Living up to expectations, especially when those expectations derive from rigidly defined social roles such as "wife," "husband," "mother," and "father," does violence to one's own needs and feelings—the feelings, according to marriage experts and other healers, with which it is so important to "get in touch." For the same reason, it is important that communication take the form of statements about those feelings rather than statements purporting to describe reality or implying an objective standard which actions—for example, the actions of one's spouse—may fall short of. Self-expression, not criticism, should prevail even in marital fights, which can serve as a form of therapy when conducted according to recognized rules of fair play.[9]

As in the twenties and thirties, marriage therapists reserve their harshest condemnation for the idea of romantic love, which gives rise to expectations no marriage can meet. Exclusive, possessive, and jealous, romantic love encourages dependency and causes lovers to make exorbitant demands on each other. It erroneously assumes that jealousy "naturally arises out of love," confuses love with power and possession, and upholds the pernicious doctrine that "true love is utterly monogamous."[10] In fact, "man is not naturally monogamous," according to the O'Neills. Like their predecessors in the twenties, the new marriage experts insist that adultery should not necessarily be considered a breach of faith. Each couple should decide for itself whether to consider it as such—"the choice is entirely up to you." But the O'Neills go further than Robert and Frances Binkley when they dismiss as an "outdated cultural hangup" the very idea that "sex without love is destructive, alienating and unpleasurable." This false dogma, they argue, derives from "the idea that sex is dirty."[11] As interpreted by the spiritual healers of the present day, the "joy of sex" derives from pure instinctual release, unadorned and unsublimated.

The sexual revolution, the revival of feminism, the emergence of the counterculture, and the growing tolerance of "alternate life-styles" have not changed the arguments for marriage or the strategies designed to make it more attractive and durable, both of which have remained essentially unaltered over the last fifty years. Advocates of "open marriage" and sexual freedom have fought the clichés of the fifties by reviving the clichés of the twenties and thirties. At the same time, the cult of undemanding interpersonal relations—the ideology of "nonbinding commitments," in the revealing phrase used by Nena and George O'Neill without any sense of its irony—has become increasingly independent of specific positions for or against marriage. Both the friends and enemies of marriage uphold divorce as a "creative act"—the friends of marriage because it provides a necessary safety valve, and its enemies because it can be seen as a step toward some new kind of family structure.[12] Both camps extol nonbinding commitments and reject as "role-playing" demands that individuals live up to predetermined expectations, whether externally imposed or self-imposed. Both sides—if one can speak of sides at all, in a debate where the points in contention have become so amorphous—seek to free the individual from guilt or failure and condemn "unrealistic" expectations that may give rise to those emotions. Both sides condemn what they call romantic love, in their view the most unrealistic expectation of all.

The ideology of nonbinding commitments, superficially optimistic about the power of positive thinking, radiates pessimism; it is the world view of the resigned. Claiming to represent the future, it regards the future with dread, having given up the hope that technology can be controlled or the social order made more just. Loss of faith in the future implies a similar loss of hope that the past can serve as a guide to the future or even become intelligible. "Living for now" is one of the main items in the therapeutic program. "Yesterday is gone; tomorrow has not arrived. But you have today, and you should make the most of it, seeking a vital awareness of . . . what is happening to you in the *now*."[13] The fear and rejection of parenthood, the tendency to view the family as nothing more than marriage, and the perception of marriage as merely one in a series of nonbinding commitments, reflect a growing distrust of the future and a reluctance to make provisions for it—to lay up goods and experience for the use of the next generation. The cult of interpersonal relations represents the final dissolution of bourgeois optimism and self-confidence.

As the world takes on a more and more menacing appearance, life becomes a never-ending search for health and well-being through exercise, dieting, drugs, spiritual regimens of various kinds, psychic self-help, and psychiatry. For those who have withdrawn interest from the outside world except insofar as it remains a source of gratification and frustration, the state of their own health becomes an all-absorbing concern. The reason such people distrust attempts to understand or describe the external world is that critical judgments interfere with the more important business of knowing "what you want and what you do not want."[14] Therapy no longer seeks merely to bring unconscious wishes to light, so as to analyze the consequences of their repression; instead, it seeks to dissolve the very machinery of repression. It assumes that psychic health and personal liberation are synonymous with an absence of inner restraints, inhibitions, and "hangups."

External inhibitions inevitably remain, but they no longer correspond to inner ones. Hence, they make themselves felt only because they rest on superior force—in the last resort, on the organized violence of the state. As long as authority was internalized in the form of conscience, people either complied with it because it appeared reasonable or resisted in the name of a higher authority. Today, however, authority appears as something altogether alien, sometimes contemptible, sometimes truly terrible, more often merely as an inconvenience, in the person of a nagging mother, teacher, or employer. It is not so much arbitrary force—the traditional enemy of bourgeois liberalism—that arouses resistance today as the attempt to hold someone up to a given set of standards. The narcissist resents being judged more than he fears being punished. He submits to punishment even when he rejects its rightness, as an arbitrary exercise of superior force in an arbitrary world, but he does not like to be asked to live up to expectations. This is why the ideology of nonbinding commitments and open-ended relationships—an ideology that registers so faithfully the psychic needs of the late twentieth century—condemns all expectations, standards, and codes of conduct as "unrealistic." It condemns the attempt to live up to expectations on the grounds that "role-playing" subverts psychic stability and health. The therapeutic community insists that only equals can enter into satisfactory interpersonal relations ("peer-bonding"); but equality in this connection means simply an absence of demands. Equals are "peers" not by virtue of common attainments but by generational default (hence the prominence of the generational theme in modern sociology, radical politics, advertising, propaganda, and promotion). Equals ask nothing, understand everything, forgive everything. The idealized comradeship of siblings, united not by undying passion or even mutual respect but merely by a common resentment of adult authority, becomes the model of the perfect marriage, the perfect affair, the perfect "one-to-one relationship," or for that matter the commune or extended family—the distinctions have become increasingly immaterial.

MAIN CURRENTS OF

SOCIOLOGICAL REVISIONISM

Summary-reviews of sociological research on the family (which appear at more and more frequent intervals as work in this field accumulates and threatens to become unmanageable) regularly announce progress "towards fundamental problems of scholarship" and away from problems of policy. Sociological scholarship, according to one such report, no longer concerns itself "with the solution of social problems as defined by administrators or by community groups."[15]

A review of recent literature shows this claim to be false. Marital adjustment, mate selection, the prediction of marital success, and the resolution of marital conflict still attract a disproportionate amount of attention. Even theoretical work continues to address problems defined by the custodians of health and morality. Thus the rise of "conjoint family therapy" has strengthened the tendency to view the family's functions therapeutically. Whereas Parsons paid more attention to "pattern maintenance" than to "tension management," recent work has revived emphasis on the family's role as an emotional refuge. "The family of the future," wrote Otto Pollak in 1967, "should be visualized as a place of intimacy in a world of loose and depersonalized relationships." In a bureaucratic society, accord-

ing to this well-worn line of reasoning, the individual "cannot afford
to have deep emotional ties outside the family circle." Since his
enemies are anonymous, the organization man cannot even indulge
his feelings of anger, and he therefore vents his pent-up feelings on
his family. Fortunately, the "pervasiveness of our growing mental
health culture" enables the members of the family to become increasingly adept in the management of interpersonal relations—in
other words, in the absorption of abuse. Husbands and wives become "co-patients," in Pollak's striking phrase, and the family "a
community of sufferers."[16]

Theorists of the sixties and seventies have regressed to the practice, so common in pre-Parsonian sociology, of treating marriage to
the exclusion of the family. It has become fashionable to argue that
parents' influence on their children should not obscure the children's influence on their parents.[17] Child rearing once again
presents itself as no more than a by-product of marriage. Do children
hold a marriage together? Posing as critics of the conventional wisdom, a number of sociologists have begun to argue that childless
marriages enjoy a better chance of success.[18] Such writings reflect
the recent shift in popular attitudes—the revulsion against "privatism" and "togetherness," the reemergence of feminism—as faithfully as earlier sociological writings reflected the attitudes of the thirties, forties, and fifties. The claim that sociology has worked out an
independent position on these issues, arising out of "fundamental
problems of scholarship," remains absurdly premature.

Another claim, that revisionist scholarship has overturned earlier
work and forced a reconsideration of the entire subject of the family,
betrays a similarly inflated estimate of progress in the field. Sociological revisionism centers on three issues: the rediscovery of the extended family, the revival of romantic love, and a broad-gauged attack on the nuclear family as the source of much that is pathological
in contemporary society. With a few important exceptions, however, work that pretends to boldness and originality turns out to be
devoid of theoretical significance, dependent on the very theories it
seeks to refute (notably those of Parsons), or worse, based on a
regression to theories already superseded by the Parsonian sociology
of the family.

A number of studies, for example, have shown that kinship plays a

larger role in American society, especially in working-class neighborhoods, than was thought. These studies would be interesting if
they showed that kinship groups actually influenced socialization
and the transmission of culture. In fact, they show merely that many
working-class families still live (not always happily) in close proxim-
ity to their kin; in particular, that daughters tend to live near their
mothers. Even those who acclaim these findings as a major discovery admit that they "beg the question of the actual influence of kin
. . . upon the culture and development of each new generation in
U.S. society." [19] It has been asserted that kinship studies call into
question the isolation of the family in modern society; but this issue
cannot be resolved by a study of kinship. The question is not
whether the nuclear family is isolated from the extended kin group,
but whether the family as a whole, an institution allegedly based on
"ascription," upholds values or works on principles opposed to the
ones that prevail elsewhere. "In a civilization of large organizations,"
as Pollak rightly observes, "even the extended family is a small
one." [20] It hardly follows, however, that the family, extended or
nuclear, protects its members from the brutalizing influence of the
market and of bureaucratic organizations, or in the lower class from
the brutalizing influence of the street. The question of whether concepts like "isolation" and "privatization" clarify the structure and
function of the contemporary family rests not on analysis of kinship—an issue of marginal importance—but on examination of the
family's relation to the dominant institutions of modern society.
Studies of residential patterns of kinship cannot refute the argument
that larger structures of domination have broken down the barriers
that once insulated the family from market relations, invading the
protected space formerly provided by the family for the young.

One reason to suspect that "privatism" no longer provides an accurate characterization of the family is that all forms of personal life,
not merely domestic relations, now embody antagonisms formerly
confined to the realm of work. Sexual relations degenerate into sexual combat, carried on beneath a veneer of glamour and sentiment.
Waller's analysis of this combat should have put an end to the sociological debate about the baneful effects of romantic love on marital
success, a debate that mistakes the trappings of romance for its substance. How can marital breakdown be blamed on romantic illusions

when it is precisely the loss of illusions, the disenchantment of love, a wary cynicism that characterize the relations between men and women?

Oblivious to the implications of Waller's research, a number of sociologists have revived the argument by suggesting after all that romantic love "may be functional in dating and marriage."[21] As early as 1950, William L. Kolb maintained that Burgess and other critics of romantic love inadvertently undermined "individualism, freedom, and personality growth." Kolb defended the "romantic complex" as the embodiment of these values but simultaneously condemned its "excesses" and "absurdities"—the cult of "continuous passion," the belief in love at first sight, and the setting up of "false dichotomies between freedom and order, society and the individual, self-love and the love of others."[22] Another writer held that the "immature ideas" often associated with romantic love "cannot be blamed on love itself." Love-marriage, he argued, offered satisfactions unavailable elsewhere: "understanding and mutual assistance in emotional conflicts, moral support and common interests, mutual confirmation and emotional security."[23] From these excerpts it can be seen that sociologists defended romantic love only after they had drained the idea of its meaning.

Sidney Greenfield's argument that rational, profit-seeking individuals would never marry at all except for the "institutionalized irrationality" of romantic love at first looked more promising; but he too reduced love to "affection, companionship, emotional security, and general happiness."[24] Such arguments did not challenge the sociological tradition that upheld marital companionship as a necessary refuge from "frustrating conditions."[25] Nor did they challenge the degradation of love, in comtemporary therapeutics, to the status of a nonbinding commitment, indistinguishable from any other relationship founded on self-interest and the manipulation of others' emotions.

A third line of revisionism, less intrinsically trivial than the first two, weighs the emotional damage inflicted by the nuclear family, the power struggles waged in the name of domestic harmony, the sufferings experienced by women and children, and concludes that earlier descriptions of the American family took too complacent a view of its functionality. Here recent work appears at first sight to have departed from, and even improved on, earlier studies. Whereas the sociology of the family used to appeal mainly to "defenders of the status quo," according to Gerald Handel, now it attracts "the attention of the unsentimental," who boldly question "longstanding assumptions."[26] On closer examination, however, recent indictments of the nuclear family owe a great deal to the Parsonian defense of its functionalism. Sociology now condemns the "isolation" of the family—precisely the condition that enabled it to operate more efficiently than ever, according to Parsons—as "privatism," escapism, and neurotic withdrawal. The theory of emotional overload—that people expect more satisfactions from the family than it can provide—grows directly out of Parsons's work. Its leading exponents, Kenneth Keniston and Philip Slater, remain loyal to the Parsonian theory of the family, even while carrying it to conclusions more critical of American society.[27] "Each family is an island," Keniston writes, "insulated from public scrutiny, control, and interference, and because of its protected isolation able to function as a haven against the demands of the rest of society." Work having been reduced to the dull business of getting a living, the family provides a necessary "escape from work" and thereby makes it "psychologically possible" for people to return to their jobs with spiritual resources renewed.[28]

Yet the isolation of the nuclear family, which enables it to serve as an emotional refuge and to train children for achievement, also creates unavoidable "strains," according to Keniston. These are sometimes devastating in their psychological consequences. "Privacy means that women . . . are unusually free to raise their children as they please," but it also means that the housewife gets little help from outside. The family's isolation cuts her off from useful work, forces her to live vicariously through her children, and thus puts "unbearable burdens" on the children themselves. As for her husband, the split between home and work, between feelings and cognition, forces him to compartmentalize his life. The delicate balance between domestic and occupational commitments often breaks down into "familism" (the husband seeks all his satisfactions at home) or compulsive careerism (he lives wholly for his work). The first puts "enormous strains" on the family, while the second "asks more of work than work can provide."[29]

The isolation of the family widens the gap between childhood

dependence and the autonomy expected of adults, and thus
lengthens the distance a child has to travel in order to grow up. In
addition to the difficulties already described by Parsons and Eisenstadt, young people suffer from the "discontinuities" in their
parents' lives. Thus a young man raised by an overly solicitous
mother and a careerist father—a pattern that Keniston encountered
in his studies of "alienated" students at Harvard in the late fifties—
may become a homosexual or develop an acute fear of homosexuality, which he tries to allay by compulsive toughness.

> Our middle-class families, despite their "goodness of fit" with many
> aspects of American society, involve inherent conflicts in the roles of
> mother and father, and produce deep discontinuities between childhood
> and adulthood. . . . Our society makes parenthood difficult, and we
> prepare our young for adulthood by accentuating needs that adulthood
> will deny. It is no wonder that many Americans—whether alienated
> or not—feel a certain ambivalence toward the adulthood our society
> offers.[30]

Slater, like Keniston, traces the contemporary malaise to the separation of home and work ("privatization"). A pervasive tendency in
middle-class culture, privatism reaches its fullest development, according to Slater, in the flight to suburbia, which carries individualism and the "unrealistic fantasy" of personal self-sufficiency to the
point of completely denying the need for "human interdependence." The suburban middle class seeks escape from alienation, itself born of excessive individualism, in a stronger dose of the same
medicine.

As a result of this desperate self-segregation, middle-class children grow up in families isolated from society, where they become
objects of intense, suffocating devotion. If this emotional overloading of child rearing produces children who can survive in the competitive free-for-all, it also exacts a psychological price which Slater
considers intolerable. Anyone raised in a middle-class suburban
family, he thinks, soon loses all capacity for spontaneity and the un-
inhibited expression of strong feeling. "Life is muted, experience fil-
tered, emotion anesthetized, affective discharge incomplete."
Through drugs and psychotherapy, the victims of this process seek
to restore the capacity to feel, but the only effective remedy lies in a
rebirth of "community." If there is a close fit between competitive
individualism and the isolated nuclear family, then for Slater that

fact becomes an indictment of individualism (and of the nuclear family as well)—the most effective argument, given the pathological consequences of the nuclear family system, for replacing individualism with a culture based on sharing and cooperation.[31]

The usual attack on romantic love tells us all we need to know about the direction this criticism of American culture comes from. Now that the coldness that prevails in the marketplace also pervades the family, a fashionable type of cultural radicalism belatedly proposes to cool off familial relations still further, as if the intensity of those relations, rather than indifference and antagonism, were the source of the tension that now characterizes relations between generations. Recognizing that sexual passion originates in the Oedipus complex, Slater would promote a healthier sexuality by diminishing the intensity of the bond between parent and child. The "only function" of romantic love, he argues, is to create sexual scarcity, to make love into "an artificially scarce commodity, like diamonds." Joining Mead, Fromm, and other celebrants of "community," he proposes to substitute a diffuse, easygoing, nondemanding warmth for the passion that fastens neurotically on a single individual, "looks backwards, hence its preoccupation with themes of nostalgia and loss," and "is fundamentally incestuous."[32] The modern organization of industry having already condemned romantic passion to a marginal position in our society, the guardians of health and morality rush boldly to the attack, justifying the suppression of passion—formerly one of the most important sources of opposition, however "incestuous," to the tyranny of convention—in the name of liberation.[33]

The line of argument foreshadowed by Keniston and made more explicit by Slater now appears in the work of "radical" sociologists who have forgotten its Parsonian origin. These revisionists, eager to flay the family without mercy, often carry the argument to ridiculous extremes. Arlene and Jerome Skolnick, drawing not only on Slater and Keniston but on Jules Henry, R. D. Laing, and other critics of the family, conjure up a fantastic picture of the isolated nuclear family as a miniature despotism in which parents enjoy "nearly absolute power." The helpless child, they write, is a "prisoner" in the family. "All activities . . . are under the total control of a single authority, empowered by the state to employ corporal punishment to enforce his rules, however arbitrary these may seem to the child. Nor is there any provision for appealing to a higher authority." The alternative to this domestic tyranny, according to the Skolnicks, lies in the recreation of the extended family, foreshadowed in the retirement villages of the elderly and the communes of the young. Revisionist sociology thus allies itself with fashionable opinion, which naïvely hopes to revive the "social solidarity that exists in the extended family, or the medieval village described by Ariès," without sacrificing equality, individuality, and personal freedom.[34]

In a more recent essay, Mrs. Skolnick reviews a number of revisionist interpretations and summarizes what she conceives to be their achievements. In the last few years, she argues, sociological scholarship has "challenged the prevailing assumption that harmony represents the natural state of family life."[35] It has overturned the myth of the nuclear family's universality. It has repudiated the view that nature and society are in conflict and given us a better understanding of childhood and socialization, one that replaces the pessimistic psychological determinism of Freud with a new appreciation of human "creativity."

These assertions can be dealt with in a few paragraphs. The claim that earlier work ignored or deplored conflict is patently false and self-serving. Ever since the twenties, sociologists have taken the position that conflict ought to be seen as a normal part of married life. Indeed, they have taken an excessively cheerful view of marital conflict and of the possibility of containing it within ground rules laid down by therapists and experts in psychodynamics. Mrs. Skolnick now restates this view, already moldy with age, and claims it as a recent discovery. We have learned, she contends, "that there has been more physical and emotional conflict in families than anyone had acknowledged, and that somehow most families have coped with these strains and children have grown up amidst them without society's 'falling apart.' "[36] This statement could have been made at any time in the last fifty years. The only surprising thing about it is that it undercuts the Skolnicks' earlier indictment of the nuclear family as a "prison." Mrs. Skolnick seems unable to adhere to any position with rigor or consistency. Her work vacillates between two clichés, the Laingian madhouse and the more familiar caricature of the family as an asylum which cures rather than causes the spiritual torments of our time.

A second accusation against structural-functionalist sociology, that it ignored the historical diversity of family forms, exaggerates the degree to which the universality of the nuclear family was a major theme in the work of Parsons and his colleagues. In any case, their work was ideological not, as Mrs. Skolnick believes, because it upheld the nuclear family as a universal norm, but because it took for granted the separation of private life and work, leisure and labor; assumed the alienation of labor as an inevitable by-product of material progress; gave scholarly support to the delusion that private life offers the only relief from deprivations suffered at work; and ignored the invasion of private life itself by the forces of organized domination. Revisionist sociology takes all this for granted too, and is equally oblivious to the erosion of the private realm. Having revived the historical relativism of the culture and personality school, it explains the present crisis of the family as a transition to new forms that will somehow preserve all the advantages of the old. The unthinking optimism of the new "radicals" makes the Parsonians look like prophets of doom.

Mrs. Skolnick rests her case for improvement in the study of socialization on two grounds. First, the study of "family interaction" has replaced the study of fantasy and the unconscious. She attributes this "advance" to the emergence of family therapy; but in fact the analysis of "interaction" has been a central theme in the sociology of the family from the beginning. Second, revisionist sociology has finally got rid of the "oversocialized concept of man," according to Mrs. Skolnick.[37] The accusation that Parsonian sociology adhered to such a concept, unlike her other accusations, is fair enough; indeed, the "oversocialized concept of man" runs through almost all modern sociology. But why is it objectionable? Because it minimizes the human potential for creativity and "innovation," or because, on the contrary, it obscures the ever-present danger of a return of the repressed? What should have been the occasion for reasserting one of the most important psychoanalytic insights—the fragility of any form of socialization in the face of the determinism of unconscious mental life—becomes in the hands of "radical" sociologists an occasion for celebrating the new awareness of "mind, consciousness, and thought." The Freudian theory of socialization, according to Mrs. Skolnick, leaves "no room for autonomy, innovation, legitimate dissent, or even the exercise of competence." Fortunately, the work of

Piaget and Chomsky has "granted the individual some autonomy from the determining grasp of family and society." These and other writers have shown that the child learns to walk and talk "without explicit adult instruction" and that socialization, moreover, does not necessarily make the child a conformist. In this way they challenge "traditional over-pessimism."[38]

Mrs. Skolnick's language betrays the impulse behind revisionist sociology: to refute pessimism and to "grant" individuals the autonomy that social conditions make it increasingly difficult for them to achieve.[39] In this respect, recent sociology harks back to the culture and personality theorists, much of whose work grew out of the same need to confer autonomy on the individual, to abrogate the conflict between nature and culture, to repudiate Freudian determinism, and to make room for human "creativity." Like their predecessors, the new critics of Freud, claiming to have revised him, have regressed to a prepsychoanalytic view of human nature, one that tries to restore the illusion of psychic freedom and choice.

PATHOLOGY OF THE "FAMILY DRAMA"

Although Parsons bowdlerized Freud, he understood that sociology could not do without a theory of socialization and that such a theory had to rest on psychoanalysis, the most impressive body of insights into the internalization of culture. Before Parsons, American sociologists had ignored socialization, concentrating instead on the dynamics of interpersonal relations—"the family as a unity of interacting personalities," in the words of Ernest W. Burgess. Revisionists now seek to revive this approach in all its crudity. "Burgess' formulation," according to Gerald Handel, "can be seen as, in effect, a charter for the study of whole families." It focuses on a problem allegedly more important than "socialization, child training, or transmission of culture"—the interaction among the "autonomous" individuals making up a given family. It undermines "the cause-effect model which locates independent variables exclusively in the parents and dependent variables exclusively in the children." Such a perspective enables us to see, according to Handel, that every family has "a culture of its own." Instead of asking how children are socialized in American culture, students of the family should "ask the more specific question of how a child is socialized into a particular family."[40]

A number of influences, all of them originating outside sociology, have hastened this retreat from theory into the particularism that was so characteristic of pre-Parsonian sociology. The "radical" insistence that all the members of a family be seen as autonomous agents in their own right, with their own peculiar needs and perceptions, encourages a preoccupation with the dynamics of interaction. The belief that domestic life imprisons people in predetermined roles, which inhibit personal growth, inspires the study of "family drama"—the mechanisms by which individual needs are stifled by the family's misguided obsession with order and stability. The feminist revival contributes additional impetus to this kind of study, which concerns itself with the distribution of marital power, the struggle for strategic advantage, and "the commonplace facts of ordinary coping" (as opposed to psychoanalytic subtleties).[41] Jessie Bernard, author of one of the standard family textbooks of the forties, has recently argued that men and women experience marriage in completely different ways. Whereas marriage satisfies the male need for sex, emotional support, and unpaid domestic service, it shuts up the housewife "in a separate isolated household," burdens her with menial labor, and deprives her of company. It is no wonder that men flourish in marriage, according to Bernard, showing better health and less tendency to crime or suicide than their unmarried counterparts, while women "deteriorate" into disease and neurosis.[42]

The growing concern with the emotional cost of marriage and family life reflects the influence not only of feminism but of recent developments in psychotherapy, notably the rise of "conjoint family therapy." In the forties and fifties, psychiatrists began to notice that treatment of a single subject inevitably alters the balance of psychic forces in the subject's entire family. If the patient begins to recover, other members of the family get sick. If the others combine to lock the patient into the sick role, his condition suffers a further decline. In view of these facts, many psychiatrists proceeded to treat the family as a unit, paying more attention to interpersonal dynamics, role-playing, and stereotyping than to psychic conflicts within a single mind. They soon evolved theories to justify this procedure. These theories, which are more interesting than the revisionist sociology that grows out of them, deserve examination in their own right. Cited by critics of "privatism" to strengthen the indictment of the nuclear family, they can be taken to quite different conclusions.

One theory growing out of family therapy holds that sick families cause or at least contribute to various forms of mental disorder; another, that even healthy families cause mental disorder—indeed, that sickness is precisely the condition of their precarious "health." Both explanations give special attention to the etiology of schizophrenia. The growing conviction that schizophrenia is the typical form of madness in modern society and that it originates in deranged familial situations has given new urgency to sociological study of domestic relations.

In the period immediately following World War II, when the outcry against "Momism" was at its height, students of schizophrenia, already convinced that their patients "always" came from "seriously disturbed families," tended to blame it on the suffocating attentions of the overprotective mother, who lives through her children and prevents them from developing differentiated identities of their own.[43] Gradually these investigators came to believe that the wrong kind of fathers, marital conflicts, and other domestic disorders could lead to equally unsatisfactory results; but they never abandoned their original emphasis on the mother. Studies of the sociocultural determinants of schizophrenia repeatedly found, according to one survey, that "mothers of schizophrenics are likely to be overprotective and sometimes rejecting, domineering, and aggressive," while the father "is usually described as weak, submissive, indifferent, negligent, or passive."[44] Students of schizophrenia concluded that the trouble lay not with mothers alone but with the "dynamics of role relationships," as Theodore Lidz put it, whereby the dominant partner uses his own neurotic symptoms to tyrannize over an acquiescent spouse, with disastrous consequences for the young.[45] Nevertheless, these writers almost always identified the mother—with good reason—as the dominant partner.[46]

Where Lidz and his disciples, following Parsons in this respect, emphasized the importance of a proper division of labor between husband and wife and found role disturbances in schizophrenic families, Lyman Wynne focused on "pseudo-mutuality." In his view, not the confusion of roles but the rigid attempt to maintain them unchanged "prevented the individual from differentiating his own identity." The families of schizophrenics showed a "desperate preoccupation with harmony," which they tried to preserve by preventing anyone from departing from his accustomed role. Often they did this by stigmatizing one member as insane and by refusing to let him escape from this part. Unless he had miraculously developed the inner resources to resist this victimization, he shared the negative valuation of himself and thus cooperated in maintaining the illusion of intimacy. "In pseudo-mutuality emotional investment is directed more toward maintaining the sense of reciprocal fulfillment of expectations than toward accurately perceiving changing expectations."[47]

Both Lidz and Wynne approached the family from the point of view of role theory. Gregory Bateson, on the other hand, was more interested in communication. According to Bateson's famous theory of the "double bind," the parents of schizophrenics send contradictory messages to their children—for example, that sons should love their mothers yet keep their distance.

> A young man who had fairly well recovered from an acute schizophrenic episode was visited in the hospital by his mother. He was glad to see her and impulsively put his arm around her shoulders, whereupon she stiffened. He withdrew his arm, and she asked, "Don't you love me any more?" He then blushed, and she said, "Dear, you must not be so easily embarrassed and afraid of your feelings."[48]

The mother's conflicting communications create a painful dilemma for the son. If he accepts her simulated warmth as genuine and approaches her affectionately, she pulls away at once; but if he pulls away himself, she reproaches him as an unloving son. She punishes him both for understanding her correctly and for falsifying his own perceptions.

After repeated experiences of this kind, according to Bateson, the schizophrenic begins to defend himself by responding literally to metaphorical messages, as a witness carefully circumscribes his answers in a court of law, or by confusing metaphor and literal speech in his own utterance. By speaking with an ambiguity that soon becomes habitual and unthinking, he leaves it up to his mother to see in his statements an accusation of neglect or abandonment, or to ignore them if she chooses; but he also prevents himself from making the accusation he wishes to make. Under extreme pressure, he removes himself still further from reality by the expedient of becoming someone else or pretending to be in some other place. The only alternative to these self-defeating strategies of self-defense would be to recognize the deliberate ambiguity not only of his own communications but of his mother's; but he would then have to face the full truth of her coldness and her simulated warmth. Terrified of emotional abandonment, the schizophrenic cannot bring himself to take this step. To develop an ability to comment critically on communications—an elementary skill "essential for successful social intercourse," in Bateson's words—carries with it the threat of insupportable loss.[49]

It will be seen that Bateson's analysis, while it differs from those of Lidz and Wynne in interpreting schizophrenia as a disturbance in communication, has much in common with explanations that trace schizophrenia to role reversal and, more specifically, to a suffocating maternal presence. Although Bateson did not assume that the double bind is inflicted by the mother alone, he seldom mentioned a case where it was inflicted by anyone else.[50] His articles leave the unmistakable impression that dominating mothers, anxious for some reason in the presence of a particular child but unable to admit their underlying hostility, drive their sons mad. In Bateson's theory of schizophrenia, fathers matter only in their weakness and passivity, qualities which prevent them from intervening in the relations between mother and child or from supporting the child against the mother's confused and contradictory communications. Bateson's description of the "basic family situation" of the schizophrenic closely resembles that of Lidz: a family in which husband and son are drawn into complicity with the madness of a powerful, dominating mother. For that matter, it is only a heightened version of the situation that generates what Talcott Parsons called "compulsive masculinity"; and Bateson's theory, like the one Parsons formulated in the late forties and then abandoned in his later writings on adolescence, invites the same objection, that although it tells us a great deal about the psychic consequences of maternal dependence, it does not explain how this form of dependence arises in the first place or why it seems to be so pervasive in our society.

The beauty of Bateson's work on schizophrenia is that it connects the sociocultural determinants of the disease—contradictory communication between mother and son—with its characteristic symptoms: confusion of literal and metaphoric speech, assumption of a false identity, an ability to "make astute, pithy, often metaphoric remarks that reveal an insight into the forces binding him" without transcending them.[51] Bateson cannot explain, however, why the schizophrenic fails to develop the critical capacities, the distance from his mother, that would release him from his torment.

All the Bateson theory can say on this point is that "his intense dependency and training prevent him from commenting upon his mother's communicative behavior."[52] But as Bateson readily acknowledged, the "double bind" arises in many forms of communication, even in many encounters between son and mother, without producing a schizophrenic response. The crucial element in schizophrenia, therefore, must be the "intense dependency" that prevents the victim from admitting the truth about his mother and thereby disentangling himself from the womblike web of her madness. What is the source of this dependency? Whatever light they throw on the psychodynamics of the family drama, neither role theory nor communications theory has an answer to this question.

A number of common themes can be extracted from the work of Bateson, Lidz, and Wynne on schizophrenia, Parsons on compulsive masculinity, and also from the work of Adorno and his colleagues on the "authoritarian personality." The theory that schizophrenia both arises from maternal dependence and seeks to recreate its earliest forms shares with the Parsonian theory of "badness" in boys a growing recognition—which manifests itself in many other phases of contemporary thought—that early relations with the mother vitally affect all subsequent stages of psychic development; that these relations have become increasingly tenuous and precarious; and that in fact, the flawed relations between mothers and their offspring (especially between mothers and sons) hold the key to the psychopathology of our society.[53]

Sociocultural studies of schizophrenia share another kind of insight with *The Authoritarian Personality*: that the illusion of intimacy, not a cloying "togetherness" brought about by the "privatization" of domestic life, is the family pattern that gives rise to pathological results. In Bateson's theory, it is the mother's fabricated warmth—not the overly solicitous attention conventionally deplored in the myth of the "Jewish mother"—that drives her son crazy. Wynne has shown that pseudo-mutuality, not mutuality itself, underlies the dynamics of schizophrenic families—a desperate effort to hold things together by a show of solidarity. In *The Authoritarian Personality*, Adorno and his collaborators found that although many of their subjects made conventional protestations of family feeling, coldness and stifled rage governed their domestic relations.[54] All these studies, then, suggest that domestic ties have frayed to the breaking point. All of them implicitly undermine the conventional glorification of the family as a "therapeutic community," an institution specializing in affection and companionship, a haven in a heartless world; but they also undermine the equally conventional criticism of the family as an institution flawed by its members' retreat into "privatism."

In order to make full use of these discoveries, we need to disregard some of the preoccupations with which they have hitherto been accompanied: the preoccupation with authoritarianism, the insistence on the nuclear family's "isolation," the attempt to substitute role theory and communication theory for analysis of unconscious mental life. The narcissist, not the authoritarian, is the prevalent personality type. Not the family's isolation but its inability to protect its members from external dangers has eroded domestic ties. As for "Momism"—the psychological dominance of the mother in the modern middle-class family—this condition arises not because the father is always "absent" at his work, as the Parsonians would have it, but because he is weak and acquiescent at home. In the schizophrenic family, moreover—which in many ways appears to represent an exaggerated version of the "normal" family—the mother's power does not originate in her effective management of the household in the husband's absence, in her emergence as the principal disciplinarian by default, or in her pressure on the children to achieve—the conditions usually adduced to explain why the American mother has become the dominant parent. It originates in the imposition of her own madness on everybody else. The other members of the family defer to her not because of the authority that goes with her commanding position in the daily life of the group, but rather because arbitrary, unpredictable, and contradictory actions are often intimidating and because a refusal to examine their meaning is the easiest way to keep a precarious peace.

According to a popular theory, echoes of which survive in much of the sociological description of the contemporary family, women have somehow gained the upper hand in the sex war, either because men are too busy or too exhausted by their work to fight back. A better hypothesis would be that men fear the dangers of close personal intercourse and prefer acquiescence to intimacy, rationalizing passivity in the form of an ideology of nonbinding commitments. As the quality of personal relations deteriorates, in spite of the cult of personal relations as the newest form of salvation, a deadly chill descends over the family. Psychic survival replaces intimacy and parental guidance as the goal of domestic life. Each member of the family attempts to protect himself from the dangers threatening to annihilate him, while as a group, the domestic circle clings to a flimsy equilibrium by attempting to exclude everything that might disturb it. Conditions in the family thus mirror conditions in society as a whole, which have created an ever-present sense of menace and reduced social life to a state of warfare, often carried out under the guise of friendly cooperation.

BLACK "MATRIARCHY": THE CONTROVERSY
OVER THE MOYNIHAN REPORT

Recent studies of the black family show, more clearly than any other example, the disintegrating impact on the family of a dangerous social environment, in which the struggle to survive creates an atmosphere of chronic antagonism, and friendship, love, and marriage are sustained only with great difficulty.

The sociology of the black family, because it touches so many sensitive issues, has given rise to bitter debates, especially since the publication of the Moynihan Report, widely accused of diverting attention from racism and poverty to the false issue of the "matriarchal" family. In March 1965, the U.S. Department of Labor sent to President Johnson and a few of his advisers a seventy-five-page report, "The Negro Family: The Case for National Action." The anonymous author of this document, Daniel Patrick Moynihan, personified the union of social science and federal policy. A political scientist with a special interest in urban sociology, Moynihan went to Washington in the great influx of intellectuals in 1961. Like other New Frontiersmen, he seems to have shared John F. Kennedy's belief that the complicated problems of modern government defied the understanding of the ordinary citizen.[55] Just as the makers of American foreign policy sought to base decisions on systems analysis and game theory, so Moynihan proposed to recast the race problem, the central domestic issue of the sixties, in the light of academic social science. His report drew on the work of E. Franklin Frazier, Frank Tannenbaum, Stanley Elkins, and other scholars, summarizing a long tradition of inquiry into the peculiarly debilitating effects of American Negro slavery. It also drew on a long tradition of social work, according to which social pathology originates in "broken homes."

Brimming with graphs, charts, and tables, the Moynihan Report argued that "the Negro family in the urban ghettos is crumbling" and that the "deterioration" of the family is "the fundamental source of the weakness of the Negro community at the present time." Even the removal of arbitrary forms of discrimination would not promote racial equality, according to Moynihan, so long as weaknesses in the structure of ghetto life prevented blacks from taking advantage of their new opportunities. Poverty had forced the ghetto into a matriarchal and highly unstable pattern of family life, which, perpetuating itself over the generations, gave rise to a complicated "tangle of pathology." For reasons that Moynihan did not explore, "Negro children without fathers flounder—and fail." Statistical correlations appeared to connect juvenile delinquency, crime, academic failure, and the "inability to delay gratification" with fatherless or otherwise "disorganized" homes. Although patrifocal families "presumably" enjoyed no intrinsic advantage over "matriarchal" families, "it is clearly a disadvantage"—for reasons, once again, that Moynihan failed to clarify—"for a minority group to be operating on one principle, while the great majority . . . is operating on another." The federal government should therefore make it an object of policy to bring Negro family patterns into harmony with the dominant pattern: "to strengthen the Negro family so as to enable it to raise and support its members as do other families."[56]

The Moynihan Report exemplified the medicalization of politics:

it was this above all that stamped it as a typical product of academic social science. Moynihan did not ignore the effects of poverty and racism, as his critics unfairly charged; nor did he argue that broken homes "caused" poverty. His insistence on the "pathology" of the matrifocal family, however, left the impression that the problem, whatever it was, required some form of therapeutic intervention. Herbert Gans feared that the Moynihan Report would "lead to a clamor for pseudo-psychiatric programs that attempt to change the Negro family through counseling and other therapeutic methods."[57] But the point is not that Moynihan proposed to substitute therapy for social action, or in the words of another critic, that he thought "it's the individual's fault when it's the damned system that really needs changing," but rather that Moynihan saw the "system" itself as an organism understood only by social pathologists and proceeded to redefine social action as a form of therapy by its very nature.[58] Thus the struggle for racial equality—which now had to take precedence, in Moynihan's view, over struggles for political freedom or a mere equality of opportunity—had to be waged not by the victims of racial inequality but by the federal government: this was the underlying import of his analysis. He sought to channel the ghetto revolt into acceptable forms and to bring it under federal leadership, and his interpretation of its origins—a diagnosis of ghetto "pathology" that would enable the right kind of doctors to cure it—admirably suited that end.

In singling out the family for special emphasis, however, Moynihan by no means diverted attention from the "real issue," as his critics charged. On the contrary, he addressed a central problem in the black revolt, addressed in quite different language by the Black Muslims and later by the advocates of Black Power: the restoration of black manhood. In effect, Moynihan proposed to forestall more radical solutions of this problem, in which a militant and deliberately exaggerated male chauvinism supported other forms of militancy, with a program of federal intervention designed, in the words of President Johnson at Howard University, "to strengthen the family, to create conditions under which most parents will stay together."[59]

Unfortunately for Moynihan, the intensification of racial conflict after the Watts riot made his report a convenient target of radicals and would-be radicals. His critics misrepresented Moynihan's views, often in a thoroughly opportunistic fashion, while leaving uncriticized his overriding concern with health and disease. Indeed they adopted his medical imagery as their own. "What may seem to be a disease to the white middle class," wrote Bayard Rustin of the matrifocal family, "may be a healthy adaptation to the Negro lower class."[60]

Moynihan's opponents pursued one or another of two strategies, both of which disclose widely held misconceptions about the family and its significance—the only reason for rehearsing a controversy so devoid of intellectual merit on either side. The first strategy denied the importance of the family altogether, reducing the plight of the ghetto to purely economic oppression or to "white racism." Poverty and racism, not the family, determined the structure of ghetto life, according to this view, whereas Moynihan's emphasis on the family encouraged the illusion that "the weaknesses and defects of the Negro himself . . . account for the present status of inequality between Negro and white."[61] Laura Carper, after announcing that she was "not prepared to argue an economic determinist thesis," argued precisely that poverty, not the matriarchal organization of the family, explained the Negro's lack of social progress.[62]

Such interpretations ignore the family's mediation between social conditions and individual experience. Few would deny that social conditions shape the structure of the family, but the family in turn shapes the individual's perceptions of the world and the psychic mechanisms by means of which he attempts to deal with it. Poverty is undoubtedly the overriding fact of ghetto life, and all interpreters of the ghetto family agree that its special characteristics originate in the father's inability to support his household. Nevertheless, the growing child experiences poverty through the intermediary of his parents, and the quality of that mediation unavoidably influences his psychic development. Although the blacks of the ghetto subscribe to a middle-class norm of marriage in which the husband "oughta be out makin' a livin' " while his wife stays home with the children, they find it impossible to sustain this ideal in the face of poverty.[63] The male, unable to find steady work, often leaves his family for the more agreeable, easygoing society of his peers. Even when he stays at home, he hesitates to make an emotional investment in relations in which he is almost certain to fail.

Even when both father and mother are present, black parents find it difficult to insulate their children against the dangers and temptations of the street. Parents complain that children "see too much" and become prematurely wise to the ways of the world.[64] Children then use this knowledge to negotiate their independence from parents. At first, when children are young, parents seek to imprison them in the house, but as these efforts inevitably fail, the parents become resigned to their own lack of influence. The sense of impotence further undermines their attempt to teach the child what he needs to know in order to master his surroundings. Elders retreat from painful confrontations by not enforcing their own standards on the young. The child learns to fend for himself and to get what he wants by manipulating, seducing, or exploiting the emotions of others. He perfects what Lee Rainwater calls an expressive style of adaptation, which depends on skill in social interaction, "competitive self-enhancement," and "dramatic self-presentation." He learns to get what he wants by taking it rather than by waiting for what he is entitled to receive.[65]

These strategies ensure survival but at the same time perpetuate the victimization of blacks by other blacks. Although the ghetto subculture—an amalgam of middle-class norms and situational responses to poverty and exploitation—serves the black community as a means of coping with everyday hardships, it also contributes in its own right to the harsh and oppressive quality of the environment. The family and other agencies of socialization toughen the young, but in doing so they not only disable the young for life in other surroundings but prevent them from mastering, instead of being mastered by, their own. Those who argue that study of the black family diverts attention from poverty and racism fail to notice the ways in which poverty and racism reverberate in every area of life, embedding themselves in cultural patterns and personality and thus perpetuating themselves from one generation to the next. The view that presents itself as clear-sighted realism about the economic basis of culture closes its eyes to the very desperation it pretends to reveal.

A second type of criticism of the Moynihan Report, instead of ignoring the family, defends the matrifocal household as a "healthy adaptation" to ghetto conditions. Herbert Gans wrote that "instability, illegitimacy, and matriarchy" may be "the most positive adaptations . . . to the conditions which most Negroes must endure."[66] Other interpreters have reminded us that two parents in conflict make "little positive contribution to the household" and that "some women with stormy marriages behind them feel that they are better off alone."[67]

According to Ray L. Birdwhistell, an authority much quoted by critics of the Moynihan Report, psychiatrists and other students of the family have set up a "sentimental model" of the family, a middle-class suburban norm which they try to impose on others by treating deviations from the model as pathological. Drawing on Birdwhistell's work, critics of Moynihan argue that culture-bound assumptions about the family prevent the middle-class observer from seeing that the ghetto has its own distinctive culture, which admirably serves its needs. "Divorce, illegitimacy, and female-headed households," according to Robert Staples, "are not necessarily dysfunctional except in the context of western, middle-class, white values."[68] The black family appears "unstable" only "when judged by the white ideals of the husband-wife-child relationship-complex."[69] Feminists condemn Moynihan for assuming that "leadership is necessarily male," Negro activists for thinking that "everyone should have a family structure like his own."[70] Instead of recognizing that Negroes "have a culture of their own," according to one scholar, critics of the black family judge it against "the nuclear family of a generalized American culture" and judge it a failure, whereas in fact "Negro families, whether headed by males or females, provide secure groups for child raising."[71]

The trouble with this line of argument is that blacks themselves regard the male-centered household as the most desirable form of the family. Far from upholding the matrifocal arrangement as a "healthy adaptation" or a "secure group for child raising," black mothers condemn their husbands for their failure to provide support. Indeed, they go so far as to blame this failure on laziness rather than on the unavailability of jobs. Most of the evidence supports Rainwater's conclusion that poor black people find it almost impossible to develop a sense of family solidarity. "They did not regard themselves," Rainwater writes of one St. Louis family, ". . . as a solitary unit separate from the outside world. Instead, their home territory was readily invaded by anyone who established a relationship with one of them, and the children were ready to derogate and demean other family members."[72] The defenders of the matrifocal family, posing as critics of cultural parochialism, have unthinkingly absorbed the rising middle-class dissatisfaction with the isolated, "privatized" suburban family, a dissatisfaction that has become especially pervasive in the very suburbs in which the "sentimental model of the family" is said to originate. Claiming to have liberated themselves from the assumptions of their own class, these writers share the fashionable concern with "alternatives to the nuclear family" and project the search for alternate life-styles onto the ghetto. They idealize the matrifocal family, exaggerate the degree to which it is embedded in a rich network of kinship relations, and ignore evidence which plainly shows that blacks themselves prefer a family in which the male earns the money and the mother rears the young.

In a study of ghetto life-styles, Ulf Hannerz attacks the "sentimental model" and its Freudian underpinnings, which allegedly assume that if the father does not serve as an example to his son, the son identifies with his mother and then develops "compulsive masculinity" as a defense against effeminacy. But the concept of compulsive masculinity derives from Parsons, not from Freud, and it rests, as we have seen, on a debased version of the theory of identification—one that confuses internalization of lost love-objects with imitation of "role models." Hannerz sets up this simplified "Freudian" interpretation and then tries to refute it with a still more simpleminded interpretation of his own. The "Freudian" view, he argues, rests on "mainstream assumptions about what a man should be like." Thus a Freudian interpretation of "joning" or the "dozens"—the ritualized verbal aggression in which ghetto adolescents claim to have had sexual intercourse, under bizarre and imaginative circumstances, with the opponent's mother—would insist that "the boys have supposedly just found out that they have identified with the wrong person, the mother. Now they must do their utmost to ridicule her and thus convince everybody . . . of their masculinity." In reality, according to Hannerz, the aggressive banter of the ghetto functions as a "rite of passage" whereby adolescent boys train for the roles they will play as adults. Even without fathers, they learn masculinity from the men of the street, and verbal "motherfucking" initiates them into the culture of the grown-up world.[73]

This interpretation fails to explain why ghetto masculinity depends to such a large degree on sexual intercourse with mothers, and why the term "motherfucker" pervades ghetto speech, both as a term of praise and as a term of contempt. The concept of compulsive

masculinity at least addresses this issue, but it does so crudely and
with little feeling for nuance. Indeed, the problem of "motherfucking" demonstrates more clearly than any other the inadequacy of the
Parsonian theory of socialization. Far from signifiying a declaration
of independence from the mother, the term directs against her the
aggression typically experienced by infants, an aggression associated
with dependence and helpless rage. It also embodies a recognition,
by no means unrealistic in a world of poverty and exploitation, that
dependence is the common fate and that "the individual is not
strong enough or adult enough to achieve his goal in a legitimate
way, but is rather like a child, dependent on others who tolerate his
childish maneuvers."[74] The term reminds those who use it that
even adult males often depend on women for support and nurture;
that many of them have to "pimp" for a living, ingratiating themselves with a woman in order to pry money from her; that sexual
relations thus become manipulative and predatory; and that satisfaction depends on taking what you want (fucking someone's mother)
instead of earning what is rightfully yours to receive.

The premature toughness of ghetto youth, like the toughness of
middle-class adolescents, conceals a deeper dependence. Detailed
analysis of the psychic origins of this need would take us beyond the
bounds of the present inquiry, but the failure to internalize parental
authority clearly lies at the heart of the problem. The well-known
distinction between "shame-cultures" and "guilt-cultures" helps to
locate the culture of the ghetto, to characterize the personality structure it tends to produce, and to clarify, if only in a preliminary fashion, the psychological processes at work. Shame—the fear of ridicule
and ostracism—originates in a primitive fear of the loss of nurture,
whereas guilt fears the loss of parental approval and its heir, self-
approval. Guilt, as Rainwater reminds us, arises only when "individuals have the opportunity to develop (in fantasy if not in reality) an
orderly, predictable and loving relationship with their parents, and
to regard the parents as themselves capable of living up to the norms
which they proffer."[75] In the absence of such experience, early
dependence on the mother dominates later development. The immediate satisfaction of wants takes precedence over future gratifica-
tions; strategies for day-to-day survival take precedence over invest-

ments in a future that presents itself as menacing and unpredictable. Expressive styles of interaction predominate over instrumental styles. A dramatic presentation of the self helps to seduce and manipulate others, even as it undermines the capacity for sustained activity and for long-term friendships and love relations. Interpersonal intercourse, at the same time that it monopolizes attention, becomes increasingly manipulative, fragile, and precarious.

These observations describe, in a schematic and tentative fashion, the personality structure produced not just by the dangerous world of the ghetto but, increasingly, by the conditions of middle-class life as well. The real objection to the Moynihan Report is that it exaggerates the distance between the ghetto and the rest of American culture, which in some ways has come to resemble a pale copy of the black ghetto. Without minimizing the poverty of the ghetto or the suffering inflicted by whites on blacks, we can see that the increasingly dangerous and unpredictable conditions of middle-class life give rise to similar strategies for survival, a similar search for nonbinding commitments, and a similar toughness (combined with an underlying dependence) in the young. Indeed, the attraction of black culture for disaffected whites suggests that it now speaks to a general condition, the most striking feature of which is a widespread loss of confidence in the future.

Middle-class "Momism," a muted version of black "matriarchy," can be understood as a product of the general deterioration of the social environment. In a dangerous world from which the family can no longer protect its members—a world, moreover, in which exploitation dominates even friendship, love, and marriage—children find it more and more difficult to form secure and loving ties to their parents. In the absence of such ties, early impressions of the mother remain the basis of personality structure. Fear of maternal abandonment underlies the frantic search for psychic survival, which has replaced the traditional virtues of work, thrift, and achievement as the essence of the bourgeois ethic. The dependence on the mother which Bateson found in schizophrenics, and which so many others have identified as a characteristic pattern in all American males (revealing itself in the cult of large breasts, a fixation on oral sex, and a tendency to regard all women as mothers)—this dependence, the key to the post-protestant personality, originates in the changes that have transformed domestic life. More precisely, it originates in the invasion of the family by the marketplace and the street, the crumbling of the walls that once provided a protected space in which to raise children, and the perversion of the most intimate relationships by the calculating, manipulative spirit that has long been ascendant in business life.

8

Authority and the Family: Law and Order in a Permissive Society

THE RISE OF BOURGEOIS DOMESTICITY
AND THE RELIGION OF HEALTH

The rise of bourgeois society enlarged the boundaries of freedom, but it also created new forms of enslavement. Capitalism created unprecedented abundance but simultaneously widened the gap between rich and poor. The conquest of nature liberated mankind from superstition but deprived it of the consolation of religion. The spread of education, designed to make the masses more critical of established authority, encouraged a certain cynicism about official protestations but also made the masses avid consumers of advertising and propaganda, which kept them in a chronic state of uncertainty and unsatisfied desire. Private property and the nuclear family, which in the nineteenth century provided new supports for political freedom and personal autonomy, contained within themselves elements fatal to their own existence. When the democratic revolutions freed property from feudal restrictions, they also removed the obstacles to its accumulation and brought about a situation in which the most characteristic form of "private" property would be the multinational corporation. As for the family, its isolation from the marketplace, from the ravages of which it provided a refuge, was precarious from the beginning.

From the moment the conception of the family as a refuge made its historical appearance, the same forces that gave rise to the new privacy began to erode it. The nineteenth-century cult of the home, where the woman ministered to her exhausted husband, repaired the spiritual damage inflicted by the market, and sheltered her children from its corrupting influence, expressed the hope that private satisfactions could make up for the collapse of communal traditions and civic order. But the machinery of organized domination, which had impoverished work and reduced civic life to a competitive free-for-all, soon organized "leisure" itself as an industry. The so-called privatization of experience went hand in hand with an unprecedented assault on privacy. The tension between the family and the economic and political order, which in the early stages of bourgeois society protected the members of the family from the full impact of the market, gradually abated.

The withdrawal into the "emotional fortress" of the family took place not because family life became warmer and more attractive in the nineteenth century, as some historians have argued, but because the outside world came to be seen as more forbidding.[1] Nor did the family's withdrawal take place without a struggle. Older patterns of male conviviality gradually gave way to a life centered on hearth and home, but in the first half of the nineteenth century, the new domesticity still met with resistance, which crystallized in protracted battles over temperance, the rights of women, and the attempt to suppress popular amusements and festivities that allegedly distracted the lower orders from familial duties.

Seasonal holidays and festivals, so important to the life of preindustrial societies, disappeared from Western Europe and the United States not because the working class suddenly discovered the delights of polymorphous sexuality but because the champions of temperance and sobriety—the prohibitionists, the feminists, the Society for the Prevention of Vice, the Society for the Prevention of Cruelty to Animals, the Animals' Friend Society—stamped them out as occasions for drunkenness, blood sports, and general debauchery.[2] Bourgeois domesticity did not simply evolve. It was imposed on society by the forces of organized virtue, led by feminists, temperance advocates, educational reformers, liberal ministers, penologists, doctors, and bureaucrats.

In their campaign to establish the family as the seat of civic virtue, the guardians of morality dwelled on the dangers lurking in the streets, the demoralizing effects of "civilization," the growth of crime and violence, and the cutthroat competition that prevailed in the marketplace. They urged right-thinking men and women to seek shelter in the sanctuary of the family. From the beginning, the glorification of domestic life simultaneously condemned the social order of which the family allegedly served as the foundation. In urging a retreat to private satisfactions, the custodians of domestic virtue implicitly acknowledged capitalism's devastation of all forms of collective life, while at the same time they discouraged attempts to repair the damage by depicting it as the price that had to be paid for material and moral improvement.

Nineteenth-century doctors, reformers, and public health officers, like missionaries, regarded themselves as agents of enlightenment, bearers of civilization to the heathen. Like their ecclesiastical counterparts, they believed it their mission to stamp out debauchery and superstition. Neither the disinterested benevolence with which they performed their duties, the dangers they suffered, nor the personal sacrifices they endured gave them an understanding of the customs they were attempting to eradicate. In rural France, doctors reported that peasant husbands unfeelingly exposed their wives to syphilis and that their wives ignored the health of their children. After the domestic revolution engineered by themselves, on the other hand, "unity reigned in the families," in the words of one practitioner, "and this true solicitousness, which means the sharing equally of trouble and joy, fidelity between the spouses, fatherly tenderness, filial respect and domestic intimacy," became the general rule.[3]

The new religion of health, though based on modern science and technology, was no more tolerant of other religions than was Christianity itself. The medical mode of salvation, no less than its predecessors, asserted exclusive rights to virtue and truth. But whereas the missionaries, for all their ignorance of the peoples to whom they ministered, sometimes defended their elementary human rights against the state's attempt to enslave or otherwise exploit them for profit, the medical profession worked hand in hand with the state to modernize the backward sectors of European and American society. This partnership proved to be more effective than Christianity in improving not only the health of the poor but their "morals" as well.[4]

The attack on disease was part of a general attack on preindustrial customs. It went hand in hand with the suppression of public executions, the movement to institutionalize the insane, and the campaign to replace public riot and licentiousness with domestic bliss. Doctors were among the earliest exponents of the new ideology of the family. They extolled domesticity on the grounds that it encouraged regular habits, temperance, and careful attention to the needs of the young. They saw the family as an asylum, analogous in its functions to the hospital, the insane asylum, and the prison. Just as doctors and penologists hoped to cure sickness, madness, and crime by segregating the patient in a professionally supervised environment devoted to his care, they hoped to mold the child's character in the home.

The therapeutic conception of insanity, disease, and crime repudiated theological assumptions of their inevitability and relieved the patient of responsibility for his actions, insisting that he was neither possessed nor willfully sinning, but sick. The new conception of the family as an asylum similarly repudiated fatalism and the assumption of original sin, insisting on the child's innocence and plasticity. The medical profession saw itself as the successor to the church, just as theorists of bourgeois domesticity for a long time upheld marriage as the successor to monasticism. Whereas the church, in attempting to stamp out sex, had merely made it an obsession, these theorists maintained, marriage put sex at the service of procreation and encouraged a healthy acceptance of the body. This affirmation of the physical side of life had demonstrably better effects on the health of the individual and the community, according to bourgeois moralists, than the church's denial of the body.

From the beginning, a medical view of reality thus underlay attempts to remodel private life. The struggle between the new remissions and the old proscriptions, between personal fulfillment and self-sacrifice, between the ideology of work and the ideology of creative leisure, began in the nineteenth century. Liberal clergymen themselves participated in the campaign to transform religion into moral and mental hygiene. They allied themselves with a nascent feminism and with the campaign to feminize society by extending the domesticating influence of women to institutions beyond the home. The religion of health had a special appeal to women because of its concern with personal relations, its attempt to substitute domestic enjoyments for the rough and brutal camaraderie of males, and its glorification of the child and of maternal influence on the child's development. The conflict between the work ethic and the therapeutic point of view, which became sharper as the century wore on, also presented itself as a conflict between masculine and feminine "spheres"—the split between business and "culture," the practical and the aesthetic, so characteristic of bourgeois society and of American society in particular. As late as the 1950s, John R. Seeley and his associates found the same division in the suburbs of Toronto, where women joined with mental health experts in combating the competitive, work-oriented values of their husbands. Middle-class Canadian men valued material objects and their production, while their wives concerned themselves with the management of personal relations. Men valued achievement; women, happiness and well-being.[5]

THERAPEUTIC IDEALS OF THE FAMILY
AND THEIR IMPACT ON PARENTHOOD

In the United States, relations between the sexes had entered a new stage by this time.[6] When social scientists replaced clergymen as the most prominent purveyors of the new ethic, male resistance, at least among the educated, gradually declined. The once-familiar alignment of domestic forces, in which the father tacitly sides with the children's war against maternally imposed refinement, now survived only in folklore. The ideology of mental health, having routed the residual opposition of American males, effectively ruled the family, thus bringing domestic life under the growing domination of outside experts. The remarkable popularity of Benjamin Spock's *Baby and Child Care*, which went through more than 200 printings between 1946 and the mid-seventies, provided merely the most obvious example of this parental dependence on outside help and advice.

Outside advice, however, weakens parents' already faltering confidence in their own judgment. Thus although Spock urges parents to trust both their own and the child's impulses, he undermines this trust by reminding them of the incalculable consequences of their actions. Words "uttered in a thoughtless or angry moment" can "destroy the child's confidence"; nagging can lead to troubles that "last for years"; and the failure to give the child love and security can cause "irreparable harm." "In the face of this forbidding awareness," Michael Zuckerman writes, "Spock's appeals for confidence fade. He may know that mothers and fathers cannot come to any assurance of their own adequacy if they have to rely on physicians and psychiatrists in every extremity, but he is nonetheless unwilling to leave parents to their own intuitions at such junctures."[7] The proliferation of medical and psychiatric advice undermines parental confidence at the same time that it encourages a vastly inflated idea of the importance of child-rearing techniques and of the parent's responsibility for their failure. Meanwhile, the removal of education and medical care from the household deprives parents of practical experience, during their own childhood, in taking care of children, nursing the sick, and housekeeping. In their ignorance and uncertainty, parents redouble their dependence on experts, who confuse them with a superabundance of conflicting advice, itself subject to constant changes in psychiatric and medical fashion. Because the "immature, narcissistic" American mother "is so barren of spontaneous manifestations of maternal feelings," according to one observer, "she studies vigilantly all the new methods of upbringing and reads treatises about physical and mental hygiene." She acts not on her own feelings or judgment but on the "picture of what a good mother should be."[8]

Thus the family struggles to conform to an ideal of the family imposed from without.[9] The experts agree that parents should neither tyrannize over their children nor burden them with "oversolicitous" attentions. They agree, moreover, that every action is the product of a long causal chain and that moral judgments have no place in child rearing. This proposition, central to the mental health ethic, absolves the child from moral responsibility while leaving that of his parents undiminished. Under these conditions, it is not surprising that many parents seek to escape the exercise of this responsibility by avoiding confrontations with the child and by retreating from the work of discipline and character formation. Permissive ideologies rationalize this retreat. When parents cannot altogether avoid disciplinary decisions, they seek to delegate them to other authorities. The father cites the demands of his work as an excuse for assigning daily discipline to his wife. She in turn avoids the most painful encounters by invoking the ultimate authority of the father, threatening children with a fearful reckoning when he finally returns to the scene. Both parents shift much of the responsibility for the child's development to his peers—against whom, in the absence of firm standards of their own, they also measure the child's academic, athletic, and psychological progress. Seeley and his associates found that upper-middle-class parents in "Crestwood Heights" hesitated to impose their own tastes on the child and left the formation of taste to the child's peers. "Crestwood parents who would deem it morally wrong and psychologically destructive to regulate the expression of their children's tastes, after self-examination realized and stated that they were able to afford these views because . . . in these areas the peer group performed a satisfactory policing function for them."[10] Permissiveness thus rests, in part, on peer-group control.

The peer group not only regulates taste, it puts forward its own version of ideal family life. It circulates information about parental regulations currently in force, about regulations that are violated with impunity, about what the world upholds as the norm of parenthood. The child's mastery of this information gives him an important tactical advantage in negotiations with his parents. If he can show that they have departed from established norms, he further weakens their self-confidence. Having made it clear that their own actions are to be submitted to the same standards of justice to which the child himself is expected to conform, parents find it difficult to specify those standards. In theory, justice derives from reason, but community practice turns out to be the only reliable guide. The child knows more about this ambiguous and constantly shifting practice than his parents do, and he skillfully exploits their uneasiness. Parental training has collapsed not because of the inevitable supersession of parents' technical knowledge but because organized interest groups, such as the health and welfare professions and the adolescent peer group, have a stake in promoting their own conceptions of the world, which compete with those of the family. Like the health industry, the peer group spreads information that parents cannot hope to master in its complexity but on which they nevertheless depend in their unsuccessful struggles to discipline their children and at the same time to retain their devotion.

Relations within the family have come to resemble relations in the rest of society. Parents refrain from arbitrarily imposing their wishes on the child, thereby making it clear that authority deserves to be regarded as valid only insofar as it conforms to reason. Yet in the family as elsewhere, "universalistic" standards prove on examination to be illusory. In American society, most rules exist only to be broken, in the words of a popular axiom. Custom has reestablished itself as in many ways the superior of reason. The administration of justice gives way, in a therapeutic society, to a complicated process of negotiation. Just as prices in the neocapitalist economy, allegedly determined by the impersonal laws of supply and demand, are really fixed by negotiations among corporations, unions, and government (with the corporations taking the leading role), so justice is fixed by means of similar bargains among interested parties. In learning to live by the law, therefore, the child actually learns how to get around the law, in the first place by getting around his parents.

PARENTS AND CHILDREN

The erosion of parental authority and the delegation of discipline to other agencies have created in the American family a growing gap between discipline and affection—something of the same result that has been brought about by deliberate design in the Israeli kibbutz and other experiments in communal living. In the kibbutz, according to its admirers, the child sees his parents only in "affectional" settings, while toilet training and other forms of discipline are entrusted to the socialized agencies of child rearing. This arrangement supposedly spares the family the conflicts that arise when the same persons exercise love and discipline.[11] In America the family still supervises the child's early development, but new modes of child care have lowered the temperature of family life and reduced overt tensions. Parents accept their obsolescence with the best grace they can muster, voluntarily relegating themselves to the background of their children's lives. They do all they can to make it easy for the younger generation to surpass the older, while secretly dreading the rejection that usually follows. The children return neither solicitude nor resentment, nor does anyone expect them to. On the contrary, everyone assumes that children will painlessly escape emotional entanglements with their parents, and the older generation cooperates in this escape by making few demands it can back up. Mothers worry about losing their sons, but sons seldom worry, at least explicitly, about losing their mothers. Fathers spontaneously abdicate in favor of sons-in-law. Parents represent the useless past. Raising and holding children, not escaping from parents, are the dominant themes of domesticity in a culture which assumes that children will put family attachments behind them without passing through an emotional crisis.

Recent studies of American youth show how closely practice conforms to this ideal, at least on the surface. Again and again, young people assure interviewers that relations with their parents are free of tension, that their families are "abnormally normal," and that even their parents' cool detachment provokes no bitterness on their own part.[12] Yet the rise in student suicide, drug addiction, and impotence immediately casts doubt on this agreeable picture. It does not require a high order of psychoanalytic sophistication to penetrate the bland surface of family life and to uncover deep-seated fears and resentment. The same students who complain of parental neglect—if indeed them complain at all—dream of their parents as devouring, murderous monsters. Some accuse their parents simultaneously of indifference and of intense, suffocating attention to the child's every whim. Young people routinely deplore the absence of their fathers, only to conjure up fantasies of relentless persecution by fathers whose knowledge of their victims' movements extends to the smallest detail.

On the surface, American youth seem to experience no strong

sexual attachment to either parent; yet their dreams and fantasies bring to light feelings of rage and desire, which can be traced back to the earliest stages of infancy. Thus while they describe their mothers as cool and remote, their deeper fears center on a completely different kind of mother, alluring and castrating at the same time: a terrifying mother with a vagina full of teeth.[13]

Popular culture embodies the same split, so pronounced in psychiatric interviews, between conflicting images of parenthood—between the untroubled emotional surface of family life and the rage beneath. Films, comic strips, and popular novels—in particular, the many novels of adolescent revolt, patterned after J. D. Salinger's *Catcher in the Rye*—ridicule the "manifest" father, and authority in general, while depicting "latent" father-figures as sinister, aggressive, and utterly unprincipled in their persecution of the hero or heroine.[14] Often the parents have divorced, leaving the child to fend for himself. Alternately, they preserve the emotional intensity of their marriage at the child's expense. In either case, they hover in the background of the child's existence. In the enormously popular comic strip *Peanuts*, parents have vanished completely from the world of childhood—an anomaly recaptured, in more sinister form, in William Golding's *Lord of the Flies*, a novel that has enjoyed a long vogue among high school students and undergraduates.

If parents attempt to intervene in their children's lives, family comedies depict them as objects of amusement or contempt. Thus Mother ineffectually attempts to uphold old-fashioned ideas of decorum and refinement, which Father collaborates with the younger generation in subverting. Father's well-meaning attempts to instruct, befriend, or discipline the young lead to situations that expose his incompetence. Having nothing of value to pass on to his sons, he reserves most of his affection, what there is of it, for his daughters.[15] Yet he makes no attempt to keep his daughter to himself. He makes way for her suitors without complaint, even encouraging their courtship. According to Martha Wolfenstein and Nathan Leites, the ease with which fathers welcome sons-in-law as boon companions exposes another important theme in American popular culture: the sharing of a woman by two friends or "buddies." As sex becomes more casual, the jealousy of the male subsides. He not only tolerates promiscuity in his women but finds it titillating, largely because women know how to keep promiscuity within the bounds of what is called sexiness.[16]

On the surface, then, children in American popular culture painlessly escape the crippling entanglements with their parents that have obsessed so much of the world's literature. On the rare occasions when a strong father appears in the story, his part of the story takes place offstage, as if Americans found it impossible to imagine a strong father in action. But things are not so simple after all—even in popular fantasies not noted for their emotional complexity and moral depth. The nighttime world of melodrama, mystery, crime, and intrigue, which alternates with the family sit-com as the setting for most popular "entertainment," projects onto the comic strip or television screen a shadowy dreamworld in which deeper emotions come to the surface. The melodrama of crime brings to quasi-consciousness a sinister father-image, buried but not forgotten, in the disguise of a criminal, a "lord of the underworld," or a law-enforcement officer who commits crimes in the name of justice. In *The Godfather*, the identification of the father with the master-criminal becomes unmistakable, but in a more tenuous form it has always provided the excitement on which the popular thriller depends for its appeal to a mass audience.

A stock situation in films and novels of crime arises when the hero is wrongly suspected and falsely accused of the very crimes committed by his surrogate father. The regularity with which crime stories return to the theme of false accusation suggests that the latent father-image consists of the son's own repressed wishes projected onto the father. The gangster-father perpetrates the crimes the son would like to commit and then blames them on his son. The unfairness of his accusation expresses the popular belief that mere wishes are harmless and should never be punished. Only incompetent or criminal authorities propose to do so. The drama of the divided self, in which the superego attacks the ego for entertaining forbidden impulses, does not interest the producers of American popular culture. Instead, they externalize not only the superego, in the form of falsely accusing authorities, but the forbidden wishes themselves, now attributed to those same authorities and vicariously gratified even as the hero remains incorruptibly innocent. Self-accusations become the accusations of others, and the son's wish to get rid of his father is translated into the father's determination to make the son one of his victims. Danger comes from without, not from within.

The externalization of dangerous impulses makes the whole world seem dangerous and forbidding; it reinforces the realistic perception that public safety has objectively deteriorated in almost every sector of American society. "The hero of the melodrama," as Wolfenstein and Leites have observed, "is surrounded by an almost completely dangerous world—danger replacing the guilt or divine vengeance which have oppressed and pursued other dramatic heroes."[17] The unpredictability of the outer world has become a recurrent theme not only in melodrama but in all of modern literature. The sense of man's isolation and loneliness reflects the collapse of public order and the loss of religion; but the waning of public order and of religion itself reflects the waning of parental authority and guidance. Without this guidance, according to Alexander Mitscherlich, the world becomes "totally inaccessible and incalculable, continually changing shape and producing sinister surprises."[18]

Modern man faces the world without the protection of kings, priests, and other more or less benevolent father-figures; but he could accept their loss if it had helped him to develop inner resources of his own. Unable to internalize authority, however, he projects forbidden impulses outward and transforms the world into a nightmare. Authorities, inevitably modeled on the divided father, present themselves as either incompetent or malevolent. Accordingly, the individual appears to be justified in his efforts, not to overthrow or succeed them, but to bypass them: to undertake "investigations" of his own, in his capacity of "private eye" or investigative reporter, into the crimes they seek to conceal; to resort to private violence in the tradition of the vigilante; or simply to make endless protestations of his own innocence.

THE NORMALIZATION OF
THE ABNORMAL

Divided perceptions of authority, which figure so prominently both in psychiatric testimony and in popular culture, presumably originate not only in the structure of American society but more immediately in the family, which mediates between society and the individual. But how can the family give rise to such deeply conflicting views of itself? The father's absence—the structural feature of the American family that has attracted the attention of so many observers—might explain why children so often complain of parental neglect and why popular fantasy relegates parents to the background, but it hardly seems at first sight to explain the fantasy of paternal persecution and revenge. The fantasy of maternal suffocation might be accounted for, on the other hand, by the hypothesis that "Mom" has emerged as the dominant parent in the father's absence; but in that case, why do her children see her at the same time as a figure remote, detached, ineffectual, and indifferent to their needs?

All such explanations make too crude and direct a connection between sociology and psychology, between the structure of the family and its reverberations in mental life. They assume that everyday perceptions of the family more or less accurately reflect its structure and emotional content. They fail to distinguish between conscious and unconscious ideas. Complaints of parental indifference, which alternate with the claim that generational conflict plays little part in domestic life, embody conscious perceptions of the family, while the fear of devouring, castrating parents survives from infancy at a deeper psychic level. The remoteness and self-effacement of the American parent, the desexualization of motherhood, and the coolness that has come to characterize domestic relations only superficially ease the younger generation's break with the older. At a deeper level, old conflicts live on. Indeed, they become more deadly, precisely because of the social changes which have diminished the emotional intensity of family life, made it easier for the young to break with their parents, and thus smoothed the transition from childhood to maturity. The softening of the more explicit manifestations of generational conflict merely guarantees the persistence of that conflict in a more primitive psychological form.

Every society imposes certain prohibitions on the young and teaches them how to cope with the ambivalent emotions those prohibitions evoke. It enforces its rules in such a way that the young make the rules their own, neither submitting to them passively nor ignoring them. When adults have confidence in their ability to instruct the young, they do not allow their children's putative needs, as defined by the young themselves, to determine the entire content of education. Nor can they afford to take the child's rights and wishes into account at every point. On the other hand, neither can they ignore those wishes. "Obedience must not be taken for granted and must not be enforced by unilateral communication from above to below; instead, conscious consideration must be given to the weaker party, [who] will one day be the stronger." [19] Without this consideration, the child experiences authority as pure force and learns only that superior strength will always prevail.

An excess of permissiveness, strangely enough, does not necessarily soften this impression. The child who scorns his parents as weak and indecisive—who forms the most tenuous ties to his parents and pushes them without much difficulty into the background of his mind—conjures up another set of parents in his fantasies. Since those other parents so largely represent the creation of the child's unconscious thought—projections of his unconscious wishes and the fears that go with them—they appear to be as vengeful and punitive, as terrifyingly arbitrary and unjust, as the real-life parents are helpless, reasonable, and bland. The remoteness of the older generation does not mean that children form no vivid impressions of their parents; it only means that those ideas will seldom be tested against everyday experience. The child's fantasies go unchecked; he invents a supremely seductive, castrating mother and a fantasy-father who is remote, vindicative, and all-powerful. He sees the world to be starkly divided between power and impotence, and reduces all questions of justice and morality to questions of strength.

The pathology of the bourgeois family, subjected to penetrating scrutiny by psychoanalysis just as the bourgeois family was giving way to a new type of domesticity, provides a glimpse into the psychic structures that are now becoming typical, normal. According to Freud, the infant's sexual feelings and fantasies center first around the intake of nourishment, then around the retention and elimination of his feces, and only later around genital sensations. The child enters the genital or phallic stage of his development only when he has been forced to give up oral and anal gratification—to feed and evacuate according to his parents' pleasure instead of his own. At this point, he becomes aware of his father as a rival for the sexual favors of his mother and dreams of taking his place.

Sometimes, however, the fear and guilt aroused by these fantasies overwhelm the child, and he represses his genital wishes with particular severity. Still enthralled by the earliest associations aroused by his mother, those of nursing at the breast, he fears that his genital desires will themselves be governed by oral-sadistic impulses. The aggressive impulses inevitably directed against the mother, which originate in her frustration of the child's oral and anal pleasures, become so intense that they threaten to dominate every other activity. Under these conditions, the penis presents itself to the child's mind as a dangerous weapon, the presence of which in the mother's vagina makes the vagina itself a dangerous place by association. In the child's fantasies, she becomes a vampire, a devouring bird with an open beak. "This dread of the mother is so overwhelming," writes Melanie Klein, "because there is combined with it an intense dread of castration by the father."[20] These fears make the thought of sexual intercourse intolerably menacing. Unable to allow himself the fantasy of taking the father's place, the child can make his mother a love-object only by disowning his phallic desires, idealizing the breast and the mother-baby relationship, and attempting to restore the oral dependence of infancy.

Having projected fears of his own destructiveness onto his parents, the child then incorporates these monsters into his own psyche. He thinks of himself as containing alien aggressors that threaten to destroy him from within. The fear of persecution coexists with hypochondria, fear of the devouring presences inside his own body. These alien forces seem to threaten not only the child's health but the internalized image of the nurturing mother. The child regresses from object-love to narcissism; this regression tends to abolish the object itself, just as it does in the similar psychic process of mourning, in which the mourner reconciles himself to the loss of a loved object by internalizing it. In both cases, however, the object not only lives on in the ego but overwhelms it. The ego itself becomes an object, not only of love but also of anger, aggression, and murderous impulses that can lead even to suicide.[21] Impotence, hy-

pochondria, depression, and suicide form part of the same psychic
configuration, which originates in the intense anxiety associated
with the child's own destructive impulses. The fear that he cannot
protect his loved internal objects from danger, and that their death
means the end of his own life, constitutes "the fundamental anxiety
of the depressive individual."[22]

In the heyday of the bourgeois family, the very structure of the
family helped the child to overcome these anxieties—the analysis
and treatment of which, accordingly, belonged to the realm of abnormal psychology. As everyday contact with the parents diminished the intensity of early fantasies about them, the child acknowledged rivalry with his father, turned his aggression outward, and
took up in fantasy (and later, in sublimated form, in actual practice)
the struggle to displace the father. The emotional structure of the
contemporary family, however, increasingly militates against such
an outcome. The parents remain too shadowy and remote to challenge the child's primitive fantasies about them. Since the content of
those fantasies reflects anxieties aroused by oral-sadistic impulses,
the child internalizes his parents not as objects of genital love but as
projections of his own destructiveness. He sees the father not as a
rival but as an all-powerful avenger, the mother alternately as breast
and *vagina dentata*. What Melanie Klein wrote of one of her patients, a ten-year-old boy who imagined his mother a "vampire,"
now has a wider application: "The fear and guilt relating to his destructive phantasies moulded his whole emotional life."[23] The students recently interviewed by Herbert Hendin, both those suffering
from severe psychic disturbances and those whom psychiatry would
consider healthy and normal, all seek to repress their aggressive impulses for fear that those impulses, once unleashed, will destroy everything in sight. These young people can "conceive of no competition that [does] not result in someone's annihilation."[24] The flight
from competition in all areas of life, so striking a feature of the youth
culture of the sixties and seventies and so often justified in the name
of principle, originates in a murderous rage.

The so-called counterculture, hailed for its subversion of established
conventions, merely gives ideological sanction to the retreat from
rage, rivalry, and strong emotions in general. The counterculture's
quest for emotional detachment, put forward as a program of emo-

tional liberation, reflects a deeply held belief, rooted in the psycho-dynamics of the contemporary family and much more pervasive than the counterculture itself, that strong feelings lead to self-destruc-tion. New ideas of sexual liberation—the celebration of oral sex, masturbation, and homosexuality—spring from the prevailing fear of heterosexual passion, even of sexual intercourse itself. The repudia-tion of monogamy expresses an accurate understanding of the de-structive effects of possessive individualism extended to the emo-tional realm, of the jealousy that confuses love with emotional ownership. Yet it also expresses a rejection of intimacy and a search for sex without emotion—the "zipless fuck" in which "no one is try-ing to prove anything or get anything out of anyone."[25]

The contemporary cult of sensuality implies a repudiation of sen-suality in all but its most primitive forms. The fascination with per-sonal relations, which becomes increasingly intense as the hope of political solutions recedes, conceals a thoroughgoing disenchant-ment with personal relations. Ideologies of impulse gratification and pleasure seeking gain the ascendancy at the very moment that plea-sure loses its savor. A narcissistic withdrawal of interest from the ex-ternal world underlies both the demand for immediate gratifica-tion—resoundingly endorsed by advertising, mass promotion, and the health industry—and the intolerable anxiety that continually frustrates this demand. The more the "liberated" man clamors for fulfillment, the more he succumbs to hypochondria, to melancholy, or to a suicidal self-hatred that alternates, not with occasional heights of rapture, but with a chronic mild depression, the dominant mood of the times.

CORRUPTION AS A FORM
OF SOCIAL CONTROL

The organized assault on the superego, which has liberated pleasure only to transform it into another form of pain, reflects the devalua-tion of authority in modern society. Those who wield authority—fathers, teachers, magistrates, and priests—have all suffered a loss of

"credibility." Unable to inspire loyalty or even to command obedience, they have had to allow their subordinates a greater range of
pleasures—and also a greater range of crimes and misdemeanors—
than they would once have tolerated. But just as the seeming
triumph of the pleasure principle masks a new submission to reality,
so a permissive society has invented new forms of political repression or perfected old ones, notably force, bribery, intimidation, and
blackmail. The dissolution of authority brings not freedom but new
forms of domination.

The crisis of authority has deep roots in recent history. Abuses of
authority by the authorities themselves have become more and
more prevalent, and these abuses have given rise to popular cynicism and distrust. In the twentieth century, official propaganda for
the first time has had to address itself to a mass audience. Official lies
and half-truths, whether they emanate from government or from the
advertising industry, accordingly excite mass disbelief. The weakening of institutional loyalties makes it possible even for the people in
charge of society to consider the corporation, the university, or the
government itself merely as avenues of self-promotion and self-
advancement. Whereas the inner-directed bureaucrat identified
himself with the institution from which he derived his status, even
when he was poorly rewarded for his services, today the corporate
executive or politician looks on his office as an opportunity to spend
public funds, to dispense perquisites and favors among his friends,
and to surround himself with luxuries.

Since authority no longer commands respect, the authorities have
to impose their will through psychological manipulation or, when
manipulation fails, through outright violence. Government becomes the art of personnel management and public relations. With
the help of industrial sociology, employers have learned to translate
collective protest into private grievances. They encourage the
worker to think, not that wages are too low, but that a given worker's
"present earnings, due to his wife's illness, are insufficient to meet
his present obligations." Instead of addressing themselves to "what
is on the worker's mind in general," in the words of a pioneering
study in industrial sociology, they address "what is on some particular employee's mind in terms of a worker who has had a particular
personal history."[26] Personnel management treats the grievance as a
kind of sickness, curable by means of therapeutic intervention.

Authorities no longer appeal to objective standards of right and wrong, which might serve to clothe power in a higher morality but might also justify resistance to it. Instead of attempting to explain or justify their power, they seek only an acknowledgment of its existence. Power no longer needs any justification beyond the fact of its exercise.

The new mode of social control avoids conflicts and direct confrontations between authorities and the people on whom they seek to impose their will. Because confrontations provoke arguments about principle, the authorities whenever possible delegate discipline to someone else, so that they themselves can pose as friendly helpers. The diffusion of discipline even within the family provides the new forms of control with a solid basis in the individual's early experience. Having been taught from infancy to measure his demands not against abstract moral standards but against reality, the child submits all the more willingly to the reality principle as an adult. His own view of the world corresponds to the view of those who seek to control him.

In a study of the American high school, Edgar Z. Friedenberg found that high school students regard social control as "a technical problem, to be referred to the right expert for solution."[27] In response to a series of hypothetical problems in social control, Friedenberg's subjects rejected both libertarian and openly authoritarian solutions, justifying their preference for social engineering on pragmatic rather than moral grounds. Thus if a teacher finds an unruly student smoking in the washroom, he should neither "beat him coolly and with emotional restraint" or publicly humiliate him, on the one hand, nor ignore the offense, on the other hand, as a minor infraction that should not add to the student's reputation as a troublemaker. Having rejected authoritarian solutions for reasons that were "cautiously bureaucratic rather than indignantly humane," the students voted overwhelmingly that the offender should be sent to the school psychiatrist. Beating him would make him more unmanageable than ever, whereas the psychiatric solution, in effect, would enlist his own cooperation in the school's attempt to control him.

When authority presents itself as benevolence and questions about the exercise of power disguise themselves in the language of psychiatry, traditional political responses become inappropriate and traditional safeguards ineffective.[28] Thus a judge who pronounces a defendant incompetent to stand trial, on the advice of professional psychiatrists, ostensibly protects the defendant's rights, although in fact his ruling may have the opposite effect. In many cases, courts have proceeded to incarcerate the "mentally incompetent," in effect, without a trial. The court assigns the defendant to a hospital for the criminally insane until he can establish his competence to stand trial, failing which he can be reconfined for an indeterminate period of time. The psychiatric perversion of the concept of incompetence nullifies the rights of the accused—the right to a trial on his guilt or innocence, the right to a sentence of determinate duration, and the right not to be tried twice for the same offense—in the name of medical assistance. Even if the "patient" sees through the disguise, he finds that medical tyranny yields to resistance even more reluctantly than political tyranny. He could prove his innocence, even in a rigged system of justice, more easily than he can establish his mental competence. The very tenacity with which he insists on his innocence may be taken as evidence of mental derangement, especially if he has what amounts to a criminal record—a history of psychic disorder. "This patient still denies or keeps on repeating his denial of having committed the crime," runs the psychiatric verdict, "and he still insists upon his innocence." In the doctors' eyes, the patient's refusal to incriminate himself becomes a form of self-incrimination in its own right.

Even acquittal may leave a suspicion of psychiatric guilt. Those who get in trouble with the law, even when the law eventually finds them innocent of the charges against them, identify themselves as troublemakers—psychiatric offenders in need of psychiatric "help." As the ideas of guilt and innocence lose their meaning, permissiveness becomes the most effective system of social control. Just as parents, instead of enforcing standards of right and wrong, leave it to the peer group to keep children in line, so upholders of law delegate much of their authority to doctors. Society no longer enforces its rules by means of the authoritative edicts of judges, magistrates, teachers, preachers, and other embodiments of the social superego. It no longer expects authorities to articulate a clearly reasoned, elaborately justified code of morality; nor does it expect the young to internalize moral standards in the form of a conscience. It demands only conformity to the rules of everyday intercourse, sanctioned by psychiatric definitions of "normal" behavior.

The younger generation itself has adopted this view of things. Friedenberg's students "believe that enforcement of regulations, rather than any internal stability or homeostasis, is what keeps society from breaking down into disorder." They regard law not as a body of authoritative commandments but as "an indispensable technique for controlling behavior." This distinction goes to the root of the contemporary situation; it explains the growing devotion to "law and order" in a permissive society. The demand for law and order, which at first sight appears to attempt a restoration of moral standards, actually acknowledges and acquiesces in their collapse. Law enforcement comes to be seen as the only effective deterrent in a society that no longer knows the difference between right and wrong. The campaign to empty law of moral content—to banish the ideas of right and wrong and to replace them with an ethic of human relations—has had an unintended consequence. Divorced from the concept of justice, the law becomes nothing more than an instrument by means of which authorities enforce obedience. In former times, men regarded law as the moral consensus of the community—a means of "setting up categories," in Friedenberg's words, "under which society could subsume and isolate those whom it defined as miscreant." Today they see law merely as a means of controlling behavior. "Neglect law enforcement and the social structure decays."[29]

The prevalence of this view does not mean, however, that subjects and citizens regard authorities as "essentially benign" or hesitate "to discuss the possibility," in Friedenberg's words, "that a social institution . . . might be hostile or destructive in its purpose."[30] On the contrary, official protestations of benevolence elicit contempt or cynical indifference. "Apathy," widely deplored by political scientists and other observers of the political scene, greets all public statements in a society saturated with public lies. The official pretense that officials only want to "help" is rightly regarded as the biggest lie of all. People submit to the rules of social life, then, because submission usually represents the line of least resistance, not because they believe in the justice of the rules or the good intentions of those who promulgate them. The public takes it for granted that power corrupts those who wield it, but it regards this fact not with indignation but with a resigned sense of its inevitability. Disbelief in official pretensions, which formerly might have aroused resistance to the state, becomes another form of obedience, another acknowledgment of the way things are. Men submit not to authority but to reality.

If submission rests not on loyalty to a moral consensus but simply on a belief in the need for law enforcement, it rests on a shaky foundation. Men break the rules whenever the opportunity presents itself, not only because infractions of the rules so often go undetected, but also because authorities themselves conspire with offenders to overlook such violations. The contempt for authority, which leads to rising rates of crime and to the "legitimation of the ripoff," originates in part in the ease with which authorities can be corrupted.[31] Yet the corruptibility of authority serves in a curious way to strengthen the hand of those who wield power. The official who winks at an offense puts the offender in his debt. Moreover, he exposes the offender to blackmail. He keeps people in line precisely by overlooking their transgressions, a technique of control that closely resembles the "flattery of the lie," by means of which industrial supervisors assert power over subordinates by tolerating falsehood and inefficiency.[32] Lawbreaking contributes to law enforcement. The complicity between the criminal and the crime fighter, the subordinate and the superior, the violators of rules and the enforcers of rules, contributes to the maintenance of order by keeping troublemakers in a state of chronic uneasiness.[33] Repeated humiliations—the other side of flattery—lower their self-esteem, while the constant threat of disclosure creates fears more painful than disclosure itself. The threat of punishment exceeds punishment in its horror.

The family serves the social order even in the dissolution of its authority. It teaches the child his first lessons in the corruption of authority and thereby exposes him, at an impressionable age, to prevailing modes of social control. The "absence of the father," so often alluded to by students of the family but so little understood in its psychic repercussions, creates in the child a chronic fear of punishment; and although the threat loses its practical force through repeated deferral, it continues to reverberate in the child's fantasies. Precisely because the father's absence allows early fantasies to persist unmodified by later experience, the child fears the terrible vengeance that his father can inflict even while he scorns the everyday father who never inflicts it. The divided perception of parental authority carries over into social action. On the one hand, authorities invite contempt because they allow so many violations of their own rules; on the other hand, they threaten to exact a terrifying revenge at some unspecified moment in the future. As the postponement of gratification loses its force as a form of social control, the postponement of punishment takes its place. Deferred retribution represents the price paid for undeferred gratification.

The only alternative to the superego, it has been said, is the superstate.[34] The eighteenth-century *philosophes*, whose benevolent despotism anticipated so many features of the therapeutic state today, recognized this fact when they sought to remove the citizen from his family and to attach his libidinal energies to the state. As Fred Weinstein and Gerald Platt have written:

> Since neither Helvétius nor Holbach conceived of a conscience, the mode of control over human activity had to take the form of psychic manipulation. . . . Virtue, therefore, became the concern of the state, not of the individual, and society was regulated by the manipulation of emotions stemming from the desire for esteem and the fear of disgrace.[35]

Far from upholding "an archaic view of authority relationships," as Weinstein and Platt argue, Holbach and Helvétius saw far into the future. Today the state controls not merely the individual's body but as much of his spirit as it can preempt; not merely his outer but his inner life as well; not merely the public realm but the darkest corners of private life, formerly inaccessible to political domination. The citizen's entire existence has now been subjected to social direction, increasingly unmediated by the family or other institutions to which the work of socialization was once confined. Society itself has taken over socialization or subjected family socialization to increasingly effective control. Having thereby weakened the capacity for self-direction and self-control, it has undermined one of the principal sources of social cohesion, only to create new ones more constricting than the old, and ultimately more devastating in their impact on personal and political freedom.

NOTES

Introduction

1. T. B. Bottomore, *Critics of Society: Radical Thought in North America* (New York, 1968), pp. 80–81.

2. I am indebted to Thomas L. Haskell for showing me chapters from his forthcoming study of the emergence of American social science, which demonstrates the central importance of the principle of interdependence.

3. Taking their cue from the social sciences, historians have recently discovered the importance of professionalization in recent American history and have turned out book after book on the subject. See, for example, Robert H. Wiebe, *The Search for Order* (New York, 1967) and Burton Bledstein, *The Culture of Professionalism* (New York, 1976). Almost all these studies, however—including the two just mentioned—treat professionalization as a historical determinant in its own right, and see professionals as a separate class with its own interests and identity. They repeat the mistake made by earlier students of the "managerial revolution," who argued that managers constituted a "new class." In reality, both the growth of management and the proliferation of professions represent new forms of capitalist control, which enable capital to transcend its personal form and to pervade every part of society.

1 / Social Pathologists and the Socialization of Reproduction

1. Mary Wollstonecraft, *A Vindication of the Rights of Woman* (New York, 1967 [1792]), pp. 31–32, 35.

2. Quoted in Bray Hammond, *Banks and Politics in America from the Revolution to the Civil War* (Princeton, 1957), p. 196.

3. Nelson Manfred Blake, *The Road to Reno: A History of Divorce in the United States* (New York, 1962), pp. 134–135; William Fielding Ogburn, "Eleven Questions concerning American Marriages," *Social Forces* 6 (1927):7.

4. Theodore Roosevelt to Cecil Spring Rice, August 13, 1897; in Elting E. Morrison, ed., *The Letters of Theodore Roosevelt* (Cambridge, 1951–1954), 1:647.

5. Brooks Adams to Robert Grant, October 15, 1900; July 20, 1909; October 13, 1915; quoted in Robert Obojski, "Robert Grant: Storist of the Old Boston and Intellectual Leader of the New," Ph.D. dissertation, Western Reserve University, 1955, pp. 201, 208–209, 240–241. See also Arthur F. Beringause, *Brooks Adams* (New York, 1955), pp. 360–362.

6. "Women and Race Suicide," *Harper's Bazaar* [sic] 45 (1900):265. The proof that

women were not to blame, according to this argument, was that college women, though they married later, had as many children as other women of the same age.

7. Jane Addams, "Why Women Should Vote," *Ladies Home Journal* 27 (1910):21–22, and her "Larger Aspects of the Woman's Movement," *Annals of the American Academy of Political and Social Science* 56 (1914):1–8; Frances E. Willard, *How to Win: A Book for Girls* (New York, 1888), pp. 48–57; Florence Kelley, "The Invasion of Family Life by Industry," *Annals Am. Acad.* 34 (1909):90–96; Olive Schreiner, *Woman and Labor* (New York, 1911), and "The Woman's Movement of Our Day," *Harper's Bazaar* 36 (1902):3–8, 22–27, 103–107; Thorstein Veblen, *The Theory of the Leisure Class* (New York, 1899), especially chap. 13; Louise Collier Willcox, "Wives as Companions," *Harper's Bazaar* 44 (1910):304 ff.

8. For example, G. V. Hamilton and Kenneth MacGowan, *What Is Wrong with Marriage* (New York, 1929); G. V. Hamilton, *A Research in Marriage* (New York, 1929); Katharine B. Davis, *Factors in the Sex Life of Twenty-two Hundred Women* (New York, 1929); Ben B. Lindsey and Wainwright Evans, *The Revolt of Modern Youth* (New York, 1925). For the use radicals made of these studies, see V. F. Calverton, *The Bankruptcy of Marriage* (New York, 1928), chap. 5.

9. Robert Binkley and Frances Binkley, *What Is Right with Marriage* (New York, 1929), pp. 215–216. Cf. Lindsey and Evans, *Revolt of Modern Youth*, pp. 192–193, describing a "pact" under which one couple agreed "not to attach the name of 'inconstancy' to anything we may do."

10. Binkley and Binkley, *What Is Right with Marriage*, pp. 227–228.

11. Abraham Meyerson, *The Nervous Housewife* (Boston, 1920), pp. 142–143.

12. Émile Durkheim, *Moral Education* (1925), translated by Everett K. Wilson and Herman Schnurer (New York, 1961), pp. 92, 235. On the mystique of society in modern social thought, see Sheldon S. Wolin, *Politics and Vision* (Boston, 1960), chap. 10.

13. Charlotte Perkins Gilman, *The Home: Its Work and Influence* (New York, 1903), pp. 165, 335.

14. Florence Kelley, *Some Ethical Gains Through Legislation* (New York, 1905), p. 96.

15. Ellen H. Richards, *Euthenics: The Science of Controllable Environment* (Boston, 1910), pp. 74–75, 78–79. Educational reformers insisted ad nauseum that changing social conditions had thrust on the schools the care of the "whole child," quite independently of the educators' own wishes. For another, equally typical disclaimer, see Katherine Glover and Evelyn Dewey, *Children of the New Day* (New York, 1934), p. 217: "[The enlarged role of the school] has come about not because the school has demanded such responsibilities or has set out to usurp those formerly adequately discharged by the home and community, but because life has changed and new conditions have forced the burden on the schools."

16. Abraham Flexner and Frank P. Bachman, *The Gary Schools* (New York, 1918), p. 17.

17. Joanna Colcord, *Broken Homes: A Study of Family Desertion and Its Social Treatment* (New York, 1919), pp. 197–198.

18. Commonwealth Fund, *Fifth Annual Report* (1922–1923), and George S. Stevenson and Geddes Smith, *Child Guidance Clinics* (1934); both quoted in Roy Lubove, *The Professional Altruist: The Emergence of Social Work as a Career* (New York, 1972 [1965]), pp. 91, 97.

19. Quoted in ibid., pp. 99–100.

20. For a representative statement, see James H. S. Bossard, *Problems of Social Well-Being* (New York, 1927), p. 569.

21. Frank Dekker Watson, *The Charity Organization Movement in the United States* (New York, 1922), p. 276.

22. Edward T. Devine, *The Spirit of Social Work* (New York, 1912), p. 120.

23. Quoted in Robert M. Mennel, *Thorns and Thistles: Juvenile Delinquents in the United States, 1825–1940* (Hanover, N.H., 1973), p. 130.

24. Ibid., p. 140.

25. Quoted in ibid., pp. 142–143.

26. Ben B. Lindsey and Rube Borough, *The Dangerous Life* (New York, 1931), p. 168. On the juvenile court movement, see, in addition to Mennel's account, Anthony M. Platt, *The Child Savers: The Invention of Delinquency* (Chicago, 1969), and Joseph M. Hawes, *Children in Urban Society: Juvenile Delinquency in Nineteenth-Century America* (New York, 1971).

27. Lindsey and Evans, *Revolt of Modern Youth*, p. 180; Ben B. Lindsey, *Companionate Marriage* (New York, 1927), pp. 151, 184–186.

28. Lindsey and Evans, *Revolt of Modern Youth*, pp. 75, 113–114.

29. Philip Rieff, *Freud: The Mind of the Moralist* (Garden City, N.Y., 1961), p. 390.

30. Glover and Dewey, *Children of the New Day*, p. 48.

31. My analysis here draws on Harry Braverman, *Labor and Monopoly Capital* (New York, 1974); Stewart Ewen, *Captains of Consciousness* (New York, 1976); and David F. Noble, *America by Design* (New York, 1977). An unpublished paper by Renate Bridenthal of Brooklyn College, "Towards a Theory of Women's History," has helped me to clarify my thoughts on the socialization of reproduction. See also John R. Seeley, "Parents—the Last Proletariat?" in his *Americanization of the Unconscious* (New York, 1967), pp. 322–330.

32. See F. J. Roethlisberger and William J. Dickson, *Management and the Worker* (Cambridge, Mass., 1947), chap. 12, especially the section, "Manifest vs. Latent Content of Complaints." For analyses of managerial modes of control, see Herbert Marcuse, *One-Dimensional Man* (Boston, 1964), chap. 4; Loren Baritz, *The Servants of Power: A History of the Use of Social Science in American Industry* (Middletown, Conn., 1960), chaps. 5–6.

33. Quoted in Ewen, *Captains of Consciousness*, p. 37.

34. On the "repeal of reticence," see Nathan G. Hale, Jr., *Freud and the Americans: The Beginnings of Psychoanalysis in the United States, 1876–1917* (New York, 1971), chap. 10. On sexual technique and the invasion of the realm of leisure by the standards of production, see Lionel S. Lewis and Dennis Brissett, "Sex as Work: A Study of Avocational Counseling," *Social Problems* 15 (1967):8–18.

2 / Sociological Study of the Family in the Twenties and Thirties: "From Institution to Companionship"

1. In 1889, U.S. Commissioner of Labor Carroll D. Wright reported that the number of divorces in the United States had risen from about 10,000 in 1867 to more than 25,000 in 1886, an increase of 157 percent. In the period between 1870 and 1900, the population as a whole increased by almost 100 percent. See Nelson Manfred Blake, *The Road to Reno: A History of Divorce in the United States* (New York, 1962), pp. 134–135.

2. Helen Bosanquet, *The Family* (London, 1906), pp. 39–40.

3. An essential feature of the evolutionary study of society was the so-called comparative method, according to which institutions observable in extant cultures could be arranged in historical sequence. While condemning the "false hypothesis" of evolution as part of the ideology of progress, Le Play made free use of the comparative method. In his view, the traveler recapitulated all of European history as he passed from Western to Eastern Europe. See below, chapter 3.

4. These points appear also in William Graham Sumner, "The Family and Social Change," *American Journal of Sociology* 14 (1909):577–591.

5. Arthur W. Calhoun, *A Social History of the American Family* (New York, 1919), vol. 3, especially chaps. 8, 14.

6. Willystine Goodsell, *A History of the Family as a Social and Educational Institution* (New York, 1915), p. 497.

7. James Quayle Dealey, *The Family in Its Sociological Aspects* (Boston, 1912), pp. 90–91.

8. J. P. Lichtenberger, "The Instability of the Family," *Annals of the American Academy of Political and Social Science* 34 (1909):103.

9. J. E. Cutler, "Durable Monogamous Wedlock," *Am. J. Sociol.* 22 (1916):226–251.

10. See William Fielding Ogburn, *Social Change with Respect to Culture and Original Nature* (New York, 1922), especially part III, chap. 1, "Conceptions of Social Evolution."

11. V. F. Calverton, "The Compulsive Basis of Social Thought: As Illustrated by the Varying Doctrines as to the Origins of Marriage and the Family," *Am. J. Sociol.* 36 (1931):702, 715–717. Note that Calverton's attack on evolution, though launched from the left, could be published as the lead article in a respectable academic journal.

It is also interesting to note that since Calverton did not seem to have the concept of ideology at his disposal (even though he used the word once), he had to resort to clumsy circumlocutions—"the theory of cultural compulsives," "the compulsive basis of social thought"—in order to explain how thought is shaped by class interests. This argues a certain underdevelopment of Marxian thought in the United States—perhaps of social thought in general. Calverton's formulas are not only clumsy but reductionist: thought is seen as a mere reflex of economic interests. Yet Calverton was one of the least rigid and dogmatic of American Marxists.

12. Ernest R. Mowrer, *The Family: Its Organization and Disorganization* (Chicago, 1932), p. 77.

13. Joseph Kirk Folsom, *The Family: Its Sociology and Social Psychiatry* (New York, 1934), pp. 117–118.

14. Ernest W. Burgess, "Topical Summaries of Current Literature: The Family," *Am. J. Sociol.* 32 (1926–1927):107–109.

15. Ernest W. Burgess, "The Family as a Unity of Interacting Personalities," *The Family* 7 (1926):3–9; Ernest W. Burgess and Harvey J. Locke, *The Family: From Institution to Companionship* (New York, 1945).

16. Charles Horton Cooley, *Social Organization* (New York, 1909), pp. 61, 81, 87. See Erik H. Erikson, *Gandhi's Truth* (New York, 1969), pp. 431–433, and *Childhood and Society* (New York, 1963), p. 270.

17. All these points are made in the excellent summary and critique of the positivist conception of society by Steven Marcus, "Human Nature, Social Orders, and 19th Century Systems of Explanation," *Salmagundi* no. 28 (1975):30–35. Marcus argues that the same view of society can be found in the novels of George Eliot and many other nineteenth-century writers. On positivism, see also Gertrud Lenzer's introduction to her collection, *August Comte and Positivism: The Essential Writings* (New York, 1975).

18. Trigant Burrow (1924), quoted in Burgess, "Family as a Unity," 8.

19. In the fifth edition of *The History of Human Marriage* (1921), Westermarck conceded that marriage was a "social institution," although he still insisted that it was "rooted in instincts" (1:26, 71).

20. Louis Wirth, "Urbanism as a Way of Life," *Am. J. Sociol.* 44 (1938):10–11, 21, 28.

21. Burgess and Locke, *The Family*, p. 337.

22. W. F. Ogburn, "The Family and Its Functions," chap. 13 of *Recent Social Trends in the United States*, Report of the President's Research Committee on Social Trends (New York, 1933), p. 661.

23. Wirth, "Urbanism as a Way of Life," p. 17; italics mine. Cf. Robert E. Park, Ernest W. Burgess, and Roderick D. McKenzie, *The City* (Chicago, 1967 [1925]), p. 22: "Human relations [in the city] are likely to be impersonal and rational, defined in terms of interest and in terms of cash"—everywhere except within the family.

24. F. Stuart Chapin, "The Lag of Family Mores in Social Culture," *Journal of Applied Sociology* (1925):248.

25. Ernest R. Groves, *The Marriage Crisis* (New York, 1928), p. 46.

26. W. F. Ogburn, "Eleven Questions Concerning American Marriages," *Social Forces* 6 (1927): 5–12.

27. Ogburn, "The Family and Its Functions," p. 663.

28. Edward Sapir, "What Is the Family Still Good For?" *American Mercury* 19 (1930):145, 149–151.

29. One of the results of this contradiction, Folsom observes in passing, is "an increase in homosexual love relationships" (*The Family*, p. 416).

30. Mowrer, *The Family*, pp. 51–52. The reference is to W. I. Thomas, *The Unadjusted Girl* (Boston, 1924), pp. 17–31.

31. M. F. Nimkoff, *The Family* (Boston, 1934), pp. 373–374. In arguing that marriage "preceded" the family, Nimkoff was attempting to reverse the order favored by Westermarck and his followers. They had argued that the family, originating in the biological dependence of the human young, gives rise to marriage, an institution that had no other purpose than to serve this basic evolutionary need. For routine restatements of this view see, among many others, Sumner, "Family and Social Change," 577–578; and Goodsell, *History of the Family*, p. 11.

32. Nimkoff, *The Family*, pp. 374–375.

33. Mowrer, *The Family*, p. 82.

34. Jessie Bernard, "An Instrument for the Measurement of Success in Marriage," *Publications of the American Sociological Society* 27 (1933):94 ff.; cited in Nimkoff, *The Family*, pp. 377–380.

35. On Hamilton and Davis, see p. 192, n. 8. See also C. G. Woodhouse, "A Study of 250 Successful Families," *Social Forces* 8 (1930):530.

36. Mowrer, *The Family*, p. 280.

37. Willard Waller, *The Family: A Dynamic Interpretation* (New York, 1938), p. 597.

38. Louis M. Terman and Paul Buttenwieser, "Personality Factors in Marital Compatibility," *Journal of Social Psychology* 6 (1935):143–171, 267–289.

39. E. W. Burgess and L. S. Cottrell, "The Prediction of Adjustment in Marriage," *American Sociological Review* 1 (1936):737–751. See also E. W. Burgess and L. S. Cottrell, *Predicting Success or Failure in Marriage* (New York, 1939); E. W. Burgess and Paul Walling, *Courtship, Engagement, and Marriage* (Philadelphia, 1954).

40. Harvey J. Locke, *Predicting Adjustment in Marriage* (New York, 1951). See also Robert Winch, *Mate-Selection* (New York, 1958).

41. Herman R. Lantz and Eloise C. Snyder, *Marriage* (New York, 1962), p. 161.

42. "He who explains divorce . . . should also be able to explain why people go on living together." Willard Waller, *The Old Love and the New: Divorce and Readjustment* (New York, 1930), p. 28.

43. Waller, *The Family*, p. 539. Calverton ("Compulsive Basis of Social Thought") also argued that serial polygamy had become the accepted form of marriage and monogamy the exception.

44. Mowrer, *The Family*, p. 280.

45. Such was the interpretation of Locke's findings offered by Ira L. Reiss in his course in the sociology of the family at the University of Iowa, according to my class notes of April 11, 1963. Locke himself does not comment on this issue.

46. Mowrer, *The Family*, pp. 265–266.

47. Folsom, *The Family*, p. 230.

3 / Roads Not Taken: Challenges to Sociological Orthodoxy

1. Disagreements over methodology similarly failed to upset underlying assumptions. Reuben Hill, in an international survey of the literature from 1945 to 1956, distinguished seven different approaches to the study of the family, but this classification gives the impression of far more variety than actually existed. Of all American publications during the years in question, only 2.5 percent adopted what Hill called the macroscopic approach—that is, discussed the family's relation to other institutions and to society as a whole. Twenty-eight percent dealt with either mate selection or marital adjustment, 17 percent with the family as a small group, 21 percent with socialization or child development, and 7.5 percent with "family transactions with societal agencies." In an earlier period, the number of studies devoted to socialization would have been even smaller. Of the two functions assigned to the family by American sociologists—"companionate marriage" and child rearing—the second began to receive attention only in the forties; but this shift of emphasis (the reasons for which will be considered later) in no way altered the tendency of "interpersonal" study of the family to treat domestic life in isolation from larger social and historical developments. See Reuben Hill, "Sociology of Marriage and Family Behaviour, 1945–56," *Current Sociology* 7 (1958):1–98; see especially p. 7 (table 2), pp. 15–19, and the compendious bibliography beginning on p. 43.

2. Samuel Dupertuis prepared an abridged translation of Le Play's chef d'oeuvre, *Les ouvriers européens,* for inclusion in Carle C. Zimmerman and Merle E. Frampton, *Family and Society: A Study of the Sociology of Reconstruction* (New York, 1935), where it appears as part 4, "European Studies." The passage quoted appears on p. 366. On Le Play, see Hans Dodds Kellner, *Frederic Le Play and the Development of Modern Sociology,* Ph.D. dissertation, University of Rochester (1972).

3. See Le Play, *The Organization of Labor,* translated by Emerson (Phila., 1872).

4. Le Play returns many times to this last theme. For example: "If rural China has prospered for forty-two centuries, it is because it has always been regenerated by immigration or by the periodic conquests of Mongol or Manchurian shepherds." The European population could no longer replenish itself from these precious patriarchal reserves, but the next best thing was to recruit Europeans from the stem-families still surviving on the fringes of industrial society. See Le Play, *Les ouvriers européens,* 2d ed. (Paris, 1879), 1:58; Zimmerman and Frampton, *Family and Society,* p. 388. In vol. 3 of *Les ouvriers européens,* Le Play studied a number of families in Sweden, Norway, Hanover, Westphalia, England, and the Netherlands—the Saxon and Scandinavian shores, as he called them—and concluded that the prosperity of these regions derived from three causes: submission to the Decalogue, the reign of the stem-family, and the abundance of natural resources.

5. Le Play, *Les ouvriers européens,* 1:78; *Family and Society,* p. 401.

6. Lewis Mumford, *The Culture of Cities* (New York, 1938), pp. 9, 351.

7. Donald Davidson, "A Mirror for Artists," in Twelve Southerners, *I'll Take My Stand: The South and the Agrarian Tradition* (New York, 1962 [1930]), p. 30.

8. See Frank L. Owsley, "The Irrepressible Conflict," in *I'll Take My Stand,* pp. 61–91; "The Economic Basis of Society in the Late Ante-Bellum South" (with Harriet C. Owsley), *Journal of Social History* 6 (1940):24–45; and *Plain Folk of the Old South* (Baton Rouge, 1949). See also Howard W. Odum, *Southern Regions of the United States* (Chapel Hill, 1936); Rupert B. Vance, *Human Geography of the South* (Chapel Hill, 1935).

9. Zimmerman and Frampton, *Family and Society,* pp. 183, 249, 291, 295.

10. Quoted in Hill, "Sociology of Marriage," 31.

11. Zimmerman and Frampton, *Family and Society,* p. 9.

12. Ibid., p. 17.

13. Ibid., pp. 41–43.

14. Ibid., p. 44.

15. Willard Waller, *The Old Love and the New: Divorce and Readjustment* (New York, 1930), p. 101.

16. William J. Goode, Frank F. Furstenberg, Jr., and Larry R. Mitchell, "Willard W. Waller: A Portrait," in *Willard W. Waller on Family, Education, and War* (Chicago, 1970), pp. 70–77.

17. The absence of a sustained tradition of criticism (such as might have developed, for example, in connection with the development of a socialist movement) goes a long way to explain "the lack of agreement or even clarity about what is being attacked in present-day society and what is to replace it." See T. B. Bottomore, *Critics of Society: Radical Thought in North America* (New York, 1968), pp. 80–81.

18. Van Wyck Brooks, *America's Coming-of-Age* (Garden City, N.Y., 1958 [1915]), pp. 100–101.

19. Quoted in Goode et al., *Waller on the Family*, p. 16.

20. Willard Waller, *The Family: A Dynamic Interpretation* (New York, 1938), pp. 362–363.

21. Ibid., p. 263.

22. Incidentally, Waller's analysis of dating and marriage may help to explain why the thirties were so fascinated by the ideas of commitment and participation. People came to perceive that they were living in a society requiring a high degree of emotional detachment not only on the job but even in personal relations, just where one would least expect such a requirement. Thus they came to see commitment and participation as positive values in themselves, no matter what that commitment or activity might be.

23. E. A. Ross, *Principles of Sociology* (New York, 1920), p. 136.

24. Waller, *The Family*, pp. 276–277. But women do write novels, and one of the favorite subjects of the novel has always been the revelation of precisely such "secrets." Of course, the point about novels of courtship and marriage is not so much that many of them have been written by women, as that even male novelists tend to write them from the woman's point of view. Richardson established this convention with *Pamela*, a work that already in 1740 revealed the "secrets" introduced to American sociology 200 years later. The novel shows how Pamela's emotional detachment, enlisted on behalf of a single-minded determination to settle for nothing less than marriage, eventually prevails over the nefarious designs of Mr. B. Note that it prevails in large part because it is supported by an effective "line"—the written account of her sufferings that melts her persecutor's heart and forces him to fall more deeply in love with Pamela than she has ever been or ever will be in love with him. Thus at the very outset, Richardson grasped the essential features of the new situation that arose when courtship was freed from certain traditional sanctions: that the prize would go to the one who could best control and manipulate his own feelings (as a prerequisite to manipulating the feelings of others); that women had a greater stake in mastering these arts than men; and finally, that part of this mastery consisted in the ability to produce a heartrending account of their own sufferings.

25. Waller, *The Family*, pp. 415–417. As the subordinate partner in love and marriage, woman, according to Waller, has to develop a superior understanding of emotional life, so that she can manipulate her partner's feelings and tightly control her own. "It is usually the subordinated member of any pair who tends to develop insight into the other," Waller remarks, citing the way in which "the Negro studies the moods of the white" (ibid., p. 356). Feminine intuition, he argues, is the insight of the underprivileged.

26. Ibid., pp. 291–292.

27. "A girl's choice of whom to fall in love with is limited by the censorship of the one-sex group. Every boy that she dates is discussed and criticized by the other members of the group. The rigid control often keeps a girl from dating at all." Willard Waller, "The Rating and Dating Complex," *American Sociological Review* 2 (1937):731. The removal of parental control over

matchmaking, too glibly associated with the popularization of romantic love, creates a situation in which the peer group controls the process instead.

28. Waller, *Old Love and the New*, pp. 6–7, 84–88, 101.

29. Waller, "Rating and Dating Complex," 731.

30. Waller, *The Family*, pp. 252–253.

31. Ibid., p. 253.

32. Edward Shils passed over Waller in silence in his survey of American sociology, *The Present State of American Sociology* (Glencoe, 1948), pp. 30–33. This omission is all the more striking since Shils recommended "family conversation" as a fruitful line of investigation—precisely the type of analysis in which Waller excelled.

The collection of Waller's writings edited by Goode, Furstenberg, and Mitchell, together with their appreciative introduction (see above, note 16), may have done something to put an end to the neglect of Waller. But I cannot accept their explanation of that neglect: that Waller lived at a time when American sociology was in a period of consolidation, and that he therefore achieved no "signal breakthrough" in his work. After World War II, they argue, the "field moved quickly past him," having been revolutionized by the work of Parsons and his colleagues at Harvard. Leaving aside the difficulty that Parsons himself was nothing if not a consolidator, the neglect of Waller seems to have stemmed from active hostility rather than indifference.

33. Ernest W. Burgess and Harvey J. Locke, *The Family: From Institution to Companionship* (New York, 1945), chap. 12.

34. John Cuber, "Changing Courtship Customs," *Annals of the American Academy of Political and Social Science* 229 (1943); reprinted in Judson T. Landis and Mary G. Landis, eds., *Readings in Marriage and the Family* (New York, 1952), p. 58.

35. Robert O. Blood, "A Retest of Waller's Rating Complex," *Marriage and Family Living* 17 (1955):41, 45; William M. Smith, Jr., "Rating and Dating: A Re-Study," ibid., 14 (1952):316.

36. Samuel Harman Lowrie, "Dating Theories and Student Responses," *American Sociological Review* 16 (1951); reprinted in Landis and Landis, *Readings*, p. 77.

37. The practice of studying cultural patterns as they appear to insiders does not have to be carried to such absurd lengths. Especially in the study of primitive cultures, there is much to be said for it. Students of dating appear to have derived the justification for their reliance on questionnaires from cultural anthropology and misapplied the method to a type of problem quite different from the problems it was originally intended to solve. Distinguishing between statements or systems of meaning provided by the actors themselves and statements, on the other hand, that are "judged appropriate by the community of scientific observers" (or more broadly, by the agreed-on conventions and standards of critical reasoning), anthropologists in the twenties and thirties assigned greater responsibility to the statements of the actors themselves. They did so for the good reason that primitive cultures had to be understood in their own terms before they could be understood "objectively." While the same thing can be said of the rating and dating complex, it is after all part of American culture, and the difficulty of deciphering its inner meaning cannot serve as an excuse for indefinitely postponing critical judgments of one's own. Even in studying primitive cultures, the preoccupation with studying them from the primitives' point of view proved to be a mixed blessing. While it probably helped to improve standards of ethnography, it encouraged the retreat from historical theory into particularism and cultural relativism. Sometimes it even led to the absurdities that characterize the study of rating and dating by means of questionnaires. Recently Rodney Needham has naïvely attempted to call into question the universality of the Oedipus complex by arguing that many primitive peoples express "never a hint of horror" when asked about "the idea of incest"! See Marvin Harris, *The Rise of Anthropological Theory* (New York, 1968), p. 575; Rodney Needham, *Remarks and Inventions: Skeptical Essays about Kinship* (London, 1974), p. 66.

38. Waller, *Old Love and the New*, p. 316.

39. Anslem Strauss, "The Influence of Parent-Images upon Marital Choice," *American Sociological Review* 11 (1946). For "cultural" determinants see, e.g., August B. Hollingshead, "Cultural Factors in Mate Selection," ibid., 15 (1950); for temperamental ones, Ernest W. Burgess and Paul Wallin, "Homogamy in Social Characteristics," *Am. J. Sociol.* 49 (1943). All these articles are reprinted in Landis and Landis, *Readings*, pp. 91–106.

4 / Culture and Personality

1. Margaret Mead to Ruth Benedict, August 30, 1924; in Margaret Mead, ed., *An Anthropologist at Work: Writings of Ruth Benedict* (Boston, 1959), p. 285.

2. Sociologists did not altogether ignore this work; indeed, W. F. Ogburn's Columbia lectures on psychology and culture influenced a number of anthropologists in the early twenties, especially the students of Boas—Ruth Benedict, Margaret Mead, and Edward Sapir—who did so much to remodel their discipline with the help of ideas derived from psychology. Those ideas, however, bore more directly on the subject matter of anthropology—the transmission of culture—than on sociology.

3. Mead, *Anthropologist at Work*, p. 207.

4. Ibid.

5. Psychoanalysis appealed to anthropologists in the twenties for the same reasons it later appealed to many cultural historians. "Psychoanalysis," wrote Donald Meyer in a review of Erikson's *Young Man Luther*, "is the most radically historical psychology. . . . Freud made the most radical effort to explain the [subjective elements of history—] 'mind,' 'spirit,' 'soul,' 'instincts,' the 'individual,' the 'self,' 'human nature' itself—in exclusively historical terms. The alternative to an historical psychology must be at some point simply to postulate the existence of something standard, normal and even normative that 'behaves' in history, and to do this, simply to postulate it, is to surrender the historical method" (*History and Theory* 1 [1961]:294). It is not surprising that historians and anthropologists found similar virtues in psychoanalysis. In repudiating evolutionary theories, cultural anthropology, unlike sociology, did not turn its back on history; under the influence of Wilhelm Dilthey and his followers, it became highly sensitive to specific historical context. "Any arbitrarily selected phase of individualized 'social behavior' or 'culture,' " according to Sapir, "is . . . the complex resultant of an incredibly elaborate cultural history, in which many diverse strands intercross. . . ." See "Why Cultural Anthropology Needs the Psychiatrist" (1938); reprinted in David G. Mandelbaum, ed., *Selected Writings of Edward Sapir in Language, Culture, and Personality* (Berkeley, 1949), pp. 572–573. Precisely their insistence on the historical uniqueness of every culture led Boas, Sapir, Kroeber, Mead, Benedict, and other adherents of the culture and personality approach to reject attempts to formulate general laws of historical "evolution." For the influence of Dilthey, see Marvin Harris, *The Rise of Anthropological Theory* (New York, 1968), pp. 268–269, 398.

6. Ralph Linton, *The Cultural Background of Personality* (New York, 1945) pp. xiii, xvi, 3.

7. Sapir, "Psychiatric and Cultural Pitfalls in the Business of Getting a Living" (1939), in *Selected Writings*, p. 579n.

8. Having outgrown "the somatic superstitions of medicine," psychiatry now recognized that its proper subject was not "the human organism at all in any fruitful sense of the word but the more intangible, and yet more intelligible, world of human relationships and ideas that such relationships bring forth" ("Cultural Anthropology and Psychiatry" [1932], in *Selected Writings*, pp. 511–512).

9. The value of psychoanalytic theory, according to Sapir, lay in the genetic analysis of neu-

rosis, the recognition of the importance of infantile experiences in adult life, the interpretation of dreams, and the "general light thrown on the problem of mental determinism" (Review of Oskar Pfister, *The Psychoanalytic Method*, originally published in *Dial* [1917]; in *Selected Writings*, pp. 522–524).

Thus Sapir, in 1917, already articulated the drastically modified and restricted view of psychoanalysis to which psychoanalytic revisionism has adhered ever since. Compare his list with Freud's own summary of the foundations of psychoanalytic theory: "the assumption that there are unconscious mental processes, the recognition of the theory of resistance and repression, the appreciation of the importance of sexuality and of the Oedipus complex." See James Strachey, ed., *The Standard Edition of the Complete Psychological Works of Sigmund Freud* (London, 1961), 18:247.

10. See the review of Pfister already cited, in *Selected Writings*, p. 522; "The Unconscious Patterning of Behavior in Society" (1927), ibid., pp. 544–545; and "Personality," an article written for the *Encyclopedia of the Social Sciences* (1934), reprinted in ibid., p. 562.

11. Review of W. H. R. Rivers, *Instinct and the Unconscious* (1921), in ibid., p. 529.

12. Sapir, "The Contribution of Psychiatry to an Understanding of Behavior in Society," *American Journal of Sociology* 42 (1937):862–863.

13. Ibid., pp. 865–866.

14. Sapir, "The Emergence of the Concept of Personality in a Study of Cultures" (1934), in *Selected Writings*, p. 592.

15. Sapir, "Emergence of the Concept of Personality," in *Selected Writings*, p. 592.

16. Bronislaw Malinowski, *Sex and Repression in Savage Society* (New York, 1955 [1927]), pp. 17–18, 73–74, 77.

17. Ibid., p. 156.

18. Ibid., p. 190.

19. M. F. Ashley Montagu, ed., *Marriage, Past and Present: A Debate between Robert Briffault and Bronislaw Malinowski* (Boston 1956), pp. 68–70. These debates were broadcast over the BBC in 1931 and originally published in *The Listener* beginning January 7, 1931.

20. "One of the most dehumanising anthropological fallacies is the notion that the savage knows no real love, that he is incapable of falling in love. . . . I maintain that among the most primitive peoples, real love, the blend of physical attraction and appreciation of personality does exist, and that many primitive marriages are based on such love" (ibid., pp. 68–69).

21. Boas to Mead, July 14, 1925; in Mead, *Anthropologist at Work*, pp. 289–290.

22. Margaret Mead, *Coming of Age in Samoa* (New York, 1949 [1928]), pp. viii, 95, 118, 122, 131. Margaret Mead's attempted revision or refutation of Freud, like so many others, rests on a misconception of the nature of the evidence psychoanalysis seeks to explain. Freud's theories about infantile sexuality, the "castration complex," and the Oedipus complex are not based on empirical observations of childhood. They are based on interpretations of memories that have been so ruthlessly repressed that they can be brought to light only with the greatest difficulty. Psychoanalytical theory cannot be refuted, therefore, by empirical observation of child development or even of family structure, but only by a countertheory that provides a more convincing explanation of the meaning of dreams, fantasies, and neurotic symptoms. This does not mean that psychoanalytic theory is impervious to any kind of empirical refutation at all. It means only that the empirical evidence has to bear on the mental phenomena psychoanalysis seeks to explain—not on the "organization of the household," variations in child-rearing practices, the physiology of the female orgasm, the history of woman's subordination, etc., which psychoanalysis does not pretend to explain and which can easily be understood without any reference to psychoanalysis at all.

In focusing her inquiry on attitudes and sentiments (for even when she speaks of household organization she is really speaking of the structure of sentiments among the various members of the household), Mead thought she was going beyond the limits of earlier anthropological writing—an illusion she shared with Malinowski and Sapir. The older writers, she believed, had confined themselves to "merely external observations," whereas she proposed to get "insight into the mental attitudes of the individual" (*Coming of Age in Samoa*, pp. vii, 152). To progress from external observations to "mental attitudes," in her view, was to leap from ethnography to anthropology, from description to analysis. Today, when anthropology has returned both to analysis of social structure and to the attempt to arrange various types of social structures in evolutionary sequence, it appears that cultural anthropology, in spite of its enormous ambitions, was on the whole a theoretical regression, justifiable (if justifiable at all) only because in demanding that cultures must first of all be understood on their own terms, ironically enough Boas and his followers at least raised the level of ethnography.

23. Mead, *Coming of Age in Samoa*, p. 117.

24. Ruth Benedict, "Continuities and Discontinuities in Cultural Conditioning" (1938), in Clyde Kluckhohn and Henry A. Murray, eds., *Personality in Nature, Society, and Culture*, 2d ed. (New York, 1954), pp. 522–531. Benedict's argument anticipates recent criticism of the family by radical Parsonians; see pp. 145–146. It also bears a close resemblance to the thesis later advanced by Philippe Ariès in *Centuries of Childhood: A Social History of Family Life* (New York, 1962), that in most societies (including European society in an earlier epoch) children are integrated very early into adult society and that the segregation of children (which Ariès, like Benedict, regards as essentially undesirable) is a peculiar feature of bourgeois society.

25. Ruth Benedict, "The Family: Genus Americanum," in Ruth Anshen, ed., *The Family: Its Function and Destiny* (New York, 1949), pp. 160, 165, 168–169.

26. Mead, *Coming of Age in Samoa*, p. 130. Yet her unflagging honesty as an ethnographer compelled her to report that Samoan males took a lively interest in the salacious, a fact she had no way of explaining. "It seems difficult to account for a salacious attitude among a people where so little is mysterious, so little forbidden" (ibid., p. 85). Once again we see the limits of an approach to culture that confines itself to purely conscious phenomena and confuses the absence of "Victorian" or "puritanical" attitudes with the absence of any sexual prohibitions at all. The repression of sexuality, in one form or another, remains the very condition of culture, and in every culture, accordingly, sexual life consists of a series of renunciations. As a result, unconscious mental life is full of forbidden objects and forbidden forms of pleasure, incest being the most obvious as well as the most important in its psychic repercussions. The prohibitions surrounding sexual life, together with the close and unavoidable connection between the erotic and the excremental, naturally give rise to a sense of the salacious. Cultural relativists are so strongly impressed by cultural differences that they overlook what human beings share simply by virtue of being human.*

27. Mead, *Coming of Age in Samoa*, pp. 91, 131. Again we hear echoes of contemporary debates and polemics. The strongest argument against the prohibition amendment then in force, and against blue laws in general, was that they created crime and other forms of antisocial behavior. As noted in chapter 1, reformers like Brand Whitlock and Ben Lindsey had long argued that by doing away with blue laws, which made pleasure a crime, society would thereby legislate a whole field of crime out of existence.

28. Mead, *Coming of Age in Samoa*, pp. 67, 125–127. This argument recalls Malinowski's contention that in Melanesia the Oedipus complex is "split" between the father and the mother's brother, thereby lessening its force.

29. Margaret Mead, *Growing Up in New Guinea* (New York, 1953 [1930]), pp. 102, 106, 128, 140, 143. For similar observations about the American family, see Geoffrey Gorer, *The American People: A Study in National Character* (New York, 1948), pp. 53–54, 56, 58–59.

30. Margaret Mead, "Social Change and Cultural Surrogates," in Kluckhohn and Murray, *Personality*, pp. 659–660.

31. Gorer, *American People*, p. 54. See also Margaret Mead, *Male and Female: A Study of the Sexes in a Changing World* (New York, 1949), pp. 302–303.

32. Mead, *Coming of Age in Samoa*, p. 119.

33. Ibid., pp. 11–12, 126; Mead, *Growing Up In New Guinea*, p. 143.

34. Max Horkheimer, "The End of Reason," *Studies in Philosophy and Social Science* 9 (1941):381.

35. Margaret Mead, *And Keep Your Powder Dry: An Anthropologist Looks at America* (New York, 1943), p. 110.

36. Horkheimer, "End of Reason," 381.

37. Edgar Z. Friedenberg, *The Vanishing Adolescent* (New York, 1962 [1959]), p. 32.

38. The term "revisionism" is used here, as earlier, for lack of a better one, but it does not accurately describe the relation between Freud and Fromm, Horney, Sullivan, Thompson, et al. Those writers did not "revise" Freudian theory; they substituted a new theory of their own, which bore only a superficial resemblance to Freud's. It has been said of Fromm (and it could be said of the others as well) that he "is a revisionist of Freud in about the same degree, if not the same direction, that the Prince of Darkness was a revisionist of the Prince of Light" (John H. Schaar, *Escape from Authority: The Perspectives of Erich Fromm* [New York, 1961], p. 8). Considering that he claimed Freud as one of his masters, Fromm took a rather cavalier attitude toward his work. When asked "Where will we land if we keep on recasting the formulations of such a pioneer as Freud—recasting them into symbolic terminology?"—he modestly replied, "Well, I think Kant was right when he once said we often understand an author better than the author understands himself." See S. Stansfeld Sargent and Marian W. Smith, eds., *Culture and Personality* (New York, 1949), p. 11.

39. For a critique of "prophylactic" interpretations of Freud, see Anna Freud, *The Ego and the Mechanisms of Defence* (New York, 1946), chap. 5. Such interpretations, she argues, derive theoretically from an exaggeration of the superego's contribution to repression and neurosis. "This notion of the super-ego as the root of all neurotic evil inspires high hopes of a prophylaxis of the neuroses," through better education and more enlightened attitudes about sex.

40. Sigmund Freud, "Some Psychical Consequences of the Anatomical Distinction Between the Sexes" (1925), *Standard Edition*, 19:249.

41. Freud, "Female Sexuality" (1931), *Standard Edition* 21:228–229.

42. The essay on "Femininity" appears in *New Introductory Lectures on Psychoanalysis*, translated by James Strachey (New York, 1933) and is reprinted in the *Standard Edition* 22:112–135.

43. Juliet Mitchell, *Psychoanalysis and Feminism* (New York, 1974), chaps. 8–12, passim. Mitchell's account in turn draws heavily on Jacques Lacan, *The Language of the Self*, translated by Anthony Wilden (Baltimore, 1968), and on Octave Mannoni, *Freud* (New York, 1971). See also the essays in *Yale French Studies*, no. 48 (1972), "French Freud."

44. Freud, "Female Sexuality," 236–237, 239.

45. This is the significance of the much-debated thesis that the girl transfers her sexual feelings from the clitoris to the vagina—a theory against which recent feminists, with the help of Masters and Johnson, have directed some of their heaviest fire. Here as elsewhere, they were anticipated by the Freudian revisionists in the twenties, thirties, and forties, who tried to show that vaginal sensitivity developed much earlier than Freud believed—indeed, that this development preceded the Oedipal crisis. See Karen Horney, "The Flight from Womanhood" (1926), reprinted in her collection, *Feminine Psychology* (New York, 1967), pp. 65–66; and "The Denial of the Vagina" (1933), in ibid., pp. 152–157. See also Clara Thompson, "Cultural Pressures in the Psychology of Women" (1942), reprinted in Jean Baker Miller, ed., *Psychoanalysis and Women* (New York, 1973), pp. 51–52; Frieda Fromm-Reichmann and Virginia K. Gunst, "On the Denial of Women's Sexual Pleasure" (1950), in ibid., p. 76. The neofeminists,

on the other hand, claim that the clitoris remains the center of sexual pleasure in women and that the vaginal orgasm is a "myth." Anne Koedt, "The Myth of the Vaginal Orgasm," in *Notes from the Second Year: Women's Liberation* (1970), pp. 37–41.

Both lines of argument take too narrow a view of what constitutes sexuality, identifying it exclusively with orgasm. Neither weakens the main point Freud wanted to make: that women have to transfer their object-love from mother to father (whereas men merely transfer their affections from the mother to a suitable substitute), and that this change also requires the transformation of female sexual energies from an active to a passive form. The Freudian theory, it must be insisted once again, rests on the interpretation of memories, fantasies, and neuroses, not on laboratory studies of "female sexual response." It cannot be refuted by the latter, for the simple reason that those studies explain physiological, not mental, phenomena. When opponents of the Freudian theory turn to psychology in search of evidence supporting their own ideas, they are likely to fall flat on their faces. Thus Marcia Cavell unwittingly provides support for the theory she is laboring to refute when she writes that in adult women "clitoral masturbation is accompanied by phantasies of all kinds, and the sensations are not those of 'mastery' [who said they were?] but typically of being overwhelmed." See Marcia Cavell, "Since 1924: Toward a New Psychology of Women," in Jean Strouse, ed., *Women and Analysis: Dialogues on Psychoanalytic Views of Femininity* (New York, 1974), p. 164.

46. Feces, penis, and baby are closely associated in unconscious thought, not only because they are physical extensions of oneself but because they represent gifts from the child to its parents. It was this kind of evidence, and more generally the connection between eroticism and excrement—not some naïve "biological determinism"—that Freud had in mind when he made his famous remark that "anatomy is destiny." See "Contributions to the Psychology of Love: The Most Prevalent Form of Degradation in Erotic Life" (1912), *Standard Edition* 11:215.

47. Freud, "Female Sexuality," 226, 229–230.

48. Freud, "Some Psychical Consequences," 256–258.

49. Freud, "Femininity," 116.

50. Horney, "Flight from Womanhood," 68.

51. Freud, "Femininity," 119.

52. In a recent essay on Karen Horney, Robert Coles twice praises her "common sense"; see Robert Coles, "Karen Horney's Flight from Orthodoxy," in Strouse, *Women and Analysis*, pp. 187, 190. This is a curious form of praise from a writer working within the psychoanalytic tradition. Because it deals with unconscious thought processes, psychoanalysis, as Freud often pointed out, repeatedly has to fly in the face of common sense, appearances, and the "illusion of psychic freedom." "A person who professes to believe in commonsense psychology," Freud is quoted as having said, "and who thinks psychoanalysis is 'far-fetched' can certainly have no understanding of it, for it is common sense which produces all the ills we have to cure" (quoted in Russell Jacoby, *Social Amnesia: A Critique of Conformist Psychology from Adler to Laing* [Boston, 1975], p. 20). Cf. Freud, *Introductory Lectures on Psychoanalysis* (1916), *Standard Edition*, 15:21–22: "We look upon consciousness as nothing more nor less than the *defining* characteristic of the psychical, and psychology as the study of the contents of consciousness. Indeed it seems to us so much a matter of course to equate them in this way that any contradiction of the idea strikes us as obvious nonsense. Yet psycho-analysis cannot avoid raising this contradiction; it cannot accept the identity of the conscious and the mental."

53. Alfred Adler, "Sex" (1927); reprinted in Miller, *Psychoanalysis and Women*, pp. 35, 42.

54. Clara Thompson, "Penis Envy in Women" (1943), in ibid., p. 47. See also her "Some Effects of the Derogatory Attitude Toward Female Sexuality" (1950), in ibid., p. 65; and "The Role of Women in This Culture" (1941), reprinted in Patrick Mullahy, ed., *A Study of Interpersonal Relations* (New York, 1949), p. 148.

55. Erich Fromm, "Sex and Character," in Anshen, *The Family*, pp. 387–388.

56. Gregory Zilboorg, "Masculine and Feminine: Some Biological and Cultural Aspects" (1944); reprinted in Miller, *Psychoanalysis and Women*, pp. 90, 107.

57. According to Fromm, the early revisionists made the mistake of thinking that in order to defend equality for women they had "to prove that there are no characterological differences between the sexes except those caused directly by existing social conditions. . . . Thus the psychologist or anthropologist was put in a position where he had to disprove that among sex or racial groups, there were any special deficiencies or vices which had anything to do with their ability to share full equality" ("Sex and Character," p. 377). The importance of this statement lies in its admission that the members of the "cultural school" were determined above all to defend women against what they took to be Freud's slanders—not in Fromm's attempt to reintroduce biological differences into the discussion. Whereas the male has to demonstrate his potency in order to carry out the sex act, Fromm argued, the woman does not have to exert herself; from this fact derive certain temperamental differences—differences, Fromm hastens to add, which by no means justify the subordination of women. In *The History of the Psychoanalytic Movement (Standard Edition,* 14:52–53), Freud noted a similar theory advanced by Adler, which "does what every patient does and what our conscious thought in general does—namely, makes use of a *rationalization,* as Jones has called it, in order to conceal the unconscious motive. Adler is so consistent in this," Freud continued, "that he positively considers that the strongest motive force in the sexual act is the man's intention of showing himself master of the woman—of being 'on top.' I do not know if he has expressed these monstrous notions in his writings."

These theories illustrate the difference between attempts to define femininity and attempts to explain how a girl becomes a woman. If only because they derive temperamental differences from an act performed only by adults, Adler and Fromm tell us nothing about the psychic processes children have to go through in order to become adults. As explanations of femininity, moreover, their theories have to compete with an indefinite number of similar theories, all of them equally plausible and equally uninformative. One of the best known is Erik H. Erikson's "Womanhood and the Inner Space," in *Identity, Youth and Crisis* (New York, 1968), pp. 261–294.

58. "The penis serve[s] as a symbol of independence." Fromm, "Sex and Character," p. 386.

59. Ernest Jones, "The Phallic Phase" (1932); reprinted in his *Papers on Psychoanalysis* (Baltimore, 1938), pp. 587–591. "Two distinct views appear to be held in respect of female sexual development," Jones wrote ". . . According to one, the girl's sexuality is essentially male to start with, . . . and she is driven into femaleness by . . . disappointment in the clitoris. According to the other, it is essentially female to start with, and she is—more or less temporarily—driven into a phallic maleness by failure of the female attitude." The first of these views, according to Jones, prevailed in Vienna, the second in London. See also "Early Female Sexuality," in ibid., p. 614.

60. Except for its glorification of the vagina, the womb, and motherhood, which many feminists would now find objectionable, this early feminist criticism of Freud anticipated all the strictures of the neofeminists. The latter, however, because they mistakenly identify all varieties of psychoanalysis with "reactionary" ideas about women, have not availed themselves of this criticism, relying instead on the seemingly more radical work of Wilhelm Reich and, to a lesser extent, of R. D. Laing.

61. Karen Horney, *The Neurotic Personality of Our Time* (New York, 1937), pp. 83–84.

62. Ibid., p. 286.

63. There were direct connections between these two movements, as well as strong similarities and parallels. Fromm, for example, was active for a time in both. In the thirties, during the first period of his American exile, Max Horkheimer, director of the Institute for Social Research, shared some of Fromm's misgivings about orthodox Freudianism, at least as they per-

tained to the death instinct and the political "resignation" it seemed to imply. According to Fromm, Horkheimer was on friendly terms with Karen Horney. Margaret Mead once published an article in the *Zeitschrift für Sozialforschung,* the Institute's journal. See Martin Jay, *The Dialectical Imagination: A History of the Frankfurt School and the Institute of Social Research, 1923–1950* (Boston, 1973), pp. 100–101.

64. Leon Bramson, *The Political Context of Sociology* (Princeton, 1961), pp. 134–139.

65. From an editorial (1916), quoted in Giuseppe Fiori, *Antonio Gramsci: Life of a Revolutionary* (New York, 1971), p. 103.

66. Ibid. See also the editorials and program from *Ordine Nuovo* and the various essays on culture and intellectuals in *The Modern Prince,* translated by Louis Marks (New York, 1967). On Gramsci's thought in general, see Eugene D. Genovese, "On Antonio Gramsci," *Studies on the Left* 7 (1967):83–107; and John M. Cammett, *Antonio Gramsci and the Origins of Italian Communism* (Stanford, 1967). See also Georg Lukács, *History and Class Consciousness* (Cambridge, 1971 [1922]); Karl Korsch, *Marxism and Philosophy* (London, 1970 [1930]).

It followed from an analysis that equated mind with consciousness (and therefore stressed the role of ideology and propaganda) that the party would have to play a leading role in breaking down the cultural inertia of the masses. Thus although Gramsci and Lukács broke with economic determinism, both remained more or less faithful to Leninism, which preserved so many features of Marxist positivism within the framework of a more voluntaristic outlook. See Jacoby, *Social Amnesia,* for an invaluable treatment of these issues and of the deterioration of psychoanalytic thought as it became associated with "humanism" and positive thinking.

67. Max Horkheimer, "Authority and the Family" (1936); reprinted in *Critical Theory: Selected Essays* [by Max Horkheimer], translated by Matthew J. O'Connell et al. (New York, 1972), pp. 58, 67, 69.

68. In doing so, they had to overcome the erroneous impression that Marxism implies a psychology of its own, which is incompatible with psychoanalysis—a psychology that insists on the primacy of the "profit motive" or the appetite for gain. "In reality, historical materialism is far from being a psychological theory; its psychological presuppositions are few and may be briefly listed: *men* make their own history; *needs* motivate men's actions and feelings (hunger and love); these needs increase in the course of historical development, thereby spurring increased economic activity." See Fromm, "The Method and Function of an Analytic Social Psychology: Notes on Psychoanalysis and Historical Materialism" (1932); reprinted in *The Crisis of Psychoanalysis* (Greenwich, Conn., 1970), p. 151. This essay originally appeared in the organ of the Frankurt school, *Zeitschrift für Sozialforschung.*

69. Wilhelm Reich, *Character-Analysis,* 3d ed. (New York, 1949), p. xxiv. The first edition of this work appeared in German in 1933, the second in English in 1945. The book is best known in the third edition, which contains much of the original text interwoven with numerous revisions.

70. Erich Fromm, "The Theory of Mother Right and Its Relevance for Social Psychology" (1934), in *Crisis of Psychoanalysis,* pp. 126–127. (This essay first appeared in *Zeitschrift für Sozialforschung.*) See also Horkheimer, "Authority and the Family," in *Critical Theory,* p. 109: "For the formation of the authority-oriented character it is especially decisive that the children should learn, under pressure from the father, not to trace every failure back to its social causes but to remain at the level of the individual and to hypostatize the failure in religious terms as sin or in naturalistic terms as deficient natural endowment. The bad conscience that is developed in the family absorbs more energies than can be counted, which might otherwise be directed against the social circumstances that play a role in the individual's failure. The outcome of such paternal education is men who without ado seek the fault in themselves."

71. Fromm, "Mother Right," pp. 131–132; "Method and Function of an Analytic Social Psychology," p. 145. In the first of these essays, Fromm argues, in a passage that shows the influ-

ence of Weber, that "the patricentric type is probably dominant in bourgeois-Protestant society, while the matricentric type would play a relatively major role in the Middle Ages and in southern European society today."

72. Fromm, "Mother Right," pp. 124–125; Wilhelm Reich, *The Mass Psychology of Fascism* (1933), translated by Vincent R. Cargagno (New York, 1970), p. 30.

73. Erich Fromm, *Escape from Freedom* (New York, 1941), p. 212n; "The Revolutionary Character" (1961), reprinted in his *Dogma of Christ and Other Essays on Religion, Psychology, and Culture* (New York, 1963), pp. 148–149. Portions of the study of German workers, which also included material on peasant and middle-class families and comparative material on Holland, appeared in a translation by A. Lissance and sponsored by the WPA (*Authority and the Family*, typescript [New York, 1937]). Both the methods and the concepts of this study were very crude. The investigators gathered most of their information in the form of questionnaires, and the questions elicited little more than a statement of political prejudices. Without any psychological probing, the investigators then simply equated political attitudes with "authoritarian," "revolutionary," and "ambivalent" character types.

74. Horkheimer, "Authority and the Family," p. 100.

75. Ibid., pp. 105–106.

76. Fromm, *Escape from Freedom*, pp. 167–168, 252; "The Present Human Condition" (1955–1956), in *Dogma of Christ*, pp. 97–98.

77. Fromm, *Escape from Freedom*, p. 250.

78. Ibid., p. 209.

79. Philip Rieff, "Fellow Teachers," *Salmagundi*, no. 20 (1972):67.

80. In Germany following World War I, according to Fromm, the decline of older symbols of authority like monarchy, the bewilderment of the older generation in the face of rapidly changing social conditions, and the economic crisis that undermined its ability to command respect by playing the role of provider, brought about a situation, in the lower middle class, in which "the younger generation acted as they pleased and cared no longer whether their actions were approved by their parents or not" (*Escape from Freedom*, p. 215). These brief observations appear in a chapter devoted to the psychology of lower-middle-class support for fascism, not the collapse of proletarian resistance to fascism.

81. Fromm, "Psychoanalysis—Science or Party Line?" (1958), in *Dogma of Christ*, p. 143.

82. Horkheimer, "Authority and the Family," pp. 112–113.

83. In a later essay ("Authoritarianism and the Family Today" [1949], in Anshen, *The Family*, p. 362), Horkheimer acknowledged that the Nazis "tried to dispense systematically with any mediation between the individual and the state and to push Jacobinism to the extreme," but he maintained that the ultimate collapse of the regime shows that even the fascist state depends on "the authority of the family." Since the Nazi regime was defeated by external invasion rather than internal overthrow or dissolution, this argument is not convincing.

84. Horkheimer, "Authority and the Family," pp. 58, 114–115.

85. Herbert Marcuse, *Eros and Civilization* (New York, 1962 [1955]), p. 86. Chap. 4 of this work examines the "technological abolition of the individual," the "decline of the social function of the family," the "premature socialization" of the young by experts and peers, and the "depersonalization" of the superego.

86. Horkheimer, "Authoritarianism and the Family Today," pp. 368–373.

87. Else Frenkel-Brunswik, "Parents and Childhood," in T. W. Adorno et al., *The Authoritarian Personality* (New York, 1969 [1950]), p. 357.

88. T. W. Adorno, "Scientific Experiences of a European Scholar in America," translated by Donald Fleming; in Donald Fleming and Bernard Bailyn, *The Intellectual Migration: Europe and America, 1930–1960* (Cambridge, Mass., 1969), pp. 356–357.

89. Horkheimer, "Authority and the Family," p. 59. This proposition has an important corollary: namely, that culture does not always play an equally indispensable role in supporting

existing social structures. There are times "when the economic decline of a specific mode of production has so undermined all the cultural forms that go with it, that the needs of the greater part of society easily turn into rebellion and it takes only the resolute will of progressive groups to win the victory over the naked force of arms on which the whole system at this point essentially rests. But such moments," Horkheimer adds, "are rare and brief."

To say that culture depends on society and that it serves in part to justify the existing relations of production does not mean that culture is to be equated simply with ideology. The highest products of culture—the sublimated rather than the repressed expression of erotic drives—contain moral and aesthetic ideas that transcend existing relations of production, indeed that often condemn them.

90. A. L. Kroeber and Clyde Kluckhohn, *Culture: A Critical Review of Concepts and Definitions* (New York, n.d. [1952]), pp. 92, 128, 176.

91. Reich, *Character-Analysis*, pp. 46, 145.

92. Reich, *Mass Psychology of Fascism*, p. 56.

93. Reich, "The Imposition of Sexual Morality" (1932), in his *Sex-Pol* (New York, 1972); see also Wilhelm Reich, *The Function of the Orgasm*, translated by Theodore P. Wolfe (New York, 1967 [1942]), p. 43.

94. S. Stansfeld Sargent and Marian W. Smith, eds., *Culture and Personality: Proceedings of an Interdisciplinary Conference Held Under the Auspices of the Viking Fund, Nov. 7 and 8, 1947* (New York, 1949), p. 5n. See also Ralph Linton et al., *The Psychological Frontiers of Society* (New York, 1945), p. 24.

95. Otto Lineberg, "Recent Studies of National Character," in Sargent and Smith, *Culture and Personality*, p. 135.

96. Henry A. Murray, "Research Planning: A Few Proposals," in ibid., p. 212.

5 / Doctors to a Sick Society

1. Harry Stack Sullivan, "Remobilization for Enduring Peace and Social Progress," *Psychiatry*, 10 (1947):239; S. Stansfeld Sargent and Marian W. Smith, eds., *Culture and Personality* (New York, 1949), pp. 203–204.

2. On the early association of psychiatry with "New Thought," see Fred Hamilton Mathews, "Freud Comes to America," M.A. thesis, University of California at Berkeley (1957); Nathan G. Hale, Jr., *Freud and the Americans* (New York, 1971), chaps. 9, 15.

3. John Money, "Delusion, Belief, and Fact," *Psychiatry* 11 (1948):36, 38. A psychiatrist who based his work on these principles, according to Money, quite properly became a "social engineer."

4. John R. Seeley, "Social Values, the Mental Health Movement, and Mental Health," *Annals of the American Academy of Political and Social Science* 286 (March 1953):19.

5. Leslie H. Farber, "Martin Buber and Psychiatry," *Psychiatry* 19 (1956):119.

6. Hanna Colm, "Healing as Participation," *Psychiatry* 16 (1953):102–107. For a cruder redefinition of religion as therapy, see Thomas A. C. Rennie and Luther E. Woodward, *Mental Health in Modern Society* (New York, 1948), p. 263: "The very persistence of the custom of worship indicates that there is mental hygiene value in it."

7. Lawrence K. Frank, *Society as the Patient: Essays on Culture and Personality* (New Brunswick, N.J., 1948).

8. Lawrence K. Frank, "The Historian as Therapist," in ibid., p. 305.

9. L. T. Fleming, review of George S. Stevenson, *Mental Health Planning for Social Action*, in *Marriage and Family Living* 19 (1957):210.

10. C. B. Chisholm, "The Reestablishment of Peacetime Society" and "The Responsibility of Psychiatrists," *Psychiatry* 9 (1946):3–20.

11. George S. Goldman, "The Psychiatrist's Job in War and Peace," *Psychiatry* 9 (1946): 273–274.

12. Harry Stack Sullivan, "The Cultural Revolution to End War," *Psychiatry* 9 (1946):87.

13. For the influence of psychiatry on social work, which began in the twenties, see Roy Lubove, *The Professional Altruist* (Cambridge, Mass., 1965), chaps. 3–4.

14. Kingsley Davis, "Mental Hygiene and the Class Structure," *Psychiatry* 1 (1938):55–65.

15. C. Wright Mills, "The Professional Ideology of Social Pathologists," *American Journal of Sociology* 49 (1943):165–180.

16. Donald Chard Marsh and Norman D. Humphrey, "Value Congeries and Marital Counseling," *Marriage and Family Living* 15 (1953):28–32.

17. John R. Seeley, R. Alexander Sim, and Elizabeth W. Loosley, *Crestwood Heights: A Study of the Culture of Suburban Life* (New York, 1967), chaps. 11–12.

18. Chisholm, "Reestablishment of Peacetime Society," 9.

19. Sidney E. Goldstein, "Aims and Objectives of the National Conference," *Marriage and Family Living* 8 (1946):57–58. "An autocratic form of family organization," wrote Goldstein, "can never prepare children for the new democratic social order."

20. Rennie and Woodward, *Mental Health in Modern Society*, p. 330.

21. Edward A. Strecker and Kenneth E. Appel, *Psychiatry in Modern Warfare* (New York, 1945), p. 71.

22. Lawrence K. Frank, "Freedom for the Personality," *Psychiatry* 3 (1940):347.

23. Gregory Zilboorg, *The Psychology of the Criminal Act and Punishment* (New York, 1954), p. 43.

24. *Durham* v. *U.S.* (1954); Bazelon's opinion in *Psychiatry* 17 (1954):286, 297.

25. *Williams* v. *New York* (1949); quoted in Nicholas N. Kittrie, *The Right to Be Different: Deviance and Enforced Therapy* (Baltimore, 1971), p. 31.

26. F. Bergan (1949); quoted in ibid., pp. 30–31.

27. Margaret Lantis, "The Symbol of a New Religion," *Psychiatry* 13 (1950):101–113.

28. Christopher Jencks, "Is It All Dr. Spock's Fault?" *New York Times Magazine*, March 3, 1968, p. 84. "Among some of the most sensitive and gifted young people," wrote David Riesman in 1959, "there has developed the tendency to withdraw altogether from the great and overriding political concerns of their elders, sometimes by choosing fields such as the humanities or the ministry which could not have a conceivable Cold War or big-project relevance, and sometimes by withdrawing any deep involvement from work in large organizations even while going through the motions. . . . The same emphasis on the affective side of life, on the family as the most important element in the good life, which has influenced the career decisions of men, has also led even the most brilliant and energetic college women to decide that they do not want to undertake long preparation for careers which might cut them off from the chance of marriage or in some subtle way defeminize them." See Riesman, "Permissiveness and Sex Roles," *Marriage and Family Living* 21 (1959):212–213.

29. Randolph Bourne to Prudence Winterrowd, April 28, 1913; quoted in Christopher Lasch, *The New Radicalism in America* (New York, 1965), p. 94. Bourne's stipulation that the women in his "salon" were "of course self-supporting and independent" suggests the important difference between the bohemian avant-garde in the period before World War I and those who domesticated its sexual program in the fifties.

30. Robert A. Harper, "Failure in Marriage Counseling," *Marriage and Family Living* 17 (1955):361–362.

31. Judson T. Landis, "The Challenge of Marriage and Family Life Education," *M. Fam. Liv.* 19 (1957):249–250.

32. Cora Kasius, "Social Resources for Families in the United States," *M. Fam. Liv.* 17 (1955):256.

33. Albert Ellis, "A Critical Evaluation of Marriage Counseling," *M. Fam. Liv.* 18 (1956): 67–68. On the growing consensus about second marriages, see Herbert Bisno, review of Philip Polatin and Ellen Philtine, *The Well-Adjusted Personality*, in *M. Fam. Liv.* 18 (1956): 88–90.

34. Ray H. Abrams, "The Contribution of Sociology to a Course on Marriage and the Family," *M. Fam. Liv.* 2 (1940):82–83.

35. David R. Mace, "What Is a Marriage Counselor?" *M. Fam. Liv.* 16 (1954):135–136. The author did not fail to point out the implications of this development for the growth of the health and welfare industry. The "decline of the family council," he argued, "in which a kinship group undertook to deal with the personal and domestic difficulties of its individual members," created the need for a new profession, which could "be expected to increase by leaps and bounds."

36. "A basic postulate held by many sociologists . . . is that the American family is in a stage of transition from the older patriarchal family to a system of a democratic, equalitarian arrangement." See William G. Dyer and Dick Urban, "The Institutionalization of Equalitarian Family Norms," *M. Fam. Liv.* 20 (1958):53.

37. Eleanor Luckey and Gerhard Neubeek, "What Are We Doing in Marriage Education?" *M. Fam. Liv.* 18 (1956):349.

38. Rachel Ann Elder, "Traditional and Developmental Conceptions of Fatherhood," *M. Fam. Liv.* 11 (1949):98.

39. Eduard C. Lindeman, "Ideals for Family Life After the War," *M. Fam. Liv.* 4 (1942):8–9.

40. Evelyn Millis Duvall, "Growing Edges in Family Life Education," *M. Fam. Liv.* 5 (1943):22–24. These ideas were popularized in Evelyn Millis Duvall and Reuben Hill, *When You Marry* (New York, 1948).

41. Mabel Blake Cohen, review of Erikson's *Childhood and Society*, in *Psychiatry* 14 (1951):351. At the same time, Cohen criticized Erikson for refusing to surrender completely to a prophylactic idea of psychotherapy. His assertion that even the most enlightened child-rearing methods could never remove a "primary sense of evil and doom" seemed to her to "make the discussion of child-rearing practices seem relatively insignificant. . . . It is, to the reviewer's mind, a somewhat stultifying assumption."

42. See, for example, Lester W. Dearborn, "The Problem of Masturbation," *M. Fam. Liv.* 14 (1952):46–55.

43. David M. Levy, "Maternal Overprotection," *Psychiatry* 2 (1939):111, 114. Levy noted, however, that children exposed to "overprotective" mothers usually read better than other children and had bigger vocabularies.

For an early statement on the dangers of maternal overprotection, see Ernest R. Groves and Gladys H. Groves, *Parents and Children* (Philadelphia, 1928), chap. 8, "The Dangerous Mother." "It is to [many mothers] the most astonishing thing that mother love has been found by science inherently dangerous, and some of them grow panicky as they let the significance of the new teaching sink into their thoughts" (p. 116).

44. Susan Isaacs, quoted in Beatrix Hamburg, review of Hilde Bruch, *Don't Be Afraid of Your Child*, in *Psychiatry* 16 (1953):410.

45. Hilde Bruch, *Don't Be Afraid of Your Child* (New York, 1952), chap. 1.

46. Jerome D. Folkman, "A New Approach to Family Life Education," *M. Fam. Liv.* 17 (1955):20.

47. Judd Marmor, "Psychological Trends in American Family Relationships," *M. Fam. Liv.* 13 (1951):147.

48. Ibid.

6 / *The Social Theory of the Therapeutic:*
Parsons and the Parsonians

1. Henry A. Murray, "Research Planning: A Few Proposals," in S. Stansfeld Sargent and Marian W. Smith, eds., *Culture and Personality* (New York, 1949), pp. 208–209.

2. Ibid., pp. 200, 203–204.

3. Edward Shils, *The Present State of American Sociology* (Glencoe, Ill., 1948), p. 45. Shils ignored the question of whether sociology had not already passed beyond the stage in which classification makes an important contribution to the field. On this issue, see T. B. Bottomore's essay on Parsons in his *Sociology as Social Criticism* (New York, 1975), p. 40: "Renouncing on one side empirical generalisations and on the other side methodological inquiry, Parsons confines himself largely to the analysis and classification of concepts; that is to say he works in a sphere which is . . . characteristic of sciences at an early stage of their development, in which theory involves no more than classifying the phenomena with which the subject deals, mapping out the problem areas, defining rules of procedure and schemes of interpretation. But this limitation seems unnecessary and undesirable in a subject which has advanced beyond this early stage, at least in the sense that the classical sociologists themselves put forward explanatory generalisations and theories which we can accept, correct, refute, discard, . . . but which we must in any case confront." This passage helps to clarify the irony that Parsons's work, which more than that of any other American sociologist appears to be a continuation of the work of the classical sociologists, actually negates it by ignoring the substance of what they accomplished. Instead of confronting that substance—that is, the interpretations put forward to explain the course of world history, the revolutions from which modern society emerged, etc.—Parsons in the name of theory undertakes an elaborate exercise in classification that would have been more appropriate as a prelude to classical sociology, not (as Parsons sees it) as its consummation.

4. Sargent and Smith, *Culture and Personality*, p. 204.

5. Shils, *State of American Sociology*, pp. 42–43 and note 80.

6. Talcott Parsons, *The Structure of Social Action* (New York, 1968 [1937]), 1:6–9. In order to understand Parsons's insistence on the primacy of theory, it is necessary to recall that many American sociologists not only neglected theory but justified this neglect as a positive virtue. In his presidential address to the American Sociological Society (1929), W. F. Ogburn demanded that sociology model itself on the natural sciences and evolve more exact techniques of measurement, relegating theory to the realm of "soft-mindedness." "Social theory," Ogburn predicted, "will have no place in a scientific sociology, for it is not built upon sufficient data." See "The Folk-ways of a Scientific Sociology," *Scientific Monthly* 30 (1930):300–306.

7. Introduction to the 1968 edition of *The Structure of Social Action*, p. xi.

8. Shils, *State of American Sociology*, p. 61: "Before psychoanalytic hypotheses and categories can become the core of sociological theory, they will, of course, have to be freed from metaphors, 'empiricized', reformulated and tested according to far more rigorous methods than psychoanalysts themselves have thus far used."

9. Robert F. Bales and Philip E. Slater, "Role Differentiation in Small Decision-making Groups," in Talcott Parsons, Robert F. Bales, et al., *Family, Socialization and Interaction Process* (Glencoe, Ill., 1955), p. 300.

10. Ibid., pp. 302–303; Morris Zelditch, Jr., "Role Differentiation in the Nuclear Family: A Comparative Study," in ibid., pp. 308–309.

11. Ibid., pp. 308–309, 321.

12. Robert F. Bales, "The Equilibrium Problem in Small Groups," in Parsons, Bales, and Shils, *Working Papers in the Theory of Action* (New York, 1953), pp. 149–150. The study of

small groups appeared to the Parsonians to provide a theoretical basis for arguing that the Oedipus complex and the nuclear family out of which it arises are universal. If the conclusion derived from small-group analysis is correct—that every small group must assign expressive and instrumental functions to different leaders—then we should expect to find in every society the division of labor characteristic of the modern family, where the male adult acts as instrumental leader and the female as tension manager and therapist-in-chief. When we survey the ethnographical literature, Zelditch argued, that is exactly what we do find. The matrilineal systems described by Malinowski, Mead, and others prove to be no exception. Even if the husband's authority is subordinate to that of the mother's brother when we consider a second social system (the extended family or lineage), the husband acts as provider and instrumental leader within the nuclear family itself. As for the mother, in every known culture her expressive role is never in doubt. See Zelditch, "Role Differentiation," 328–333, 341.

13. For radical criticism of Parsonian theory, see pp. 147–150. Mark Gerzon has aptly written: "It is not 'liberation' from the technological society to escape from a dying home, but acquiescence to it. The very idea of a home is radical in an era when private identity, to use Marcuse's phrase, is being absorbed 'by the function of the individual in the state—by his public existence.'" See Mark Gerzon, *A Childhood for Every Child: The Politics of Parenthood* (New York, 1973), p. 137.

14. Parsons, *Family*, p. 32. See also Parsons, Bales, and Shils, "Phase Movement in Relation to Motivation, Symbol Formation, and Role Structure," in their *Working Papers*, pp. 265–266.

15. Talcott Parsons, "The Social Structure of the Family," in Ruth Nanda Anshen, ed., *The Family: Its Function and Destiny* (New York, 1949), p. 190.

16. Parsons, *Family*, pp. 25–26.

17. Ibid.

18. Ibid., pp. 60–61.

19. The ingenuity with which the Parsonians worked out a structural-functionalist interpretation of the Oedipus complex and furnished "proofs" of its universality cannot be denied. Nevertheless, it is more convincing (and more consistent with the psychoanalytic theory the Parsonian interpretation claims to incorporate) to see the small group as a special type of family, rather than the reverse. Instead of viewing role differentiation as the product of interaction "over a very broad range of situations," we might argue the opposite: "role differentiation" arises out of the family and then tends to recapitulate itself elsewhere. Early experiences tend to repeat themselves in later life, and adulthood patterns itself in many ways after childhood. All wielders of authority are in some ways extensions of the father, all nurturing figures extensions of the mother. This much seems so obvious, in fact, that it is tempting to turn Freud into Jung and to see all experience as an endless proliferation of mother-symbols and father-symbols, a proliferating dualism based on sex, the most elementary form of "role differentiation." Interpreting the sexual division of labor as a special case of a division allegedly more pervasive than sexuality, on the other hand, gives rise to all sorts of unnecessary difficulties, the solution of which requires more effort than the result justifies. Not the least of these difficulties arises from the argument's circularity: small-group theory provides the concepts with which the Parsonians fashion their own version of psychoanalysis, which they then claim is verified by the very evidence—the study of small groups—from which it derived. So much for the rigorous "testing" and "reformulation" of psychoanalytic concepts by means of empirical research.

20. Talcott Parsons and Renee C. Fox, "Illness, Therapy, and the Modern Urban American Family," *Journal of Social Issues* 13 (1953); reprinted in Norman W. Bell and Ezra F. Vogel, eds., *A Modern Introduction to the Family* (Glencoe, Ill., 1960), pp. 347–348.

21. Talcott Parsons, *The Social System* (Glencoe, Ill., 1951), chap. 10; Talcott Parsons, "Illness and the Role of the Physician: A Sociological Perspective," in Clyde Kluckhohn and Henry A. Murray, eds., *Personality in Nature, Society, and Culture*, 2d ed., (New York, 1954), pp. 609–617.

22. Parsons and Fox, "Illness," 351–355.

23. Ibid., 352.

24. Ibid., 353.

25. Ibid., 350.

26. Ibid., 350–351.

27. Parsons, *Family*, p. 161.

28. Ibid., p. 104.

29. Parsons, "The Incest Taboo in Relation to Social Structure and the Socialization of the Child" (1954), in Talcott Parsons, *Social Structure and Personality* (New York, 1964), p. 70.

30. Parsons, *Family*, p. 72.

31. Parsons and Winston White, "The Link Between Character and Society" (1961), in *Social Structure and Personality*, p. 216.

32. Parsons confuses identification with conscious imitation. His analysis of socialization boils down to the proposition that girls learn to become women by imitating their mothers and boys learn to become men by imitating their fathers. Men find it more difficult to grow up, according to Parsons, because they too at first "identify" with their mothers, whose role they must later learn to renounce. They do this by going through a period of routine "badness" or "compulsive masculinity." See Parsons, "Age and Sex in the Social Structure of the United States," *American Sociological Review* 7 (1942):606, 614–615; "The Social Structure of the Family," in Anshen, *The Family*, pp. 187–188, 190–193. For similar views, see O. Hobart Mowrer, "Identification: A Link between Learning Theory and Psychotherapy" (1950) in his *Learning Theory and Personality Dynamics* (New York, 1950), p. 607; Robert F. Winch, "Some Data Bearing on the Oedipus Hypothesis," *Journal of Abnormal and Social Psychology* 45 (1950): 481–491; and Winch, "Further Data and Observations on the Oedipus Hypothesis," *American Sociological Review* 16 (1951):784–795. Like Parsons, Mowrer argues that both sexes initially identify with the mother. While "this provides a path of development which the female child can follow indefinitely, the male child must, in some way, abandon the mother as a personal model and shift his loyalties and ambitions to his father."

Freud saw things in just the opposite way. Both sexes at first identify with the father, according to his analysis, and this identification differs from conscious imitation in that the ego seeks not simply to play a learned paternal role but to be exactly like the father in all respects—to take his place, above all to take his place in the marriage bed. Children of both sexes soon "learn" that such wishes are not to be gratified, but boys in some ways accept this knowledge more easily than girls, according to Freud, since they know that eventually they will find women of their own and in this and other ways succeed to the father's estate. Having "introjected" the mother he has lost, a young man unconsciously seeks to regain her in his subsequent relations with women, in the course of which he also sees himself, unconsciously, as taking his father's place.

Women, on the other hand, must not only renounce the mother as an object but must also renounce identification with the father—a more complicated process, in Freud's view, because the active side of female sexuality has to be repressed in favor of the passive. The Parsonian theory of identification, which purports to be a modification of Freud's, represses the ideas that are essential to psychoanalytic theory: infantile sexuality, the existence of unconscious thoughts, and the Oedipus complex. In Parsons's view, the Oedipus complex becomes a transition (necessarily somewhat painful, to be sure) from infantile dependence on the mother to the assumption of adult roles. The child models his actions on those of the parent of his own sex, thereby learning to play the sex role which society expects him to play. In other words, he becomes a sexually "differentiated" adult.

33. See Alexander Mitscherlich, *Society Without the Father*, translated by Eric Mosbacher (New York, 1970), p. 286: "If [the mass man] makes a mistake, there is no conscience to prick him; at the worst, a new outside authority . . . delivers a sentence to which the accused sub-

mits as passively and reluctantly as a child accepts a punishment it believes to be unjust. He still sees the world in terms of the power-impotence relationship."

34. David Riesman, *Faces in the Crowd* (New Haven, 1952), p. 7. It might be further argued along these lines that the sociology of interpersonal relations is the scientific reflection of this change. As society comes to be seen not as man's collective transformation of nature but as a web of interpersonal relations, social science takes those relations as its special subject and treats man as wholly formed by them, repudiating every vestige of the supernatural and of "biological determinism."

35. David Riesman (in collaboration with Reuel Denney and Nathan Glazer), *The Lonely Crowd: A Study of the Changing American Character* (New Haven, 1950), p. 26.

36. Ibid., pp. 51, 62, 83.

37. Parsons, "The Link between Character and Society" (1961), in *Social Structure and Personality*, p. 195. As he put it in another essay on youth, the values of the older generation "are intact and are by and large shared by the younger generation" ("Youth in the Context of American Society" [1962], in ibid., p. 165).

38. Parsons, "Character and Society," p. 235. Parsons sees the "production of personality" as a positive development: the triumph of all those forces in modern society which encourage the development of personal autonomy. Others see this emphasis on "personality," on the other hand, as part of a growing trend toward conformity and the "commercialization of friendliness." "Early in his education, the child is taught . . . to like people, to be uncritically friendly to them, and to smile. What education may not have accomplished is usually done by social pressure in later life. If you do not smile you are judged lacking in a 'pleasing personality'—and you need to have a pleasing personality if you want to sell your services, whether as a waitress, a salesman, or a physician. Only those at the bottom of the social pyramid, who sell nothing but their physical labor, and those at the very top do not need to be particularly pleasant.' " See Erich Fromm, *Escape from Freedom* (New York, 1941), p. 241.

In all of his work, Parsons appreciates the growing importance of the therapeutic professions and the emergence of a therapeutic model of personality; but this too he sees as a step toward autonomy, whereas others associate it precisely with the waning of the sense of personal responsibility. See Philip Rieff, *The Triumph of the Therapeutic: Uses of Faith After Freud* (New York, 1966); *Fellow Teachers* (New York, 1973).

39. Parsons, "Character and Society," pp. 212–217.

40. S. N. Eisenstadt, *From Generation to Generation: Age Groups and Social Structure* (Glencoe, Ill. 1956), p. 43.

41. Parsons, "Character and Society," pp. 219–221.

42. Eisenstadt, *From Generation to Generation*, p. 47.

43. Ibid., p. 214.

44. Parsons and Shils, *Toward a General Theory of Action* (Cambridge, Mass., 1962 [1951]), p. 177.

45. Frankfurt Institute for Social Research, *Aspects of Sociology* (Boston, 1972 [1956]), pp. 139–140.

46. Parsons, "Social Structure and the Development of Personality: Freud's Contribution to the Integration of Psychology and Sociology" (1958), in *Social Structure and Personality*, p. 78. He refers to Kazin's essay, "The Freudian Revolution Analyzed," *New York Times Magazine*, May 6, 1956, pp. 22 ff, reprinted in Benjamin Nelson, ed., *Freud and the 20th Century* (New York, 1957), pp. 13–21; and to Lionel Trilling's *Freud and the Crisis of Our Culture* (Boston, 1955).

47. Trilling, *Freud*, p. 35, 38.

48. Dennis H. Wrong, "The Oversocialized Conception of Man in Modern Sociology," *Am. Sociol. Rev.* 26 (1961):187.

49. Mitscherlich, *Society Without the Father*, p. 303.

7 / *The Attack on the Nuclear Family and the Search
for "Alternate Life-styles"*

1. See R. D. Laing, *The Politics of the Family* (New York, 1971); David Cooper, *The Death of the Family* (New York, 1971).

2. For an introduction to some of these movements, see Anthony J. Sutich and Miles A. Vich, *Readings in Humanistic Psychology* (New York, 1969). See also Thomas S. Szasz, *The Myth of Mental Illness* (New York, 1961); Robert Boyers and Robert Orrill, eds., *R. D. Laing and Anti-Psychiatry* (New York, 1971); Richard A. Schwartz, "Psychiatry's Drift away from Medicine," *American Journal of Psychiatry* 131 (1974):129–134; John A. Talbott, "Radical Psychiatry," ibid., 121–128. On the controversy between "protestant" and "catholic" conceptions of psychiatry, see Christopher Lasch, "Sacrificing Freud," *New York Times Magazine,* February 22, 1976, pp. 11 ff.

3. The imperial implications of these arguments appear with particular clarity in E. Fuller Torrey, *The Death of Psychiatry* (Radnor, Pa., 1974). For criticism of this position, see my review in *Hastings Center Report,* August 1975, pp. 15–17.

4. B. M. Brown, quoted in Torrey, *Death of Psychiatry,* p. 135.

5. Abraham Meyerson attacked the "medical model" of mental disorder as early as the twenties, and on grounds superior to those on which Szasz and others attack it today. Whereas Szasz naïvely assumes a sharp dichotomy between the body, which gets sick, and the mind, which has "problems in living," Meyerson held that "there is no theory of separation of the organism into mind and body which has a medical-biological reason for existing" (quoted in James H. S. Bossard, *Problems of Social Well-Being* [New York, 1927], p. 531). His argument that "mind . . . is a function of the entire organism" anticipated the position now taken by Horacio Fabrega, George L. Engel, and others. See, for example, Horacio Fabrega, Jr., "The Study of Disease in Relation to Culture," *Behavioral Science* 17 (1972):183–203.

6. Clayton C. Barbeau, ed., *Future of the Family* (New York, 1971), pp. 20, 27, 30, 67–70. For the views of Denis de Rougemont, see his *Love in the Western World,* translated by Montgomery Belgion (New York, 1940).

7. Proposals to extend the family can easily coexist with proposals to reduce it to marriage because both originate in a belief that the nuclear family no longer trains children to face the future. For the arguments just summarized, see Alvin Toffler, *Future Shock* (New York, 1970); Nena O'Neill and George O'Neill, *Open Marriage: A New Life Style for Couples* (New York, 1972), Robert Francoeur and Anna Francoeur, *Hot and Cool Sex: Cultures in Conflict* (New York, 1975); Robert Francoeur, *Eve's New Rib* (New York, 1972); Margaret Mead, "Marriage in Two Steps" (1966), in Robert F. Winch and Graham B. Spanier, eds., *Selected Studies in Marriage and the Family,* 4th ed. (New York, 1974), pp. 507–510. On humanist psychology, see Rollo May, *Love and Will* (New York, 1969); Carl Rogers, *On Becoming a Person* (Boston, 1961). As the title of the Francoeurs' book suggests, Marshall McLuhan, with his distinction between "hot" and "cool" media, has also influenced the ideology of open marriage. Francoeur, incidentally, is a former Catholic priest and an admirer of Teilhard de Chardin.

8. O'Neill and O'Neill, *Open Marriage,* pp. 47, 63, 69, 72–73, 203.

9. Ibid., pp. 40, 82, 126. See also George R. Bach and Peter Weyden, *The Intimate Enemy: How to Fight Fair in Love and Marriage* (New York, 1968). For a penetrating discussion of the voluminous writing on awareness and psychic self-help, see Russell Jacoby, *Social Amnesia: A Critique of Conformist Psychology from Adler to Laing* (Boston, 1975); also Edwin Schur, *The Awareness Trap: Self-Absorption Instead of Social Change* (New York, 1976).

10. Albert Ellis, *The American Sexual Tragedy,* 2d ed. (New York, 1962), pp. 113–122,

145. See also William J. Lederer and Don D. Jackson, *The Mirages of Marriage* (New York, 1968), pp. 54–55.

11. O'Neill and O'Neill, *Open Marriage*, pp. 147, 241, 249, 254. See also, on the redefinition of marital fidelity, the essays in Roger W. Libby and Robert N. Whitehurst, eds., *Renovating Marriage: Toward New Sexual Life-Styles* (Danville, Calif., 1973), and James R. Smith and Lynn G. Smith, *Beyond Monogamy: Recent Studies of Sexual Alternatives in Marriage* (Baltimore, 1974).

12. For the first type of argument see Mel Krantzler, *Creative Divorce: A New Opportunity for Personal Growth* (New York, 1974); for the second, Susan Gettleman and Janet Markowitz, *The Courage to Divorce* (New York, 1974).

13. O'Neill and O'Neill, *Open Marriage*, p. 75. Cf. Frederick S. Perls, a Gestalt psychologist: "The past is no more and the future not yet. Only the *now* exists" (quoted in Schur, *Awareness Trap*, p. 43).

14. Dr. Eric Berne, quoted in O'Neill and O'Neill, *Open Marriage*, p. 159.

15. John Mogey, "Sociology of Marriage and Family Behavior, 1957–1968," *Current Sociology* 17 (1969):48. For other assessments of the state of the field, see Reuben Hill, "An Inventory of Research in Marriage and Family Behavior," *Marriage and Family Living* 19 (1957):89–92; Nelson Foote, "The Appraisal of Family Research," ibid., 92–99; Robert F. Winch, "Theorizing about the Family," *Journal of Comparative Family Studies* 3 (1972):5–16. Articles of this type have been characterized as "increasingly critical of family sociology, viewing it as a disconnected and theoretically-retarded part of sociology"; see Ronald L. Howard, "A Social History of American Family Sociology, 1865–1970," unpublished Ph.D. dissertation, University of Missouri (1975), p. 222. It is true that these articles were often defensive about the degree to which work in family sociology was still dominated by issues growing out of marriage counseling, but they claimed that the field was mellowing with age and that its problems were being overcome.

16. Otto Pollak, "The Outlook for the American Family," *Journal of Marriage and the Family* 29 (1967): 198–199, 204. Other sociologists urge the profession to concern itself more actively with "the ability of family members to tolerate conflict, to accept the hostility of others within the family with understanding and compassion, to develop and communicate a true commitment and genuine sense of care and respect to each other." See James Walters and Nick Stinnett, "Parent-Child Relationships: A Decade Review of Research," *JMF* 33 (1971):103.

Perhaps the simplest way of distinguishing my own views from those that prevail among academic sociologists is to point out that whereas they assume that people cannot afford to establish deep ties outside the family and must therefore take emotional refuge in the domestic circle, I contend that it is precisely the menacing character of the outside world which prevents most people from establishing deep ties within the family.

17. Walters and Stinnett, "Parent-Child Relationships," 204–205; Jessie Bernard, *The Future of Marriage* (New York, 1973), p. 61.

18. Ibid., pp. 60–63.

19. Bert N. Adams, "Isolation, Function, and Beyond: American Kinship in the 1960's," *JMF* 32 (1970):579. See also Eugene Litwak, "Occupational Mobility and Extended Family Cohesion," *American Sociological Review* 25 (1960):9–21; Eugene Litwak, "Geographic Mobility and Extended Family Cohesion," ibid., 385–394; Marvin B. Sussman and Lee Burchinal, "Kin Family Network," *M. and Fam. Living* 24 (1962):231–240; Michael Young and Peter Willmott, *Family and Kinship in East London* (London, 1957).

20. Pollak, "Outlook for the American Family," 198.

21. Graham B. Spanier, "Romanticism and Marital Adjustment," *JMF* 34 (1972):485.

22. William L. Kolb, "Family Sociology, Marriage Education, and the Romantic Complex: A Critique," *Social Forces* 29 (1950):66, 71.

23. Hugo G. Beigel, "Romantic Love," *Am. Sociol. Rev.* 16 (1951):332–333.

24. Sidney M. Greenfield, "Love and Marriage in Modern America: A Functional Analysis," *Sociological Quarterly* 6 (1965):375–376.

25. Beigel, "Romantic Love," 326.

26. Gerald Handel, ed., *The Psychosocial Interior of the Family: A Sourcebook for the Study of Whole Families*, 2d ed. (Chicago, 1972), p. v.

27. Although their dependence on Parsons will become unmistakable in what follows, it should be noted at the outset that Slater collaborated with Parsons on his study of the family, while Keniston acknowledges his debt to Parsons in the notes to chaps. 9 and 10 of his *The Uncommitted: Alienated Youth in American Society* (New York, 1965).

28. Ibid., pp. 277, 279, 281. Keniston's debt to Parsons appears also in his analysis of family structure, where he describes the wife as "executive manager" and the husband as "chairman of the board," the same terms used by Parsons.

29. Keniston, *The Uncommitted*, pp. 277, 293, 296–297, 299. Emphasis on the family's isolation prevents us from seeing that the "strains" uncovered by this kind of analysis often derive precisely from the intrusion of the outside world. The statement that the housewife gets little help in raising her children, a statement formulated solely with help from servants and relatives in mind, ignores the "help" she gets from psychiatrists, doctors, child guidance specialists, and legions of other experts. Their advice, even when it is not confusing and contradictory, undermines her self-confidence because of its inherent tendency to invite measurement of her child's development against a normative standard to which it rarely conforms.

It could be argued that all this expert advice arose in the first place because the family was isolated and the help of relatives no longer available. But in all likelihood the proliferation of professional advice itself hastened the "decline of the extended family." Experts regarded their own counsel as scientifically superior to that of ignorant laymen and deliberately sought to intrude themselves between the housewife and the "home remedies" she learned from her kin.

30. Keniston, *The Uncommitted*, pp. 309–310.

31. Philip Slater, *The Pursuit of Loneliness: American Culture at the Breaking Point* (Boston, 1970), pp. 24–25; see also chap. 3, passim. Compare the evidence in Herbert Hendin, *The Age of Sensation* (New York, 1975), which shows that students use drugs not to intensify feelings but to stifle them, in particular to stifle the murderous rage which the superficially easygoing relations in the middle-class family drive underground but by no means eliminate.

32. Slater, *Pursuit of Loneliness*, pp. 86–87.

33. "Our age has silently but massively resolved against the conceptions of love which dazzled the Western imagination . . . for centuries. We have ended both the epic of Christian love and the dream of romantic love which succeeded it. We have chosen sympathy-love over the stern imperatives of Christian love [the paradoxical commandment to love all mankind even though love is by nature exclusive and discriminatory], and we have chosen sentimental love over the agony of romantic love. In these respects, Fromm's work is an appropriate epilogue to the story of Western love. In Fromm's pages, Christian love appears only as a bland residue of sympathy and benevolence left over after all the stringent elements of duty, debt, and sacrifice have been distilled out. Romantic love, too, has lost its perfume, its mystery, and its terror in his work, and remains only as a wispy haze of sentiment for the brotherhood of all mankind." John H. Schaar, *Escape from Authority: The Perspectives of Erich Fromm* (New York, 1961), pp. 136–137, 141. What Scharr says of Fromm applies equally to Slater.

34. Arlene S. Skolnick and Jerome H. Skolnick, eds., *Family in Transition* (Boston, 1971), pp. 22–23, 30.

35. Arlene Skolnick, "The Family Revisited: Themes in Recent Social Science Research," *Journal of Interdisciplinary History* 5 (1975):714.

36. Ibid., p. 718.

37. She refers here to the well-known article by Dennis Wrong, "The Oversocialized Con-

cept of Man in Modern Sociology," *Am. Sociol. Rev.* 26 (1961): 183–192, but carries his argument to conclusions opposite to his own. As we have seen, Wrong's article is a discussion of the "forces in man that are resistant to socialization," not a celebration of human "creativity."

38. Skolnick, "Family Revisited," 708–709, 711.

39. As the ego disintegrates under the pressures that assail it (both from without and from within), sociology insists all the more desperately on its integrity. See Jacoby, *Social Amnesia*, p. 40: "It is hardly accidental that ego psychology . . . emerges just when the ego as an autonomous unit turns openly suspect."

40. Gerald Handel, "Psychological Study of Whole Families," in Handel, ed., *Psychosocial Interior of the Family*, pp. 519–520, 524–525.

41. Bernard, *Future of Marriage*, p. 67.

42. Ibid., pp. 46–51. Bernard quotes with approval Slater's strictures on the modern folly "of imprisoning each woman alone in a small, self-contained, and architecturally isolating dwelling."

43. These observations are based on Theodore Lidz's account of the development of his own work, "The Influence of Family Studies on the Treatment of Schizophrenia," *Psychiatry* 32 (1969):240–241.

44. Victor D. Sanua, "Sociocultural Factors in Families of Schizophrenics: A Review of the Literature," *Psychiatry* 24 (1961):247. Sanua adds the qualification that "all psychotherapists, however, do not take the stand that mothers are largely responsible for the deviancy of their children, and the role of the mother seems to have been overemphasized in the literature without sufficient justification" (ibid., 256–257). Such qualifications often appear in the literature on schizophrenic families, but they always seem to be disregarded in analysis of actual cases and in the theory based on it. There is a good reason for this: the emotional dominance of the mother in the modern middle-class family.

45. Lidz, "Schizophrenia and the Family," *Psychiatry* 21 (1958):25–26.

46. The following articles all emphasize the combination of dominant mothers and passive fathers: Ruth W. Lidz and Theodore Lidz, "The Family Environment of Schizophrenic Patients," *Am. J. Psychiatry* 106 (1949):332–45; Suzanne Reichard and Carl Tillman, "Patterns of Parent-Child Relationships in Schizophrenia," *Psychiatry* 13 (1950):247–257; Joseph C. Mark, "Attitudes of Mothers of Male Schizophrenics toward Child Behavior," *Journal of Abnormal and Social Psychology* 48 (1953):185–189; C. W. Wahl, "Some Antecedent Factors in the Family Histories of 568 Male Schizophrenics of the United States Navy," *Am. J. Psychiatry* 113 (1956):201–210; Melvin L. Kohn and John A. Clausen, "Parental Authority Behavior and Schizophrenia," *American Journal of Orthopsychiatry* 26 (1956):297–313. The important conclusion to which these studies seem to point is that psychosis arises out of maternal dependency and seeks to recreate a still more primitive form of it. See William McCord, Judith Porter, and Joan McCord, "The Familial Genesis of Psychoses," *Psychiatry* 25 (1962):70.

47. Lyman C. Wynne et al., "Pseudo-Mutuality in the Family Relations of Schizophrenics," *Psychiatry* 21 (1958):207, 210–211. See also Lyman C. Wynne et al., "Maintenance of Stereotyped Roles in the Familes of Schizophrenics," *American Medical Association Archives of Psychiatry* 1 (1959):93–98; Lyman C. Wynne, "The Study of Intrafamilial Alignments and Splits in Exploratory Family Therapy," in Nathan W. Ackerman, ed., *Exploring the Base for Family Therapy* (New York, 1961); Lyman C. Wynne, "Communication Disorders and the Quest for Relatedness in Families of Schizophrenics," *American Journal of Psychoanalysis* 30 (1971): 100–114.

48. Gregory Bateson et al., "Toward a Theory of Schizophrenia," *Behavioral Science* 1(1956): 258–259.

49. Ibid., 258.

50. Ibid., 253.

51. Ibid., 261.

52. Ibid., 259.

53. "[The] shift in emphasis from the pregenital organization of the libido to object relations, ego formation, and the mother's role is strikingly evident no matter where one turns in the recent post-Freudian literature." Fred Weinstein and Gerald M. Platt, *The Wish to Be Free: Society, Psyche, and Value Change* (Berkeley, 1969), p. 188. The stress on the mother is striking indeed; but it takes us still deeper into the pregenital stage of psychic development, not into later childhood, as the reference to "ego formation" implies. It is misleading to claim, as Weinstein and Platt do, that the neo-Freudians and ego psychologists were the first to discover the importance of the pre-Oedipal mother. Her significance was already understood by Melanie Klein, "The Oedipus Complex in the Light of Early Anxieties" (1945), in *Contributions to Psycho-Analysis* (New York, 1964), pp. 339–390; and by Géza Róheim, *Magic and Schizophrenia* (New York, 1955). Indeed, it was Freud himself, in his essays on the psychology of women, who first uncovered this buried layer of psychic development, the psychic equivalent of "the Minoan-Mycenean civilization behind the civilization of Greece."

54. See pp. 92–93.

55. In one of his characteristic pronouncements, Kennedy proclaimed the end of ideology in the following carefully chosen words: "Most of the problems . . . that we now face, are technical problems, are administrative problems. They are very sophisticated judgments which do not lend themselves to the great sort of passionate movements which have stirred this country so often in the past. [They] deal with questions which are now beyond the comprehension of most men. . . ." These comments were made in a press conference, May 22, 1962, quoted in David Eakins, "Policy-Planning for the Establishment," in Ronald Radosh and Murray Rothbard, eds., *A New History of Leviathan* (New York, 1972), p. 198.

56. U.S. Department of Labor, Office of Policy Planning and Research, "The Negro Family: The Case for National Action" (March 1965), unpaginated preface; pp. 5, 35, 39, 47. The text of the report is reprinted in Lee Rainwater and William L. Yancey, *The Moynihan Report and the Politics of Controversy* (Cambridge, Mass., 1967), pp. 39 ff.

57. Herbert J. Gans, "The Breakdown of the Negro Family," in ibid., p. 450.

58. Quoted in ibid., p. 200.

59. Ibid., p. 130. Regarding the male chauvinism associated with black militancy, it is enough to recall a remark variously attributed to Eldridge Cleaver and to Stokely Carmichael. When asked to comment on the position of women in the black movement, the black leader replied "prone."

60. Quoted in Rainwater and Yancey, *Moynihan Report*, p. 200.

61. William Ryan, "Savage Discovery: The Moynihan Report," in ibid., p. 458.

62. Laura Carper, "The Negro Family and the Moynihan Report," in ibid., p. 474.

63. Lee Rainwater, *Behind Ghetto Walls: Black Families in a Federal Slum* (Chicago, 1970), p. 89. His study of the Pruitt-Igoe housing project in St. Louis impressed Rainwater with "the conventionality and ordinariness" of ghetto conceptions of good family life. The man should be the head of the family and bring in a steady income. Sex should be confined to marriage. Marriage should be based on love, not interest, convenience, or the threat of pregnancy. Wife and husband should be companions; the husband should not drink, gamble, or hang out with his friends. "The realization of these Pruitt-Igoe ideals would produce a style of life hardly distinguishable from other working-class life" (ibid., p. 50). But the ghetto does not have the resources to sustain them.

64. Ibid., p. 80.

65. Ibid., pp. 225, 231, 285–286, 288. See also Elliot Liebow, *Tally's Corner: A Study of Negro Streetcorner Men* (Boston, 1967), chaps. 3–6, passim.

66. Gans, "Breakdown," p. 450.

67. Ulf Hannerz, *Soulside: Inquiries into Ghetto Culture and Community* (New York, 1969), p. 93.

68. Robert Staples, letter to the editor, *JMF* 33 (1971):7. See also Jerold Heiss, *The Case of the Black Family* (New York, 1975), p. 121. Birdwhistell's article, "The American Family: Some Perspectives," appears in *Psychiatry* 29 (1966):203–212.

69. Roger D. Abrahams, *Positively Black* (Englewood Cliffs, N.J., 1970), p. 6.

70. Quoted in Rainwater and Yancey, *Moynihan Report*, pp. 186, 200. In view of this last criticism, voiced by Floyd McKissick of CORE, it should be noted that Moynihan grew up in a mother-centered family in the Irish slum of Hell's Kitchen. According to Rainwater and Yancey, this experience helped to alert him to the importance of the matrifocal family in the first place (ibid., p. 22). It also prevented him from seeing it as a structure peculiar to blacks. The same type of family, he believed, could be found in the "wild Irish slums of the 19th Century Northeast" (ibid., p. 17) and in many other lower-class neighborhoods.

71. Virginia Heyer Young, "Family and Childhood in a Southern Negro Community," in John H. Bracey et al., *Black Matriarchy: Myth or Reality?* (Belmont, Calif., 1971), pp. 194, 198–199.

72. Rainwater, *Behind Ghetto Walls*, p. 213.

73. Hannerz, *Soulside*, pp. 133–134.

74. Rainwater, *Behind Ghetto Walls*, pp. 388–389. On this last point, on the interpretation of the significance of the term "motherfucker," and on the interpretation of the ghetto family in general, my account draws heavily on Rainwater's. Of all treatments of the subject, his is the least afflicted by the new middle-class sentimentalism about "alternatives to the nuclear family." For another interpretation of the "dirty dozens," one much closer to that of Hannerz, see Abrahams, *Positively Black*, pp. 39–42. See finally, the highly regarded study by Carol B. Stack, *All Our Kin: Strategies for Survival in a Black Community* (New York, 1974), which demonstrates the importance of kinship networks and mutual exchange in the life of the black family. This study does not challenge the view that blacks hold "mainstream values" (p. 27); nor does it present any evidence to show that parents have enough authority over their children to protect them from outside influences.

75. Rainwater, *Behind Ghetto Walls*, p. 227.

8 / Authority and the Family: Law and Order in a Permissive Society

1. For the view criticized here, see Edward Shorter, *The Making of the Modern Family* (New York, 1975).

2. For the suppression of popular amusements, see Robert W. Malcolmson, *Popular Recreations in English Society, 1700–1850* (Cambridge, England, 1973).

3. Quoted in Shorter, *Making of the Modern Family*, p. 228.

4. Practitioners of the "new social history" think it is a waste of time to read novels, but an acquaintance with Homais, the village chemist in Flaubert's *Madame Bovary*, might prevent them from being taken in by medical ideologues posing as men of science—on the testimony of whom Shorter, for example, has built his fantastic account of the "surge of sentiment" that created the modern family. Homais can be taken as exemplifying the emerging alliance between medical ideology, republican anticlericalism, and the new machinery of mass promotion. He is full of enlightened ideas about child rearing: "For my own part, I think that mothers ought themselves to instruct their children. That is an idea of Rousseau's, still rather new perhaps, but that will end by triumphing, I am certain of it, like mothers nursing their own children and vaccination."

Homais's book, *General Statistics of the Canton of Yonville, Followed by Climatological*

Remarks, is just the sort of book Shorter relies on for allegedly objective evidence; but we would do better to see productions of this kind, as Flaubert saw them, as expressions of the ideology of the therapeutic, which from the beginning directed itself not merely against disease but against superstition, backwardness, and popular "immorality." "The statistics," Flaubert writes, "drove him to philosophy. He busied himself with great questions; the social problem, moralization of the poorer classes, . . . railways." Gustave Flaubert, *Madame Bovary*, translated by Eleanor Marx Aveling, Universal Library edition, (New York, n.d.), p. 376.

5. John R. Seeley, R. Alexander Sim, and Elizabeth W. Loosley, *Crestwood Heights: A Study of the Culture of Suburban Life* (New York, 1956), chaps. 11–12.

6. See David Riesman's introduction to *Crestwood Heights*, pp. xi–xii, where he argues that the divergence between male and female spheres, which Seeley and his collaborators observed in Canada, recalls an earlier period of American history when males read only the newspaper and women supervised the realm of art, religion, and leisure.

7. Michael Zuckerman, "Dr. Spock: The Confidence Man," in Charles E. Rosenberg, ed., *The Family in History* (Philadelphia, 1975), pp. 187–188.

8. Beata Rank, "Adaptation of the Psychoanalytical Technique for the Treatment of Young Children with Atypical Development, *American Journal of Orthopsychiatry* 19 (1949): 131–132, 138. See also, on the "necessarily experimental manner" in which the American child is raised, Geoffrey Gorer, *The American People* (New York, 1949), p. 74. Because of her dependence on experts, according to Gorer, the American mother "can never have the easy, almost unconscious, self-assurance of the mother of more patterned societies, who is following ways she knows unquestioningly to be right."

9. Seeley et al., *Crestwood Heights*, p. 165. This ideal "is sponsored first and foremost by the child-rearing experts active in Crestwood Heights."

10. Ibid., pp. 165–167, 367–368, 400. On the delegation of discipline to the peer group, see also Herbert Hendin, *The Age of Sensation* (New York, 1975), p. 315.

11. Bruno Bettelheim, *Children of the Dream* (New York, 1969), pp. 36, 74n, 97, 130, 171, 262; see also Melford E. Spiro, *Children of the Kibbutz* (New York, 1965 [1958]), chaps. 2, 4. According to Bettelheim, the founders of the kibbutz movement misunderstood Freud to be saying that "parents should never have any but good times with their children." The same fear of ambivalent attachments, based in part on the same misunderstanding of Freudian theory, can be seen in the American family today. But it is precisely the conjunction of love and constraint that enables a child to grow up and to accept the constraints of adulthood without losing the capacity for love. It is true that children do grow up in the kibbutz and in fact develop into remarkably "well-adjusted" adults; but it is precisely their "adjustment," their "ability to work well with others," their attachment to the peer group, their fear of being alone, their alienation from the past (since "there is no permanence in human relations except with the peer group"), and their lack of introspection and of a highly developed inner life which may provide an ominous foretaste of our future.

12. Hendin, *Age of Sensation,* p. 34.

13. Ibid., pp. 34, 47, 72, 75, 79, 96–98, 108, 116, 129–130, 215, 267, 289, 292, 297.

14. The distinction between "manifest" and "latent" images of parents derives from Martha Wolfenstein and Nathan Leites, *Movies: A Psychological Study* (New York, 1970 [1950]), chap. 2, a penetrating psychoanalytic interpretation on which I have relied heavily in the following argument.

15. It may be objected that the strength of the father-daughter connection is nothing new in American culture. According to Page Smith, *Daughters of the Promised Land: Women in American History* (Boston, 1970), it has been a prominent theme ever since the eighteenth century: "The father-daughter relationship . . . was the principal source of much of the energy and ambition that American women displayed" (p. 66). The novelty lies in the father's unpos-

sessive attitude toward his daughter. The attack on jealousy, focused initially on the relations between lovers, now extends to the relations between parents and children as well.

16. Wolfenstein and Leites, *Movies*, pp. 25–46.

17. Ibid., p. 168.

18. Alexander Mitscherlich, *Society Without the Father* (New York, 1970), p. 160.

19. Ibid., pp. 174–175. See also Jacques Ellul, *The Political Illusion*, translated by Konrad Kellen (New York, 1967), p. 211: "The contemporary orientation is that the child must learn without pain, that it must have agreeable, seductive work, that it must not even notice that it is working, and that in class the teacher must be really a sort of game leader, a permissive leader with whom there is no conflict." Ellul goes on to argue that the elimination of conflict between teacher and pupil, or between parent and child, "radically falsifies the child's participation in social life and keeps his personality from developing." It is in the course of such conflicts that the pupil learns and grows, providing, of course, that "in this conflict the teacher knows that his role is not to bully, crush, or train children like animals."

20. Melanie Klein, "Early Stages of the Oedipus Complex" (1928), in *Contributions to Psycho-Analysis, 1921–1945* (New York, 1964), p. 206.

21. See Sigmund Freud, "Mourning and Melancholia" (1917), *Standard Edition* 14: 161–163.

22. Klein, "The Oedipus Complex in the Light of Early Anxieties" (1945), in *Contributions*, p. 362. I have made heavy use of this essay in the foregoing analysis.

23. Ibid., p. 346.

24. Hendin, *Age of Sensation*, p. 167.

25. Erica Jong, *Fear of Flying* (New York, 1973), pp. 10–14.

26. F. J. Roethlisberger and William J. Dickson, *Management and the Worker* (Cambridge, Mass., 1947), pp. 267, 591. "The important consideration was not whether his complaint was justified but why he felt the way he did" (p. 269). The methods of social control first worked out by industrial sociologists bear a close resemblance to the advice given to parents by experts in child guidance and "parent-effectiveness" training. In both cases, superiors are advised that it does no good to argue with subordinates. "As a rule, it is wise never to argue with the speaker about his opinions, prejudices, or irrationalities" (p. 288). The point is to find out why he holds them. In order to do so, the superior must try "to help the person talk," "to relieve . . . fears or anxieties," and "to praise the interviewee for reporting his thoughts and feelings accurately" (p. 289).

27. Edgar Z. Friedenberg, *Coming of Age in America* (New York, 1965), p. 76.

28. Both Thomas S. Szasz, *Psychiatric Justice* (New York, 1965), and Nicholas N. Kittrie, *The Right to Be Different* (Baltimore, 1971), discuss this problem in detail. But the liberal, pluralist critique of "psychiatric justice" and its underlying "medical model" of mental disorder need to be deepened, extended, and in some ways revised. Not only does this argument depend on an indefensible distinction between somatic sickness (regarded as genuine sickness requiring medical intervention) and social deviance (which Szasz contends is misleadingly labeled sickness for purposes of social control), but it also assumes that the answer to the medicalization of justice is to make society more tolerant of deviance—for example, by getting psychiatrists to admit that homosexuality is not a "sickness." What looks at first like a radical attack on the therapeutic sensibility turns out to be an objection merely to a particularly rigid form of it. By redefining psychiatry not as medicine but as the management of interpersonal relations, these revisionists would extend what remains a therapeutic view of life into all social relations. Their cure is that staple of post-Freudian psychiatric practice, universal understanding. But it is precisely this universal understanding, sympathy, and tolerance (which in any case does not conceal the persistence of intolerance at a deeper level) that reflect the collapse of moral consensus, the collapse of distinctions between right and wrong, the collapse

of moral authority, and the shift from the old civic religion to the new antireligion of the therapeutic.

How and why the critique of "psychiatric justice" needs to be revised is suggested by a sentence from the introduction to Kittrie's *Right to Be Different*, which, as its title indicates, adopts the perspective of Szasz, but with a dawning awareness of its inadequacy. Kittrie first notes that the "therapeutic state" redefines crime as sickness in order to enforce conformity in the guise of benevolence (against which we have no legal defenses). He then goes on to say that although his book is addressed to the problems growing out of this medical revolution, "as this volume neared completion, the fear of societal excesses, which still remains very real, is somewhat dulled by yet another and opposite surge toward a 'permissive society,' where even fundamental needs of social order and organization fail to achieve broad public consensus and support." It remains only to note that it is precisely the collapse of "public consensus" that turns law into an agency for the mechanical enforcement of rules and regulations. Such a concept of law is quite compatible with the notion that those who get out of line are sick and need "treatment."

29. Friedenberg, *Coming of Age*, p. 77.

30. Ibid., p. 82.

31. See Arnold A. Rogow, *The Dying of the Light* (New York, 1975), chap. 2, "The Decline of the Superego," on the legitimation of the ripoff, the collapse of corporate loyalties, new patterns of child rearing based on bribery, and the increasing prevalence of language associated with primary-process thinking.

32. On the "flattery of the lie" in the enforcement of bureaucratic patterns of superordination and subordination, see Thomas S. Szasz, *The Myth of Mental Illness* (New York, 1961), pp. 275–276.

33. Thus law reinforces advertising, which tries to keep the consumer chronically anxious, uneasy, and fearful.

34. Rogow, *Dying of the Light*, p. 79.

35. Fred Weinstein and Gerald M. Platt, *The Wish to Be Free: Society, Psyche, and Value Change* (Berkeley, 1969), pp. 67–68.

INDEX